A Kingdom Within
The Conversion of King David

A Kingdom Within
The Conversion of King David

Douglas G. Bushman

Published by Douglas G. Bushman

Copyright © 2024 by Douglas G. Bushman
All rights reserved.

ISBN: 978-1-7349094-2-5

NIHIL OBSTAT
    Rev. Lawrence C. Brennan, S.Th.D.
    Censor
    June 19, 2020

IMPRIMATUR
    Most Rev. Michael J. Sheridan, S.Th.D.
    Bishop of Colorado Springs
    June 15, 2020

Except where otherwise noted, all biblical quotations are taken from *The Holy Bible, Revised Standard Version; Second Catholic Edition* (San Francisco: Ignatius Press, 2006).

Excerpts from the English translation of the *Catechism of the Catholic Church* for use in the United States of America Copyright © 1994, United States Catholic Conference, Inc. – Libreria Editrice Vaticana. Used with Permission. English translation of the *Catechism of the Catholic Church*: Modifications from the Editio Typica copyright © 1997, United States Conference of Catholic Bishops—Libreria Editrice Vaticana.

Cover Art: "Nathan Admonishes David" pen drawing (19 × 25 cm) by Rembrandt van Rijn (1606 – 1669) c. 1653, The Metropolitan Museum of Art, New York; see 2 Samuel 12:13.

Contents

	Introduction	1
1	David Prior to His Sin and Conversion: A Spiritual Profile	20
2	David's Sins: A King Betrays His God, His Mission, and His People	42
3	David's Conversion: A King Participates in God's Judgment	55
4	David After His Sin and Conversion: The Kingdom Within	94
	Conclusion: Conversion as Descent into Humility in Order to Ascend to the Inner Kingdom of Prosperity Measured by Divine Mercy	201

Introduction

Why a book of meditations on the conversion of the second king of Israel, David the son of Jesse, at this moment in the Church's pilgrimage of faith? We are now more than fifty years after the close of the Second Vatican Council, which intended to foster a renewal of the Church for the sake of a reinvigoration of the Church's mission. Guided by St. John XXIII and St. Paul VI, Council participants realized that a new missionary ardor can only be the fruit of a profound interior conversion, which Pope Paul did not hesitate to call *metanoia*. For him and his successor, St. John Paul II, the Council's call to holiness is the core of its plan for the renewal of the Church. For, holiness is the perfection of charity, and charity is the animating force of mission, the soul of the apostolate.[1]

It is tempting to think of conversion as a step towards holiness. In reality, because it is cooperation with God's grace, conversion is the manifestation of holiness already possessed yet in the process of becoming more mature, more ardent. Conversion is the movement of man back to God, but in order for this movement to occur there must be an already existing communion with God, even if it is only partial. Conversion is communion with God in the truth about man's sins and God's mercy. It is a movement, a series of actions that take place in the depths of man's being. It is precisely what God wills and man wills with Him when man is aware of his sins and returns to God, knowing in advance that he will be welcomed and forgiven because he knows that God is merciful.

Conversion into a deeper communion with God and thus into a more ardent charity is the irreplaceable foundation for the revitalization of the Church's mission, for mission is nothing other than charity in action: "For the love of Christ urges us on" (2 Cor 5:14). To insist that everything depends on holiness, and therefore on ongoing conversion, is no exaggeration. It is another way of saying that the Church most perfectly fulfills her vocation when her members are docile to the prompting of the Holy Spirit. By their responsiveness to the Spirit's movement, holy men and women—saints—assure that it is not merely human calculations but the Spirit Who guides the Church.

The aim of this book is to present the conversion of King David as a paradigm of conversion and to identify and to examine a number of essential truths about man's sin and God's mercy. Presuming the faith and working of grace in readers, the hoped-for fruit is a renewed confidence in God's mercy. God's mercy is His greatest attribute in relation to us; it is the truth that sets us free to face our sins, to turn to God for forgiveness, and through this conversion to give glory to God. For, the glory of God is the manifestation of His holiness, and nothing manifests His holiness more than the conversion of sinners. And since conversion into deeper

---

1   The phrase, "soul of the apostolate," occurs in Vatican II's *Lumen gentium*, 33 and *Apostolicam Actuositatem*, 3.

communion with God in holiness and charity produces the fruit of reinvigorated mission, mission for the sake of leading others to God is also His glory. The participation of people of faith in God's holiness, His charity, is the glory of God, but holiness is inseparable from the conversion that flows into it and from the mission that flows from it.

To sustain the Church in her ongoing conversion into more perfect holiness and more vigorous mission, the Holy Spirit, "the Church's living memory,"[2] not only inspired the sacred authors of Scripture to consign the account of King David's conversion to Sacred Scripture. He also guided the Church to recognize the books that narrate this event as the word of God and He continually calls David's conversion to mind in a public way through the Church's liturgy. Complementing this objective presence of David's conversion in the Church's life, the graces by which the Holy Spirit continually brings faith to perfection[3] have assured and continue to assure that the conversion of David bear the fruit of ongoing conversion in the lives of the faithful. The Fathers of the Church bear witness to this impact, for example, in St. Augustine's commentaries on the psalms and in St. Gregory the Great taking David's conversion as a paradigm of humility. In the Byzantine Liturgy, the faithful hear of God's forgiveness of David's sins through the Prophet Nathan in the words of absolution pronounced by the priest in the Sacrament of Penance.[4]

This book can be thought of as an extended meditation on Psalm 51. In the course of his commentary on Psalm 51, in which King David expresses experience of confronting sin and encountering God's mercy, St. Thomas Aquinas observes that the Church incorporates Psalm 51 into her life of prayer more than any other psalm.[5] The reason he gives for this predilection is that this Psalm so beautifully and simply implores God's mercy that everyone with faith can easily make it his own. This Psalm expresses the distress of a heart burdened by the weight of sin with such simplicity and clarity that men and women of all cultures and all times discover in it a most precise expression of their own experience of sin and conversion. Every Christian generation finds in David's words the most adequate correspondence to their own interior reality, as if they were to say: "These are the right words; I cannot find any better. I would have written precisely this, had I the skill."

St. Thomas' comment about the prominence of Psalm 51 in the Church's life can be taken as an indication of the *sensus fidei*, that supernatural instinct of faith by which the Church's members are able to distinguish the true currency of the Church's faith from counterfeit representations of that faith. In every age, the Psalm's description of the

---

2   *Catechism of the Catholic Church* (hereafter *CCC*), 1099.
3   "To bring about an ever deeper understanding of revelation the same Holy Spirit constantly brings faith to completion by His gifts" (Vatican II, *Dei Verbum*, 5).
4   See *CCC*, 1481.
5   In the Liturgy of the Hours, Psalm 51 is the first Psalm for Friday Morning Prayer for all four weeks. It is the first psalm for Morning Prayer for the Office of the Dead. In the Lectionary, Psalm 51 is the Responsorial Psalm nineteen times.

movement from the desolation of a soul burdened by sin to the joy of receiving forgiveness and restoration to communion with God resonate in the souls of believers. Since the paschal mystery is the permanent foundation of Christian faith, this must mean that believers of all ages perceive a relation between Psalm 51, and thus David's conversion, and redemption through Christ's sacrifice for sins, which definitively reveals the depths of human sin and the corresponding depth of divine mercy. It is no different in our own age, because what God has revealed about sin and mercy are timeless, and the faith that lives by this revelation is essentially the same in every age. Therefore, it is a theological certitude that the Holy Spirit will work in our age as He has in former ages, so that the faithful who are called to holiness and conversion in our own time will derive consolation, insight, inspiration, and encouragement by prayerfully reading and meditating on the conversion of King David, the essence of which Psalm 51 expresses. This psalm's unique place in the Church's life means that it has a unique contribution to make to the spiritual renewal through conversion, based on God's mercy, called for by Vatican II.

What is it, then, that explains that the words of an ancient king of an ancient people possess the power to be the occasion of consolation, insight, inspiration, and encouragement, and to make people feel so thoroughly understood? By allowing readers to view the state of his own soul, David makes it possible for them more accurately to view their own souls. Though the experience is universal, only a few have been given the grace and the mission to describe it precisely so as to enlighten others. St. Paul's depiction, in chapter seven of Romans, of the battle between his desire to accomplish God's will and his inability to do so, has had this impact, as have St. Augustine's *Confessions*, the *Dark Night of the Soul* of St. John of the Cross, *The Way of Perfection* of St. Teresa of Avila, and St. Thérèse of Lisieux's *Story of a Soul*.

By describing his own experience with such accessible imagery, St. David gains credibility with his readers. If his words have the effect of revealing people to themselves, then they realize that in a way he knows them better than they know themselves. In God's plan, this is vitally important, for if David is right in how he describes a soul in turmoil over unreconciled guilt, then there is every reason to be confident that he is right about the remedy. The credibility that he gains through making people feel understood justifies a transference of this confidence to what he says about turning to God for mercy and forgiveness. David is among the most credible witnesses to the truth about sin and the truth about God's mercy. But his credibility is more than this. He is credible because he exudes precisely what every conscience burdened by guilt seeks, the joy of having received God's mercy. This is the reason that St. Thomas Aquinas gives for the prominence of the Psalter in the Church's life: "it is to give us hope in the divine mercy, since although David sinned, he was nevertheless restored through penance."[6]

---

6   Aquinas, *Commentary on the Psalms*, Prologue.

David is like a leper whom Jesus has healed. The charism of a poet allows him to describe the anguish and hopelessness of living with spiritual leprosy, so that other lepers see themselves in his description. And when he describes the ineffable joy of having encountered God's healing power in Jesus and the new life that comes with being healed, he bears witness not to a fantasy but to the fulfillment of every leper's hope. It is above all hope that people need when they cooperate with the grace of God to acknowledge their sins.

Fr. Dominique Barthélemy elaborates on this affinity that Christian believers have with Psalm 51. Though his focus is on the Old Testament as a whole, not on any particular book or passage, what he says certainly applies to Psalm 51. His insight hinges on the undeniable reality that the battle against sin continues after Baptism. A passage of the *Catechism of the Catholic Church* succinctly summarizes what he says: "Baptism, by imparting the life of Christ's grace, erases original sin and turns a man back towards God, but the consequences for nature, weakened and inclined to evil, persist in man and summon him to spiritual battle."[7] This theme of the Christian life as a battle runs throughout the *Catechism*.[8] Particularly relevant for the current discussion is its link of the battle with holiness: "The way of perfection passes by way of the Cross. There is no holiness without renunciation and spiritual battle."[9]

This is the foundation for Fr. Barthélemy's insightful description of the tactics of the "old man," who battles against the "new man" that each has become in Baptism.

> He does not attack the new man openly; the old man is too subtle for that. He knows very well that, should he show himself as an atheist in the heart of one baptized, the latter would promptly take steps to exterminate him. And so the old man, atheist though he is, puts on the guise of religion.... The old man does not present himself as an atheist but as an idolater, which is something much more delicate and cunning. In other words, realizing his inability to drive God away, he seeks instead to take him in hand and fashion him to his own image. The old man never yields himself into the hands of the living God, for that would be his death.[10] He prefers instead to make for himself a comfortable God, easy to live with; while the new man, who is seldom very shrewd when he is young, is capable of living for a long time without suspecting that somebody else is gradually fashioning his

---

7 *CCC*, 405.
8 See: *CCC*, 407–409, 410, 921, 979, 1496, 2015, 2516, 2520–27, 2573, 2577, 2592, 2612, 2757–45.
9 *CCC*, 2015.
10 It is the old man who says, "It is a fearful thing to fall into the hands of the living God" (Heb 10:31), while the new man cries out, "My heart and flesh sing for joy to the living God" (Ps 84:3).

God for him; so that instead of being placed in the hands of the living God, he finds in his own hands a dream-God. Thus he tries to placate and ease his conscience by remaining faithful to a God ... not perhaps a God of his own invention, but one far removed from the living God. And therein lies the drama: the old man turns monk with a taste for a gospel that has become insipid. There is nothing he will not do to make sure he is not recognized, so that he can go on living as a parasite in the bosom of those good intentions which pave the way to hell, in the bosom of all that passes for what is noblest in man's heart. For there is nothing he cannot make use of or twist to his ends.[11]

The value of the Old Testament, Fr. Barthélemy concludes, is that it is a witness to the earliest interactions between God and the people He chose to be His own. It records the whiles of the "old man" as he is slowly being unmasked. In other words, the Old Testament chronicles the divine pedagogy according to which God's people progressively become aware of their sins, so that they are prepared for the definitive revelation of God's mercy in Jesus Christ.

This time of preparation for Christ is a time of discovering the deepest poverty that man can experience, the poverty of being cut off from God's love. For, sin is always a rejection of God's love. "Sin sets itself against God's love for us and turns our hearts away from it."[12] Sin reduces man to a state of spiritual destitution. By sinning, man deprives himself of the love for which he is made, and his life becomes unbearable. "Man cannot live without love. He remains a being that is incomprehensible for himself, his life is senseless, if love is not revealed to him, if he does not encounter love, if he does not experience it and make it his own, if he does not participate intimately in it."[13]

The propensity of sinful man is to be suspicious of God's love and to turn elsewhere for the fulfillment of his aspiration to live a fully human life. As a result, he is reduced to the state of destitution that Jesus depicts in the Parable of the Prodigal Son. But, in God's plan, such poverty is ordered to the cultivation of humility and becomes the beginning of a new openness to receive God's love. Here, again, the *Catechism of the Catholic Church* magnificently summarizes God's wisdom at work in the history of His people:

> The People of the "poor" (cf. Zeph 2:3; Ps 22:27; 34:3; Is 49:13; 61:1; etc.)—those who, humble and meek, rely solely on their God's mysterious plans, who await the justice, not of

---

[11] Dominique Barthélemy, *God and His Image* (San Francisco: Ignatius Press, 2007), xxiv–xxv.
[12] *CCC*, 1850.
[13] John Paul II, *Redemptor hominis*, 10.

men but of the Messiah—are in the end the great achievement of the Holy Spirit's hidden mission during the time of the promises that prepare for Christ's coming. It is this quality of heart, purified and enlightened by the Spirit, which is expressed in the Psalms. In these poor, the Spirit is making ready "a people prepared for the Lord" (Lk 1:17).[14]

The Holy Spirit is constantly at work to bring people to be meek and humble. He thereby prepares them for the definitive revelation of God's justice in His Messiah, Who is "meek and humble of heart" (Mt 11:29 DRA). This justice is His fidelity to His promises, and this means it is His mercy. By recounting the struggles of great personalities and of God's people as a whole, as well as God's mighty works, the Old Testament discloses God's gradual education of His people about their sins in order to purify and strengthen their faith in His mercy.

This is why a Christian reading of the Old Testament serves to deepen self-knowledge. Self-knowledge here is taken not in the modern sense of psychological introspection, but rather in the sense of the Carmelite doctors of the Church, St. John of the Cross and St. Teresa of Avila. For them, self-knowledge is above all knowledge of one's weakness and misery due to sin. St. John of the Cross tells us that this awareness of sin is the chief fruit of the dark night of purification of faith because it deepens the foundation of humility.[15] Progress in the spiritual life is progress in receiving God's transforming graces, and humility is the condition for increased receptivity to grace. This correlativity between humility and mercy-grace is the law of the spiritual life. The depth of one's faith in God's mercy and love for Him is a function of the depth of one's awareness of the evil of sin and one's own captivity to it. Jesus confirms this when He explains to Simon, the Pharisee, "He who is forgiven little loves little" (Lk 7:47).

Master of the biblical mindset and vocabulary, Fr. Barthélemy is attentive to what can be called the doctrinal and liturgical dimensions of the process of purification of faith through ongoing conversion. Because man is made in the image of God, the way he understands himself depends on how he understands God. A distortion of the truth about God necessarily results in a distortion of the truth about man. This is precisely what we see in the first sin recorded in the Bible, that of Adam and Eve. As the *Catechism* puts it, "they conceived a distorted image of God—that of a God jealous of His prerogatives."[16] At the suggestion of the serpent, Adam and Eve come to doubt God's love as the motive for giving the commandment. This error about God's love entails an error about man:

---

14   *CCC*, 716.
15   See John of the Cross, *Dark Night*, Bk. I, ch. 12, 2.
16   *CCC*, 399.

Man is not lovable for his own sake,[17] but only as useful for something or someone else. The Bible is the story of God's efforts to rehabilitate in men the truth that He is love and that all He does for man He does out of love. God does not look at man as a tool to be used but as a partner, a friend in communion of life. The drama is that so long as man is doubtful about God's love he cannot come to grips with his sins. He cannot approach God for forgiveness because he expects only punishment—which is rightly expected, if God is not love. Only a God of mercy will receive the sinner with the joy of the father of the prodigal son.

In the Bible, man's relation to God is considered above all in terms of worship. A right relation to God and a right worship of God are virtually identical. For, man's knowledge of God cannot remain merely theoretical. Since for man to live is to move, to be on a journey, faith has to be walking with God.[18] Faith must also be worship, but worship can no more be isolated from daily life than faith can. The mission of the prophets is to be the conscience of God's people by constantly reminding them that ritual worship and religious practices are a judgment against them if they are cut off from a daily life of fidelity in observing God's precepts.[19] Thus, the terms in which the Bible conveys the dependence of man's knowledge of himself and his manner of living on his knowledge of God are liturgical. The worship of God must be based on the truth about His love and His fidelity to His covenants with man; in a word, it must be based on the truth about His mercy. This is why St. Augustine said that anyone who desires to praise God should praise Him above all for His mercy, or remain silent. Apart from the revealed truth about God's mercy, religion is idolatry.[20]

The culmination of Israel's progressive education regarding idolatry comes at the time of Exile. Estranged from their land and temple, God's chosen people observe others make representations of other gods, "but in

---

17 The Second Vatican Council teaches that "man is the only creature on earth that God wanted for its own sake" (*Gaudium et spes*, 24). "For his own sake" is opposed to "for the sake of someone or something else." Man's dignity derives not from his value as a means to the perfection of some other creature, but rather directly from his relation to God and his capacity for communion with God.

18 St. Paul equates walking in the love of Christ with offering oneself with Him and in Him as a fragrant sacrifice (see Eph 5:2). The theme of walking with God is frequent in the Old Testament (see Gen 6:9; 17:1; Deut 13:4; 1 Kings 8:23, 25; 2 Chron 6:14; Ps 56:13; Mic 4:5; 6:8). To walk with God is to walk in His paths or according to His statutes (see Deut 5:33; 10:12; 13:5; 26:17; 28:9; Lev 18:4; Josh 22:5; 2 Chron 6:16; Neh 10:29; Is 2:3; Jer 7:23; Ezek 11:20; 20:19; Mic 4:2). Man's walking with God is made possible by God's initiative to walk with man (see Gen 3:8; Lev 26:12; 2 Cor 6:16). In Jesus Christ, God walks with men, and He is especially close to them in their walking when they confront the challenges to hope resulting from the mystery of God walking with men (see Lk 24:13).

19 Isaiah conveys this by defining what a true fast is (see Is 58:1–7). Jeremiah conveys the same by calling for circumcision of hearts (see Jer 4:4), and Joel by calling for the rending of hearts (see Joel 2:12–13). Jesus quotes Hos 6:6 in Mt 9:13 and 12:7. He perfectly fulfills the inseparability of worship and life by offering Himself in a sacrifice of obedience. See Heb 10:1–10, showing that Jesus' sacrifice is the fulfillment of Ps 40:5–8.

20 Augustine, *Confessions*, 6.7.12.

reality they do not truly exist but are only the inventions of men.... Instead of adoring the Creator, the creature adores his own creation."[21] Being fabricated by man is the element that this idolatry of the nations has in common with Israel's sin of making a golden calf to represent God. Religions that are not based on God's revelation are human constructs. They are philosophies of life, the fruit of man's effort to decipher the meaning of his existence and to "seek God, even perhaps grope for him and find him" (Acts 17:27 NAB).[22] The Church can and does affirm what is true in them, but she also realizes that what is false in them is harmful to man's dignity. What is false in religions is vanity, emptiness, nothingness.[23] To make idols to represent a force of nature or an idea of the origin of all things is to excavate cisterns (typically a good thing) that cannot hold water (never a good thing).[24]

Idolatry is perhaps easiest to spot when there is some kind of image, like a golden calf, used as a symbol. But the essence of religion is interior,[25] and so having a symbol is accidental. "Idolatry," the *Catechism* reminds us, "consists in divinizing what is not God. Man commits idolatry whenever he honors and reveres a creature in place of God."[26] Since God is man's origin and end, the definitive meaning of his life and source of happiness, this means that idolatry consists in looking to something created as the ultimate answer to the fundamental questions that man cannot avoid asking about the meaning his life, about his happiness, and thus in entrusting one's freedom to it.[27]

Idolatry "remains a constant temptation to faith."[28] Faith can be tempted to "domesticate" God, that is, "to interpret" what He has revealed in a manner that eliminates the Gospel's "hard sayings" (Jn 6:60). These are the truths that make the greatest demands on us, truths that call for the death of the "old man." In other words, they are truths that call for conversion. The temptation of our age is "to reinterpret" the traditional teaching of the Church in order to make it comport with current sensibilities and above all to the prevailing "definition" of love. The reshaping of doctrine in order to void it of all that is "offensive" and

---

21 Claude Wiéner, "Idols," in *Dictionary of Biblical Theology*, ed. Xavier Léon Dufour (Frederick, MD: The Word Among Us Press, 1988), 252a.
22 Our age of dialogue among religions has largely dropped the language of idolatry. The Church sees the various religions as so many manifestations of man's innate desire to discover the purpose and meaning of his life. At the same time, the Church recognizes that apart from God's revelation there is bound to be error that needs to be corrected if men are to come to the fullness of truth about God and thus to worship Him in the truth.
23 See Jer 2:5.
24 See Jer 2:13.
25 "[T]he exercise of religion, of its very nature, consists before all else in those internal, voluntary and free acts whereby man sets the course of his life directly toward God" (Vatican II, *Dignitatis humanae*, 3).
26 *CCC*, 2113.
27 "It is right and just to entrust oneself wholly to God and to believe absolutely what he says. It would be futile and false to place such faith in a creature (cf. Jer 17:5–6; Pss 40:5; 146:3–4)" (*CCC*, 150).
28 *CCC*, 2113.

contrary to every kind of "right thinking" is yet another way in which the "old man" still tries to mold God to his own expectations rather than to allow God to mold him to His.

As an example of this kind of doctrinal idolatry—of projecting on to God our own understanding of the words of revelation—the *Catechism* considers the first word of the Lord's Prayer, "Father." With profound insight, it recognizes that our first experience of love and authority comes with our interactions with our parents. Parents are God's first representatives to their children.[29] Because of sin, they cannot represent Him perfectly, and for this reason it is necessary to purify our concepts of paternal and maternal love and authority. "The purification of our hearts has to do with paternal or maternal images, stemming from our personal and cultural history, and influencing our relationship with God."[30] We may use the words that God uses in revelation. We may think of His love being like that of a mother caring for her children. We may address Him as Father. But what we expect from God in answer to our petitions will depend on how we understand the maternal character of His love and His Fatherhood. To the extent that our concepts are erroneous, there is a projection on to God of our own expectations, and this precisely what makes them idolatrous: "To impose our own ideas in this area 'upon him' would be to fabricate idols to adore or pull down."[31]

Treatises and discussions about conversion often overlook this doctrinal dimension of idolatry. In our age, the great question is whether the understanding that Christians have of love and mercy is taken from the culture around us or from divine revelation. Is there a place in this understanding for a properly understood divine punishment? And what of the understanding of sin? Is the understanding that Christians have of the evil of sin and of personal responsibility for rejecting God's love sufficient to account for the extreme measure that God has taken—becoming a man and dying on the Cross—in order to forgive sins and to reconcile men to Himself? As one astute observer puts it:

> Christianity is a high calling. One of the obstacles to seeing this is our distorted view of who God is. Some of us have succumbed to the idea that if He exists at all, He must be made in the image and likeness of our more understanding and good-natured therapists. This, of course, reduces us to the image and likeness of clients and hospital patients. It is only as we begin to realize the utter purity and holiness of God that we begin to appreciate that He simply cannot wink at sin.... Selling sin short is only the reverse side of selling God

---

29 See *CCC*, 239.
30 *CCC*, 2779.
31 *CCC*, 2779.

short.[32]

There is a profound logic in St. Paul's taking over of Moses' equation of idolatry with the worship of demons.[33] Demons are opposed to the good of man and to the fulfillment of God's plan of love. They perpetuate the first and most fundamental lie of the father of lies, namely, that God is not love, that He is more interested in preserving His divine prerogatives than in serving man and providing for his fulfillment and happiness. Christians who take their faith seriously cannot avoid confronting in themselves the lingering effects of this lie, the residue as it were of Adam and Eve's suspicion about God's love. For, this is precisely the "doctrine" of the old man, namely, that God is not for man and so man must be for himself. For the "old man," idolatry is the logical corollary of self-love. I must build a life for myself, he reasons, because I cannot count on God to do it for me. By listening to the lie of the prince of demons and acting on it by disobeying God's one commandment, Adam and Eve renounce the "rational worship" (Rom 12:1) of God that previously characterized their lives and embraced the irrational worship of the father of lies. The obedience of faith given to God is the rational worship of Him. Its contrary, disobedience, is sin, the irrational worship of a creature.

Everything hinges on seeing that obedience is rooted in the conviction that God is love and that love is His motive for giving His commandments. Certainly, Christians learn from the liturgy, from the Bible, and from the *Catechism* that God is love and that His love has been fully revealed in the paschal mystery of Jesus Christ. Man's rational worship, then, his obedience, is the doctrine of God's love projected into his action. This understanding of worship being grounded in the truth about God and its opposite, idolatry, being based on a false image of God, is at the heart of Fr. Barthélemy's case for the Christian relevance of the Old Testament. For, in the Old Testament

> we may clearly see the craftiness, the ruses that the old man made use of when he fled from God and was not yet disguised as a sheep of the Good Shepherd. For the Old Testament is above all the great exposure of idolatry, the great exposure of caricatures of the living God. There is a risk that we Christians, by a sort of quietism, may let ourselves be lulled to sleep in the hands of what we imagine is "the good Lord", instead of trying to let ourselves be formed by him who is the living God. The Old Testament brings vividly before our eyes our idolatry, our running away, and helps us to realize our wretchedness, our poverty, enabling us thus to rediscover ourselves among those poor for whom the

---

32 William Kirk Kilpatrick, *Psychological Seduction: The Failure of Modern Psychology* (Nashville/ Camden/New York: Thomas Nelson Publishers, 1983), 83–84.
33 See Deut 32:17 and 1 Cor 10:20.

Kingdom of heaven was made.[34]

Once the caricatures have been exposed and denounced, God reveals His truth, His power, and His holiness preeminently by forgiving sins. The Prophet Hosea depicts this in terms of God overriding His justice by His mercy. God is likened to a husband who discovers that his wife has been unfaithful. He could respond by repudiating her, or, as justice stipulated at the time of Hosea, by delivering her to the penalty of being stoned. But what if this husband, whose wife looked for a more meaningful love with other men, really loves his wife? What if he has defined his happiness in relation to her? What if he simply cannot image any meaningful existence, any semblance of happiness, without her? He cannot bear the thought of living without her, and so he cannot derive any satisfaction at all from the justice that would bring their relationship to an end. Her death would be a death to his love.

The only solution is to forgive her. This is the truth about mercy. Mercy is love that continues to love in the context of its having been rejected. This is what Hosea reveals about God's love for His unfaithful people, and God's holiness is the explanation for it: "I will not execute my fierce anger, I will not again destroy Ephraim; for I am God and not man, the Holy One in your midst" (Hos 11:9). To men to live the call, "be holy, for I am holy" (Lev 11:44), means to "be perfect as your heavenly Father is perfect" (Mt 5:48), and this means to "be merciful, even as your Father is merciful" (Lk 6:36). Man's vocation is to love with the very love of God, to be capable of making a gift of oneself that is so complete and so perfect that two become one and as a result the beloved enters into one's very definition of happiness. It is a love that expresses itself in the words, "I do not want to live without you. I cannot live without you. I will not live without you. I will not accept your rejection of me as an end. I will make it a new beginning by forgiving you."

The only way that descendants of Adam and Eve can arrive at this participation in the holiness of God, which manifests itself as mercy to sinners, is to know themselves as sinners and to receive God's mercy. In order to live by the new commandment that Christ enjoins on His disciples, "that you love one another as I have loved you" (Jn 15:12), it is necessary to have a precise understanding of His love. And because Jesus defines His love as forgiveness of sins—the "no greater love" (Jn 15:13) poured out as "the blood of the covenant ... for the forgiveness of sins" (Mt 26:28)—it is not possible to keep the new commandment without first confronting one's own sins, encountering His mercy, and living in the certainty of having been loved by Him. For, this is what it means to be loved by Him. Only this personal experience of being forgiven can assure that mercy is the daily bread that sustains the Church's life and animates all mission, ministry, apostolate, and service in the Church. For, mercy restores the highest good of man, namely, communion with God, and desiring this

---

34 Barthélemy, *God and His Image*, xxvi.

highest of good for others is the "love of Christ [that] urges us on" (2 Cor 5:14) for mission.

The confrontation with sin and the encounter with God's mercy produce two dispositions that at first glance seem incompatible: humility and audacity. Humility derives from the confrontation with sin, and audacity from the encounter with divine mercy. They interact with one another so as to be a check on one another. By itself, humility might be misconstrued as timidity, as if because I myself am weak and totally dependent on God's grace I am disqualified from saying anything to anyone else about sin. In reality, it is precisely the opposite. Because I am certain of having been efficaciously loved, I know from personal experience the difference between living with the leprosy of sin and enjoyment of being restored to the full health of love. How could I not let others know that there is a power that is greater than leprosy, that there is hope? Whence, the audaciousness of presuming to know others better than they know themselves and to proclaim to them the Good News of God's mercy. I could no more refrain from this proclamation than I could deny my own healing. But, since I did not heal myself, this audacity is tempered by humility. If it must be the case that I am part of the Good News because God's mercy has reached me before reaching others, my role is only as a witness, an exhibit that proves that God's love really does change the human condition. The message is only indirectly about me and directly about God's mercy. By necessity, God and I are found in the same sentence, but He is the acting subject. The Virgin Mary and St. Paul show us the way: "for he who is mighty has done great things *for me*, and holy is his name" (Lk 1:49); "it is no longer I who live, but Christ who lives in me; and the life I now live in the flesh I live by faith in the Son of God, who *loved me* and gave himself *for me*" (Gal 2:20).

The faith resulting from the encounter with God's mercy, necessarily simultaneously a combination of profound humility and audacious boldness, provides Christ's disciples with an interior principle of judgment (*sensus fidei*) that unmasks the idolatrizing propensities of the old man. They instinctively know that any proclamation of the mystery of Christ that avoids the question of sin cannot lead to the paschal mystery and the Eucharist, unless these are rethought or refashioned according to the logic of the old man. The old man strives to disfigure true religion by dismissing sin. But if sin is dismissed then Christ's mission and mercy must be rethought and refashioned accordingly, since He defines them in terms of the forgiveness of sins. And so the old man molds the Church's mission into a facile affirmation of man and of his dignity, and he does this in the name of his own definition of love.

More than fifty years after Vatican II's call for renewal for the reinvigoration of mission, it is necessary once again to recall that charity is the soul of the apostolate, the soul of holiness, and thus the goal of renewal, and that the conversion that consists in the encounter with God's mercy is the single path to holiness. Christ is the only hope for those who need to be loved, and He brings His mercy to them through those who themselves have been saved by it. We are in great need of men and women of deep faith, whose experience of their own sin and of God's mercy is the reality in light of which they assess every activity of the Church, and who are therefore able to call true reform and false reform by their proper names, and to denounce the numerous pseudo-ecclesial activities for what they truly are: so many forms of idolatry. Of course, the Council's renewal entails more than personal *metanoia*. It also concerns the updating (*aggiornamento*) of ecclesial structures. But it is a ruse of the old man to pass off the renewal of structures as an end in itself. The new man must see through this, and take his cue from Jesus' response to those who are shocked at His declaration that He does not know them, that they must depart from Him, and that they are evildoers: "Lord, Lord, did we not spend ourselves on liturgical, institutional, and theological renewal in your name?"[35]

For the participants in the Council, the renewal of structures is entirely subordinate to the holiness that grows through the renewal of hearts through conversion. Their entire value derives from their relation to holiness,[36] the heart of which is charity.[37] Structures are means to the end of holiness; they are also expressions of holiness. The Council puts it this way: "It is of the essence of the Church that she be both human and divine, visible and yet invisibly equipped, eager to act and yet intent on contemplation, present in this world and yet not at home in it; and she is all these things in such wise that in her the human is directed and subordinated to the divine, the visible likewise to the invisible, action to contemplation, and this present world to that city yet to come, which we seek."[38]

Might the temptation to reverse this order and to expend oneself on institutional and even theological renewal at the expense personal renewal of the heart be counted as one of those tactics that the old man employs in order to preserve for himself zones of freedom that in reality are so many forms of enslavement to idolatry? Might it be that until the image of God is sufficiently restored through the conversion of broken and contrite hearts this will necessarily affect the image that we have of Christ's Church, reducing it to an institution that we desire to manipulate to our own expectations rather than to see the Church as the Spouse of Christ and as the Body of Christ? Is there not a risk that the old man offers to Christians of our age a new ecclesiological idolatry?

The hope that drove the writing of this book is that renewed contact with the divinely inspired witness to King David's conversion might contribute in its own modest way to the realization of Vatican II's call to holiness through conversion, and in this way bear the fruit of

---

35 See Mt 7:21.
36 See *CCC*, 773.
37 "Charity is the soul of the holiness to which all are called: it "governs, shapes, and perfects all the means of sanctification (*Lumen gentium*, 42)" (*CCC*, 826).
38 Vatican II, *Sacrosanctum Concilium*, 2.

reinvigoration of the Church's mission to proclaim the Good News of God's mercy and the fulfillment of His plan for mankind.

The Witness of David

The life of King David bears witness to a twofold truth concerning God's plan of love. The first is that, for the accomplishment of His plan, God calls upon human beings to cooperate with Him, to be His fellow-workers.[39] Moses is the preeminent example of this in the Old Testament. God desires to save His people from slavery in Egypt, and He "calls Moses to be his messenger, an associate in his compassion, his work of salvation."[40] As with all the great intercessors and collaborators with God, the *Catechism* emphasizes that Moses must share in God's motive, and this is compassion, or mercy.[41]

The revelation of God's esteem for human dignity and His desire to call those whom He loves to be His collaborators reaches its zenith in the Blessed Virgin Mary. God proposes to her that she be the mother of the Messiah, the Son of God, and she consents by declaring herself the Lord's handmaid.[42] She is the Mother of Mercy, for Jesus is God, and God is love, and in a world marked by sin love reveals itself as mercy:[43] "He [Jesus] Himself, in a certain sense, is mercy."[44] By consenting to be the mother of the Messiah, Mary consents to His entire mission of mercy. Her *fiat* is a "Yes" to every grace of every conversion. In her mission as Mediatrix of all graces, she implores God's mercy for the conversion of sinners. By her maternal love for all of her Son's brothers and sisters, Mary accompanies them every time they rise from falling into sin.[45] Her intercessions correspond to our own: "Holy Mary, Mother of God, pray for us sinners ..." God always answers her prayers because they arise from a heart attuned to God's mercy as no other heart has been or ever will be, and the reason is that she "obtained mercy in a particular and exceptional way, as no other person has."[46] Her participation in Christ's mission of mercy begins with her own experience of mercy. In this way, her mission is simply the fulfillment of the commandment to love others as she has been loved. In Mary, the beatitude for the merciful is most perfectly realized. She whose experience of God's mercy is without equal receives the mercy of her prayers for sinners being answered. The Fatima prayer that is widely attached to the Rosary as the final word of each decade perfectly

---

39 See *CCC*, 306–307.
40 See *CCC*, 2575.
41 See *CCC*, 2571, 2575, 2635, 2844.
42 See Lk 1:38.
43 "[I]n the temporal phase, in human history, which is at the same time the history of sin and death, love must be revealed above all as mercy and must also be actualized as mercy" (John Paul II, *Dives in misericordia*, 8).
44 Ibid., 2.
45 See John Paul II, *Redemptoris Mater*, 52.
46 John Paul II, *Dives in misericordia*, 9.

complements Mary's role as Mother of Mercy: "O my Jesus, forgive us our sins, save us from the fires of hell, lead all souls to Heaven, *especially those most in need of Thy mercy.*"

The conversion of King David and his experience of God's mercy places him among those whose hearts that are attuned to God's mercy and whose mission is essentially to proclaim that mercy to those for whom it is Good News, that is, to those who are "wasting away" (Job 7:16 NJB) and whose "bones are crushed" (Ps 51:8 NJB) by unreconciled guilt. David's praise of God's mercy is not at all an abstract praise of a divine attribute discovered by applying his mind to search the mystery of God. It is a praise that rises from his experience of that mercy, from what God in His mercy has done *for him*. David's praise of God is essentially the same as Mary's: "He Who is merciful has done great things *for me*."

The Penitential Psalms (Psalms 6, 32, 38, 51, 102, 130, 143) bear witness to the working of God's mercy in the life of a sinner, and thereby they give hope to sinners. David is conscious of this. His worship of praising God for His mercy also has a missionary dimension. He is aware that others are observing, waiting to see how things will turn out for the Lord's anointed. David knows that his liturgy of praise to God is simultaneously the fulfillment of his mission to love others has God has loved him when he declares that with the restoration of joy and the sustaining power of God's grace he will teach transgressors the way of God's mercy so that sinners will repent and return to Him.[47]

Like David's liturgy of praise of God for His mercy, the Church's liturgy has a missionary dimension. "For the liturgy," Vatican II teaches, "'through which the work of our redemption is accomplished,' most of all in the divine sacrifice of the Eucharist, is the outstanding means whereby the faithful may express in their lives, *and manifest to others*, the mystery of Christ and the real nature of the true Church."[48] The liturgy is not only the source of the grace that strengthens the faithful's participation in the paschal charity of Christ, which is the soul of the apostolate. The faithful's participation in the liturgy bears witness to what they hold to be the central event in all of history, namely, the paschal mystery of Christ. By participating in the liturgy the faithful show the world that Christ is the cause of their new way of living, of that fully human life that all desire. In this way, the liturgy "shows forth the Church to those who are outside as a sign lifted up among the nations (cf. Is 11:12)..."[49] The liturgy is not just the source of the graces for bearing witness to Christ throughout the daily lives of the faithful. For Vatican II and its renewal, the liturgy is the summit of the mission to proclaim the most wondrous of all His deeds (Ps 71:17), the paschal mystery of Jesus Christ, which fully reveals God's mercy.

---

47 "Restore to me the joy of your salvation, and uphold me with a willing spirit. Then I will teach transgressors your ways, and sinners will return to you" (Ps 51:12–13).
48 Vatican II, *Sacrosanctum Concilium*, 2.
49 Ibid.

This testimonial dimension of liturgy might be compared to the one leper who returned to praise Jesus for having healed him.[50] For someone who did not witness the actual healing, his return to Jesus provides the explanation. His restored health is a gift, and the full truth about it, precisely as a gift, is not known until people know that it was Jesus Who healed Him. And they discover this by observing praise God by thanking Jesus. It is similar with the liturgy. We come to worship God by thanking Him for the mercy He has shown to us. And, just as by returning to praise God by thanking Jesus the one leper receives even more—He is the only one of the ten to whom Jesus says, "Rise and go on your way, your faith has made you well" (Lk 17:19).—so when we return to Jesus in the liturgy to worship Him by thanking Him, we are blessed anew by the mercy of an increase in faith. For, *"through giving thanks for benefits received we merit to receive yet greater benefits."*[51]

David's conversion and mission bear witness to a second truth about God's plan of love. It is that the cooperation with God in the mission of mercy is also for the sake of the cooperator's own sanctification. God does not use human beings as carpenters use saws and hammers, or even as a landowner makes use of servants. Rather, God considers men to be His friends,[52] that is, informed and conscious co-workers, whose collaboration with Him flows from a profound communion with Him in vision and motivation. By making men His partners in mission, God crowns the dignity that He bestows upon them by creating them in His image. That dignity consists in participating in the divine prerogative of communicating goodness to others. The *Catechism* refers to this as the dignity of being causes:

> To human beings God even gives the power of freely sharing in his providence by entrusting them with the responsibility of "subduing" the earth and having dominion over it (cf. Gen 1:26–28). God thus enables men to be intelligent and free causes in order to complete the work of creation, to perfect its harmony for their own good and that of their neighbors.[53]

Active participation in Christ's mission of mercy is not something in addition to communion with God in life, truth, and love. Mission is that communion in action, extended to others.

The Blessed Virgin Mary is the model of these two dimensions of relating to God—personal communion in knowledge and love, and collaboration in mission. This is seen in the relation of the grace of the Immaculate Conception to the grace of Divine Maternity. By the former,

---

50 See Lk 17:12–19.
51 Aquinas, *ST* II-II, Q. 83, a. 17.
52 "No longer do I call you servants, for the servant does not know what his master is doing; but I have called you friends, for all that I have heard from my Father I have made known to you" (Jn 15:15).
53 *CCC*, 307.

Mary is free from all sin; there is nothing in her that can impede the reception of God's love. As a result, she enjoys the most profound personal communion with God, and for this reason she receives the privilege of the most sublime of all missions bestowed on men by God. Her mission is to collaborate with God in the final act of the drama of history of salvation, by being the Mother of the Redeemer. The relation of these two dimensions of Mary's relation to God is seen in Jesus' mysterious words that were occasioned by an anonymous woman shouting out, "Blessed is the womb that bore you, and the breasts that you sucked!" (Lk 11:27). Hearing this, Jesus draws attention to Mary's faith: "Blessed rather are those who hear the word of God and keep it!" (Lk 11:28). Mary's mission as mother is rooted in the faith by which she places herself totally at the disposition of God, in her communion with God, in her holiness. Her mission is that communion, that holiness, in action, extended to others.

The preceding shows that Vatican II's renewed call to holiness and its renewed call to mission are not two separate calls. At the same time, there is a logical priority of the call to holiness. For, the missionary activity of bearing witness to Christ presupposes an encounter with Him, just as the Mary's maternity presupposes the Immaculate Conception and the leper's return to praise Jesus presupposes being healed by Him in a first encounter. Thus, the Council's call to holiness enjoys a certain primacy in relation to the call to the revitalization of the Church's mission. And because conversion is the path to deeper holiness, the indispensable path to the implementation of Vatican II is the path of conversion.

In the New Covenant, there is only one kingdom. It is a kingdom that is not of this world,[54] an interior kingdom resulting from God's reign in men's hearts through the faith by which they freely submit to His will.[55] The boundaries of this kingdom are not geographic but spiritual; they are determined by the influence of the Holy Spirit.[56] During the time of preparation for the definitive revelation of Christ's kingship, His interior kingdom is present and realized through the same faith that constitutes His kingdom as it is fully revealed and established through the paschal mystery.[57] At the same time, another kingdom, an earthly one, accompanies the interior kingdom of Christ during the time of preparation. This is the kingdom of Israel, the geographic area occupied by God's people, the Promised Land. During the time from Israel's taking possession of this land, Christ exercises His kingship through the Law of the covenant, which includes a succession of kings, as well juridical and ceremonial institutions, which visibly distinguish Israel from all other peoples.

The drama of King David's conversion occurs during the time of the coexistence of these two kingdoms. To grasp its unique place in God's

---

54 "My kingship is not of this world" (Jn 18:36).
55 "... the kingdom is within you" (Lk 17:21 DRA).
56 "For the kingdom of God does not mean food and drink but righteousness and peace and joy in the Holy Spirit" (Rom 14:17).
57 Profoundly aware of the unity of God's plan, Aquinas holds that the faith of those in the Old Testament is the same as the faith of those in the New Testament.

plan requires seeing it in relation to two kingdoms, the temporal kingdom of Israel and the kingdom of Christ that is not of this world. The relation of these two kingdoms to one another is an indispensable interpretive key for unlocking the door to the fullness of what God desires to reveal through the conversion of the king whom He chose because he is "a man after His own heart" (1 Sam 13:14).

To bring the inner reality and impact of his conversion to light, it will be useful to divide the life of David into two parts.[58] The goal is to sketch two spiritual profiles of the great king of Israel, one prior to his sin and conversion, and the other following them. The contrast between these two profiles points to a profound transformation that takes place in David's heart. From a young man whose unshakeable confidence in God masks an underlying blindness to sin, the king of Israel becomes a *summa cum laude* graduate of the school of humility, a man whose life becomes a liturgy of praise to God's mercy.

Bold confidence in God's providence is certainly laudable in itself, but when it becomes presumption it obviously calls for a purifying intervention by God. For King David, this will take the form of God allowing him to become aware that his own weakness and sin constitute a far more serious—as well as more insidious—threat to his vocation than any merely external threat. Having relied on the power of the Lord for victory over his earthly enemies, David must learn to trust in the Lord's mercy when he is defeated by the interior enemy of sin.

The passage from the first to the second period is David's sin involving Bathsheba and Uriah, and the conversion resulting from his experience of God's merciful love. The biblical account, along with David's psalms, gives every indication that David's heart had become severely hardened and that, left to himself, he would have remained a ruthless ruler preoccupied with safeguarding his reputation and authority. God's love for David is too great for Him to leave the king in such a state. In God's plan, the sins that David commits, especially the second sin of murder (with the intention of saving face before the people and preserving his prestige), are the occasion for him to become a paradigm of the words of Jesus: "For every one who exalts himself will be humbled, and he who humbles himself will be exalted" (Lk 14:11). By his own sins, David is brought low and humbled; by God's merciful love, his name is exalted to the point of being a title of the Messiah, a title that is associated with God's saving mercy.[59]

The doctrine of the Communion of Saints assures us that King David's mission continues in heaven as he participates in the intercession of the

---

[58] This division of David's life is a slight modification of that given by Fr. Barthélemy in *God and His Image*, 128–145. The following reflections on the conversion of King David draw heavily from this book and Fr. Barthélemy's lectures at the University of Fribourg from 1976–1981.

[59] See multiple texts in which Jesus is hailed as "son of David", with special attention to those texts in which He is called upon to show mercy: Mt 9:27; 12:23; 15:22; 20:30, 31; 21:9, 15.

true King of Israel, the Son of David, Jesus Christ. In heaven, by virtue of the light of the beatific vision, David sees his place in God's plan of salvation. He sees how God makes use of his conversion and his psalms, especially the penitential psalms, to impart to sinners hope in His mercy. David's intercession is the heavenly version of the prayer offered on earth, in faith and hope, "Thy kingdom come, Thy will be done on earth as it is in heaven." This must mean that David's prayers are for the building up of the Church, which in God's plan "is the goal of all things."[60] The Church of Christ is the Kingdom of Heaven, it is the Kingdom that is not of this world, as that Kingdom is realized in faith and in the hope that strains toward heavenly fulfillment. With all the saints, David's intercession expresses his desire to love others as God has loved him. He prays for the fulfillment of the Church's "intimate vocation" of "partaking, in foretaste, in the liturgy of consummate glory."[61] For, it is above all in the liturgy that God's will is done on earth as it is in heaven, as the Church makes the eternal hymn of the Kingdom of Heaven resound when she sings God's praises and gives Him glory Him for the most marvelous of His works of His mercy, the paschal mystery of Jesus Christ.

---

[60] *CCC*, 760.
[61] Vatican II, *Lumen gentium*, 51.

1.
David Prior to His Sin and Conversion: A Spiritual Profile

Prior to examining David's life before and after his conversion, it will be constructive to reflect on his vocation to be king of Israel. For, this vocation establishes the fundamental terms of David's relation to God, and of the drama of his purification and conversion. This will allow us to form some idea of both the gravity and the inner motive of his sins.

The Call of God

Like all vocations, David's to be king of Israel has its origin in the utterly gratuitous choice of God. God had determined the precise day of the event "from before the foundation of the world" (Eph 1:4).[1] God is alone in knowing this plan, until he confides it to the prophet, Samuel, who receives it as a revelation. In His wisdom, God has decreed that David should have absolutely no awareness of it, until the day that God makes it known to him through Samuel. On the day that Samuel anoints him, the future king is preoccupied with his daily duty of tending his father's sheep.[2] Minding one's business, that is, diligently applying oneself in fulfilling the present duties of one's vocation, seems to be a condition most favorable for a divine visitation and the reception of a new vocation. One need only think of God's interventions in the lives of Abraham or Noah, the prophets, the Blessed Virgin Mary, or the fishermen that Jesus first called as disciples. Jesus reveals God's high regard for conscientious attention to the present duties that disclose God's will: "Blessed is that servant whom his master when he comes will find so doing" (Mt 24:46). Fidelity to the God-given responsibilities of today is the best preparation for being faithful to the responsibilities that come from heaven for tomorrow. For the Lord, it is a principle, "He who is faithful in a very little is faithful also in much" (Lk 16:10). David had not been haughty, he did take an initiative, he did not position himself in any way. He was quite simply content in his current state.[3]

The unexpected nature of David's call thrusts him into a personal experience of the divine sovereignty, which takes an absolute initiative at the beginning of all things in the act of creation, and at the beginning of the

---

1   The expression, "before (from, since) the foundation of the world," occurs several other times in the New Testament (Mt 13:35; 25:34; Jn 17:24; 1 Pet 1:20; Rev 13:8). It conveys the sovereignly free plan of God that He conceived without any dependence on creation, a plan that He fulfills in history.
2   See 1 Sam 16:11.
3   "I have learned, in whatever state I am, to be content" (Phil 4:11).

creation of His people, in the call of Abraham. A thousand years later, Jesus will confirm this pattern of God's sovereign initiative-taking in His dealings with the apostles: "You did not choose me, but I chose you" (Jn 15:16). On the day that David becomes aware of God's call, there were, no doubt, numerous conscientious Hebrews intent on fulfilling the responsibilities of their vocation. From among them all, the Lord chose David. What appears capricious to us and takes David, his father, and even Samuel by surprise, is supremely ordered in God's wisdom. The leap from shepherd to king is something that no human mind could conceive;[4] it is something that is impossible for man yet possible for God.[5] For that very reason it is due solely to the Lord's sovereign initiative. God is king over all creation.[6]

David does not make himself king, nor is this privilege an honor due to him. He has done nothing out of the ordinary to prepare for it, other than to be faithful in fulfilling the Lord's will in the household of his father, Jesse. Precisely in this his call reproduces the pattern of Israel's origins and initiates him into the line of Abraham's faith, not merely his genetic line. Suddenly, the story of Abraham's call becomes much more than a lesson of history stored in the memory of things that occurred long ago but have no meaning for the present. The God Whose interventions shape that history intervenes again, in the life of this young man, David, and what he knows and believes about Abraham makes it possible for him to grasp something of what is now happening to him. As a member of God's chosen people and a man destined to represent God as their king, David's spirituality must be based on a profound awareness of the mystery of divine election, that God did not call him because of his righteousness,[7] and that his strength and successes are not his own, but the gifts of God.[8]

God's election of David as king is so far beyond the calculus of men that it takes even Samuel by surprise. Sent by God to the house of Jesse, the prophet knows that God has chosen one of his sons. Upon seeing one of them, perhaps the eldest, Samuel thinks he has discovered God's choice, but God corrects him. He closely examines the seven sons who are present, and one at a time God leads him to understand that none of them is His choice. Samuel is brought to ask if Jesse has any other sons, and he learns that there is one other. It is Jesse's youngest, named David, and he was busy tending the sheep. Upon seeing him, God makes Samuel realize that he is the one, and Samuel bestows on David the sacred anointing.[9]

The biblical narrative about the choice of David conveys a fundamental truth about the way of God. Samuel needs divine guidance in discerning who the future king of Israel will be because God desires a king whose heart is like His own, and only God can discern which human heart

---

4   See 1 Cor 2:9.
5   See Lk 18:27; 1:37.
6   See Judg 9:12.
7   See Deut 9:6.
8   See Deut 8:17–8.
9   See 1 Sam 16:5–13.

reflects His own. As Samuel well knows regarding the Lord's choice of David, "The Lord has sought out a man after his own heart" (1 Sam 13:14). God sees more deeply than Samuel, who can only judge by appearances. God alone can read the hearts of men.[10] The heart is a symbol for the very mystery of man, made in God's image.[11] It is the place of decision, truth, encounter, covenant,[12] and judgment, where truth is discerned and its rights are recognized and upheld. In seeking a king with a heart after His own heart, God is looking for a man who will judge as He judges, that is, in keeping with the truth. It will be a full millennium before God's own Son fully reveals what it means for a man to make the judgment of God a reality on earth. "I judge; and my judgment is just, because I seek not my own will but the will of him who sent me" (Jn 5:30). With David, we are in the period of preparation, the time of expectation of the Lord coming "to judge the world with righteousness, and the peoples with truth" (Ps 96:13). This time arrives with Jesus, Who says to Pilate: "My kingship is not of this world... For this I was born, and for this I have come into the world, to bear witness to the truth" (Jn 18:36–37).

The king's office and prerogative is to assure justice, and truth is the assurance of justice. The king's task, then, is to determine the truth, "to discern good and evil" (2 Sam 14:17), and the act by which he does this is called a just judgment. A pure heart is necessary if a king is to avoid being influenced by anything other than the truth itself. Such an act of judgment by David's son and heir to the throne, Solomon, is etched in the memory of Israel, and thus in the memory of the Church.[13] When two women were brought to him, both claiming to be the mother of an infant, Solomon displays his wisdom by the manner in which he arrives at the truth. By ordering a soldier to cut the child into two pieces, one for each of the claimants, he creates a situation calculated to bring out into the open the self-sacrificing nature of the real mother's love. He knows the heights of self-renouncement to which a mother's love can rise.[14] He knows that, if necessary, a mother will forego all the joys of the maternal bond and of watching her child grow. Solomon knows that the real mother will choose a lifetime in grief being deprived of her son rather than to see her child

---

10 See 1 Sam 16:7; Jer 11:20.
11 On this John Paul II observes, "In its penetrating analysis of 'the modern world', the Second Vatican Council reached that most important point of the visible world that is man, by penetrating like Christ the depth of human consciousness and by making contact with the inward mystery of man, which in Biblical and non-Biblical language is expressed by the word 'heart'" (*Redemptor hominis*, 8).
12 See *CCC*, 2563.
13 See 1 Kings 3:16–28.
14 This mother's love renounces her just claim as the child's true mother, for the sake of embracing a higher demand of her maternal love. Her love is totally focused on her child's well-being, despite the cost to her, that is, despite the wound inflicted on that very love as a result of being separated from her child. In this, the mother is conformed to the heart of God, which recoils within Him at the thought of being separated from His people (see Hos 11:8–9). Benedict XVI comments on this text, that God's love is "so great that it turns God against himself, his love against his justice" (*Deus caritas est*, 10).

harmed. When the true mother cedes her rights and asks that the baby be given to the other woman, Solomon hands over her child to her. "And," as Scripture relates, "all Israel heard of the judgment which the king had rendered; and they stood in awe of the king, because they perceived that the wisdom of God was in him, to render justice" (1 Kings 3:28).

When a judgment is truthful it is called a just or righteous judgment.[15] This is the judgment awaited by those who are confident that they are on the side of the truth, like the mother of the disputed infant. It is the judgment that David expects from God when Saul persecutes him. In these cases, the measure of the truth of justice is the person who is wronged and whose only hope is in a just judge. But what a difference there is when it is a question of a judgment concerning sinners! If sin is the measure of a just judgment, if sinners are to be awarded what they truly deserve, then a just judgment can only bring punishment and despair. Only if there is a different measure for a just judgment can sinners have any hope when they appear before their King and Judge.

Jesus is the king who judges justly,[16] and thus He fulfills the Psalm: "Give the king your justice, O God, and your righteousness to the royal son! May he judge your people with righteousness" (Ps 72:1–2). In one of the greatest messianic texts of the Old Testament, Isaiah foresees that "with righteousness shall [the Messiah] judge the poor, and decide with equity for the meek of the earth" (Is 11:3–4). Jesus judges not by appearances, but "with right judgment" (Jn 7:24). The just judgment of Jesus establishes the kingdom that is "not of this world" (Jn 18:36) because the truth that is the basis of His judgment is not of this world. It is the truth about God's merciful love. This mercy can be revealed on earth, but its origin is heavenly. Only Jesus, who is from heaven, can reveal it on earth, and He does so definitively in the Paschal Mystery of His sacrifice for the forgiveness of sins.

In the bible, the king's throne stands as a symbol of authority to make such just judgments.

> [4] For you have maintained my just cause;
> you have sat on the throne giving righteous judgment....
> [7] But the Lord sits enthroned for ever,
> he has established his throne for judgment;
> [8] and he judges the world with righteousness,
> he judges the people with equity. (Psalm 9:4, 7–8)

This throne-symbolism invites us to see the theme of Christ's just judgment, based on the truth about God's mercy, in a number of New Testament texts. Jesus' mission to reveal His heavenly Father's merciful love is inseparable from the throne He receives as the son of David and the corresponding office to judge: "the Lord God will give to him the throne of

---

15 See Deut 16:18; Is 1:21; Sir 32:20.
16 See Jn 5:30.

his father David" (Lk 1:32). When the one who has been appointed "to judge the living and the dead" (1 Pet 4:5) returns, it will be "in his glory, and all the angels with him, then he will sit on his glorious throne" (Mt 25:31). To take his seat on this throne conveys His authority to judge. He is about to execute the just judgment of God. Indeed, what follows in Matthew's Gospel is the vivid description of the separation of sheep from goats, according to the truth of people's actions in relation to the poor and needy, that is, the unloved. The same symbolism of the throne occurs in a profoundly reassuring passage in the Letter to the Hebrews:

> [12] For the word of God is living and active, sharper than any two-edged sword, piercing to the division of soul and spirit, of joints and marrow, and discerning the thoughts and intentions of the heart. [13] And before him no creature is hidden, but all are open and laid bare to the eyes of him with whom we have to do. [14] Since then we have a great high priest who has passed through the heavens, Jesus, the Son of God, let us hold fast our confession. [15] For we have not a high priest who is unable to sympathize with our weaknesses, but one who in every respect has been tempted as we are, yet without sinning. [16] Let us then with confidence draw near to the throne of grace, that we may receive mercy and find grace to help in time of need. (Hebrews 4:12–16)

Jesus sits on a throne of grace, and the just judgment that He issues from this throne is one of mercy. Mercy is the hidden truth about God, and only Jesus can reveal it through His just judgments. This is why His kingdom, established on the basis of this truth, is not of this world. Even though it is realized in this world, its dynamic force is entirely heavenly. The truth that guides all judgment in this kingdom is the truth that God is "rich in mercy" (Eph 2:4). This is why there is no room for fear in facing His judgment,[17] for even when our hearts are conscious of sin, it is not sin that has the last word but God's merciful love. St. John insists on this point:

> [19] By this we shall know that we are of the truth, and reassure our hearts before him whenever our hearts condemn us; [20] for God is greater than our hearts, and he knows everything. [21] Beloved, if our hearts do not condemn us, we have confidence before God. (1 John 3:19–21)

David's place in God's plan, his vocation, is to represent God, the true King of Israel, to the chosen people of his time, and to foreshadow the kingship of Jesus Christ. His vocation is to assure a reign of justice so that

---

17 "In this is love perfected with us, that we may have confidence for the day of judgment" (1 Jn 4:17).

every member of God's chosen people could enjoy the blessings of the covenant that God established with them.

It should not be forgotten what having a king means for the first generations of Hebrews who took possession of the land that God had promised to Abraham. It signifies that they are constituted in the freedom that is God's gift to them. They are free from subjugation to a foreign power. The purpose of this freedom is that they can serve God, that is, worship Him, without fear.[18] So long as they have a king, they are slaves to no one. This explains the thinking of the people when they insist on having a king: they want to be like the other nations.[19] They desire assurance that they will not fall into slavery again. So, they choose Saul, apparently because of his virility and imposing stature.[20]

God reacts to this seemingly reasonable request by revealing that the desire for a king is a rejection of Him.[21] God is the One Who alone can assure the freedom from domination that they seek. For, this freedom is His gift, and His gift alone, to them. God interprets the people's rejection of Him as their failure to live according to the logic of gift. The land that they occupy is theirs only by reason of His utterly gratuitous promise to Abraham and His fidelity to that promise by liberating them from slavery in Egypt. They should live with a consciousness that this land and the freedom they enjoy in it is pure gift. All they need do is recall the mighty works that God performed in order to deliver them from slavery and to lead them into the Promised Land. The people's desire for a king is, in the end, no different than turning to other gods. Both are rooted in the people thinking that there is something they must do, other than to observe the terms of covenant, in order to assure their freedom and abundance.[22]

Through Samuel, God responds to His people's lack of faith in Him by acquiescing to their desire to be like the other nations by having a king.

---

18 See Lk 1:74. God liberates Israel from slavery in Egypt so that His people could offer Him worship "without fear," and Israel looks forward to a definitive liberation from fear. The Canticle of Zechariah sings praise for this definitive liberation being heralded in the birth of John the Baptist and fulfilled in the mystery of Christ. Because the opposite of fear is *parrhesía* (bold confidence), this links the Canticle of Zechariah with the *parrhesía* of 1 Jn 3:21, 1 Jn 4:17, and Heb 4:16. The NJB translates *parrhesía* in these verses as "fearless," "fearlessly," and "no fear." In this way, these texts carry forward a biblical theme that actually begins with the perfect harmony and lack of fear that Adam and Eve enjoyed prior to their sin, which because of their sin was lost and replaced by fear (Gen 3:10). The *Catechism* interprets this fear as the effect of an erroneous concept of God. Assenting to the serpent's accusation against God, Adam and Eve come to think of God as jealous of His prerogatives, and this causes them to be afraid of Him (see *CCC*, 399). Because Christ vanquishes sin, He thereby vanquishes fear. He does to by revealing God's merciful love.

19 See 1 Sam 8:5, 7, 20.

20 See 1 Sam 9:2; 10:23–24. The juxtaposition of these indicators of the criteria for the acclamation of Saul as king with the Lord's instructions to Samuel regarding the choice of David is poignant: "But the Lord said to Samuel, "Do not look on his appearance or on the height of his stature ...; for the Lord sees not as man sees; man looks on the outward appearance, but the Lord looks on the heart" (1 Sam 16:7).

21 See 1 Sam 8:7–8; 10:19.

22 1 Sam 8:8; 10:18–19.

They will, indeed, be just like other nations, the kings of which lord it over their people rather than serve them. Samuel details how the people will suffer under their kings.23 This is a superb illustration of a principle set forth in the Book of Wisdom, that "one is punished by the very things by which he sins" (Wis 11:16). Faithful to His first covenant with men, the covenant of creation, God will always respect men's free will, even to the point of handing them over to their own erroneous ideas about what constitutes human fulfillment, or happiness.24 For Israel, the negative consequences of having their will for a king fulfilled will be to make them long for a truly virtuous, righteous king. Ultimately, this longing will be fulfilled in Jesus Christ.

David's assumption of his royal office comes at the outset of this developing theology of kingship in Israel. He does so under a sign of contradiction, that is, under the sign of sin. This means, first, that Israel's desire for a king is rooted in the people's desire to be like the other nations, so that it entails a rejection of God as Israel's true king. Second, David's place is to succeed Saul after the Lord rejects him because of his sins of disobedience. Third, it means that his mission is to protect Israel from the surrounding enemies. He must defend Israel against the aggressions of the neighboring peoples, whose military success is a function of Israel's fidelity or infidelity. David is charged with leading the people in observing all of the terms of the covenant, lest the cyclical history depicted in the Book of Judges repeat itself and the Lord permit Israel's defeat as a punishment for the people's sins.25

The third aspect of David being king under the sign of sin takes center stage in these reflections. David will learn that he must protect Israel from himself, from the misuse of his authority. But this is the one thing that he is incapable of doing. He cannot fulfill his vocation, for he is a son of Adam, and the mystery of iniquity as at work in him. God had warned that Israel's kings would subject the people to slavery. This warning is fully realized when David is defeated, for a time, by a twofold lust, for another man's wife and for the power of his office as king. David exhibits the same domination over another that characterizes Adam's relation to Eve as a

---

23 1 Sam 8:11–18.
24 See Rom 1:24, 26, 28.
25 See Judg 2:10–23. The full logic of this correlation between infidelity to God and defeat by Israel's enemies will become clear only with the return from the Exile. Prior to that, God raises up judges, through whom He brings military victory over Israel's enemies. In contrast, there is no military victory that brings about the return of the Exiles and the restoration of Jerusalem. Rather, the people's captivity, their "period of service" (Is 40:2 NJB), ends when their purification and conversion are complete. Even with the armed victories of the judges, God makes it clear that He is the author of those victories (see Judges 2:18), that only He can deliver His people from their enemies. Similarly, the edict of Cyrus is the result of the Lord "stirring up the spirit of Cyrus" (2 Chr 36:22). The return to national sovereignty, as a result of all of these events, is the sign of the Lord's continuing favor and of His forgiveness. In the New Testament, the sign of Christ's victory is life in the Holy Spirit.

consequence of their sin.26 The root cause of this domination is a disordered love of self. An internal domination—which St. Paul so graphically describes as a war between the desires of the body and the law in one's mind, resulting in being held captive by the law of sin27—lies at the root of David's external domination vis-à-vis Bathsheba, Uriah, and his fellow soldiers. This twofold lust overpowers the order of love in the interior kingdom of David's heart, and this results in an overthrow of the order of justice in the exterior kingdom. The king's office is to serve, even as the vocation of husbands is to serve their wives.28 But such kingly service presupposes an interior self-mastery.29 For Bathsheba, Uriah, and the men along with him who are the victims of David's domination, David's own words are verified: "Let us fall into the hand of the Lord, for his mercy is great; but let me not fall into the hand of man" (2 Sam 24:14).30

All of this must be kept in mind in order to grasp something of the divine wisdom in God's choice of David to rule His people. God is faithful even when His people are not, and His merciful love is greater than the worst sins. God's choice of David bears a striking resemblance to Jesus' selection of Peter to be the rock upon which He builds His Church.31 Both men betray the one who called them, and fail, for a time, in their mission. Their actions appear to nullify their vocations. Grace and mercy, however, triumph over their sin. Both David and Peter undergo a profound conversion, though not without equally profound suffering. The terms of Peter's conversion are more obviously christological, since he denies his King just hours after Jesus' royal entrance into Jerusalem, and Peter will eventually be configured to his crucified Lord most literally through his own crucifixion. Christian faith can already detect the dynamics of the mystery of Christ in the drama of King David's conversion, and this is a key to unlocking the role that Israel's second king is called to play in divine revelation, which is moving toward its culmination in Jesus Christ. Jesus is the definitive and perfect King, but His kingship does not exclude that His people participate in it, even if there will be shortcomings. In fact, participation in His mystery is precisely what God has always intended. As the *Catechism* puts it: "Christ enables us to live all that he himself lived, and he lives it in us."32 Everyone is called to be a king in and with the King of kings.

David's conversion teaches us what is required if we are to reign with Christ.33 This is why it is important to attend to the transformation of his heart through the conversion that begins with a profound awareness of his sin

---

26 See Gen 3:16.
27 See Rom 7:23.
28 See Eph 5:25–27.
29 See John Paul II, *Redemptor hominis*, 21.
30 See Ps 118:9: "It is better to take refuge in the Lord than to put confidence in princes."
31 See Mt 16:18.
32 *CCC*, 521.
33 See 2 Tim 2:12; Rev 20:6.

and ends with an equally profound discovery of the depths of God's mercy. In the first part of his life, David is especially aware of the external threats to his reign, and he exhibits a deep trust in God to defend his cause. His sin and conversion inaugurate a second phase, wherein he becomes painfully aware that there is another order of threat to his vocation as king, namely, the interior threat of sin. David's conversion entails a transformation in his hope in God, from trusting in God for protection from his external enemies to relying on His merciful and forgiving love so that he not be vanquished by the internal enemy of sin.

David in Israel's Tradition of Faith and Prayer

The chief characteristic of David's profile from the first period, from his anointing by Samuel until his sins of adultery and murder, is bold confidence in God's help and protection. His faith is summed up: "This I know, that God is for me" (Ps 56:9). With God on his side, he receives the anointing to be king, slays Goliath, and he prospers in all that he does. The first Psalm sketches this profile:

> ¹ Blessed is the man
> who walks not in the counsel of the wicked,
>   nor stands in the way of sinners,
> nor sits in the seat of scoffers;
> ² but his delight is in the law of the Lord,
> and on his law he meditates day and night.
> ³ He is like a tree
> planted by streams of water,
>   that yields its fruit in its season,
> and its leaf does not wither.
> In all that he does, he prospers. (Psalm 1:1–3)

David enjoys God's favor, and his exploits bring with them the favor of the people.[34] Yet, as so often happens, God's blessings show themselves to be a two-edged sword. David's life of divine blessing is lived under the sign of contradiction. On the one hand, the Lord has called him to be king, and with this call David can rightly assume that the Lord will be his guardian, the guarantor of success. On the other hand, the Lord's definition of success confounds human expectations. David is a man of prayer, as the psalms attest. Still, the lesson to be learned is that God measures success in terms of love, and thus in terms of the condition of one's heart. While men look exteriorly for evidence of God's blessings, God looks to the heart. While our prayers are often directed to heaven for deliverance from external enemies, God's concern is with relationships of love. "Transformation of the praying heart is the first response to our petition."[35]

---

34   See 1 Sam 18:7; 21:11; 29:5.
35   *CCC*, 2739.

The great lesson that David must learn is that there are two enemies whose aim is to overthrow his kingship. One is external, taking the form of the military threat of the Philistines, Saul's jealousy and persecution, the rebellion of his own son, Absalom, and later the attempt at usurpation of his throne by another son, Adonijah. The second enemy is internal; it is David's own weakness, his capacity to be blinded by desires of the flesh and ambition. His propensity to sin will cause him to fail to live up to the high demands of his office. It is the transition from the first preoccupation with external threats, to focus on the internal threat of sin, which interests us here.

Regarding external enemies, the psalms preserve precious witnesses to David's prayers. To grasp their significance, it is essential to keep in mind that the prayer of David (and the Psalmist) is situated within a tradition. The foundation of that tradition is the history of God's initiatives of love and power in behalf of the people He has chosen to be His own. David is able to voice his desires to God because He knows that God has responded to the cries of His people in the past.

> Deliver me from my enemies, O my God,
> protect me from those who rise up against me. (Psalm 59:1)

> My God in his steadfast love will meet me;
> my God will let me look in triumph on my enemies. (Psalm 59:10)

> Hear my voice, O God, in my complaint;
> preserve my life from dread of the enemy. (Psalm 64:1)

> Though I walk in the midst of trouble,
> you preserve me against the wrath of my enemies;
> you stretch out your hand,
> and your right hand delivers me. (Psalm 138:7)

> Deliver me, O Lord, from my enemies!
> I have fled to you for refuge! (Psalm 143:9)

> Arise, O Lord, in your anger,
> lift yourself up against the fury of my enemies;
> awake, O my God; you have appointed a judgment. (Psalm 7:6)

The judgment to which David appeals here is God's just judgment in favor of the poor (himself) and against his enemies. David is petitioning the Lord to act in a way that exposes the truth about his special relation to the Lord and his enemies' opposition to the Lord's plans for him, as God had done when He executed His judgments in Egypt *in behalf of* His people and *against* the Egyptians.[36]

And when it appears that his prayers have not been answered and that all is lost, his soul is filled with questions to put to God:

> [9] I say to God, my rock:
> "Why have you forgotten me?
>   Why do I go mourning
> because of the oppression of the enemy?"
> [10] As with a deadly wound in my body,
> my adversaries taunt me,
>   while they say to me continually,
> "Where is your God?" (Psalm 42:9–10)

As always, prayer of petition is rooted in doctrine, in the truth about God. David can pray for deliverance from his enemies, or complain that God appears to have forgotten him and the covenant between them, because he knows his history. He knows of God's mighty works that have accompanied Israel, from the exodus out of Egypt to the conquest and taking possession of the Promised Land. "How great are your works, O Lord!" is the constant refrain.[37] To remember the great things that He-Who-is-mighty has done for His people[38] is to make an act of faith that leads to encouragement and confident hope.

> [1] The Lord is my light and my salvation;
> whom shall I fear?
>   The Lord is the stronghold of my life;
> of whom shall I be afraid?
> [2] When evildoers assail me,
> to devour my flesh,
>   my adversaries and foes,
> they shall stumble and fall.
> [3] Though a host encamp against me,
> my heart shall not fear;
>   though war arise against me,
> yet I will be confident. (Psalm 27:1–3)

For David to find himself assailed by enemies is to find himself in the same position as Israel under the oppression of the Egyptians. For David, as for all the people of Israel, to make an act of faith is above to call to call to mind that when Israel cried out under the yoke of slavery, God heard

---

36   See Ex 12:12.
37   See Ps 92:5; 104:24; 105:2.
38   See Lk 1:49.

their cry and intervened to set them free.[39] Prayer of petition is the expression of the hope that God will act today as He has in the past.

> [1] Incline your ear, O Lord, and answer me,
> for I am poor and needy.
> [2] Preserve my life, for I am godly;
> save your servant who trusts in you.
>   You are my God; [3] have mercy on me, O Lord,
> for to you do I cry all the day.
> [4] Gladden the soul of your servant,
> for to you, O Lord, do I lift up my soul.
> [5] For you, O Lord, are good and forgiving,
> abounding in mercy to all who call on you.
> [6] Give ear, O Lord, to my prayer;
> listen to my cry of supplication.
> [7] In the day of my trouble I call on you,
> for you do answer me.
> [8] There is none like you among the gods, O Lord,
> nor are there any works like yours.
> [9] All the nations you have made shall come
> and bow down before you, O Lord,
> and shall glorify your name.
> [10] For you are great and do wondrous things,
> you alone are God. (Psalm 86:1–10)

To think that the way of the Lord has changed, that His great works are a thing of the past and that the Lord no longer stretches forth His strong arm to protect His people—this is the cause of desolation and sorrow:

> [1] I cry aloud to God,
> aloud to God, that he may hear me.
> [2] In the day of my trouble I seek the Lord;
> in the night my hand is stretched out without wearying;
> my soul refuses to be comforted.
> [3] I think of God, and I moan;
> I meditate, and my spirit faints.
> [4] You keep my eyelids from closing;
> I am so troubled that I cannot speak.
> [5] I consider the days of old,
> I remember the years long ago.
> [6] I commune with my heart in the night;

---

39 "And God heard their groaning, and God remembered his covenant with Abraham, with Isaac, and with Jacob" (Ex 2:24); "I have heard the groaning of the people of Israel whom the Egyptians hold in bondage and I have remembered my covenant. Say therefore to the people of Israel, 'I am the Lord, and I will bring you out from under the burdens of the Egyptians, and I will deliver you from their bondage, and I will redeem you with an outstretched arm and with great acts of judgment" (Ex 6:5–6). See Acts 7:34.

> I meditate and search my spirit:
> ⁷ "Will the Lord spurn for ever,
> and never again be favorable?
> ⁸ Has his steadfast love for ever ceased?
> Are his promises at an end for all time?
> ⁹ Has God forgotten to be gracious?
> Has he in anger shut up his compassion?"
> ¹⁰ I say, "It is my grief
> that the right hand of the Most High has changed." (Psalm 77:1–10)

There is only one thing to do, and that is to recall the Lord's fidelity, as seen in His great works in the past.

> ¹¹ I will call to mind the deeds of the Lord;
> yes, I will remember your wonders of old.
> ¹² I will meditate on all your work,
> and muse on your mighty deeds.
> ¹³ Your way, O God, is holy.
> What god is great like our God?
> ¹⁴ You are the God who works wonders,
> who have manifested your might among the peoples. (Psalm 77:11–14)

The great temptation against faith and hope is to doubt whether God will be faithful to His covenant and continue to intervene when His people are in straits. To fail to so recall the past fidelities of the Lord and to derive from this remembering a patient but firm hope is to rebel against God by taking one's life into one's own hands.[40] Calculating and acting as if the future depended entirely on one's own providence is, in effect, to forget the abundant evidence of God's fidelity and to proceed "as if God does not exist"[41] and thus as if one has to rely solely on one's own wisdom and power to shape a meaningful future.

Such is the faith and prayer of David at the time when his very life is threatened by Saul, Israel's first king, whose jealousy becomes a consuming fire. Living his vocation in the midst of opposition and threats, David is resolute in trusting in the God who called him to be king. In this he personifies the faith and spirituality of Israel. It is a spirituality of resolute hope in the face of seemingly insurmountable threats to that hope's fulfillment. This same resolution was previously seen in the testing of Abraham, as he confronts the contradiction of being directed to sacrifice his son, Isaac, who is the son of God's promise. In the face of this contradiction, Abraham clings to what he knows of God: "God will

---

40   See Ps 106:7.
41   "To live as if God does not exist" is the description of John Paul II and Benedict XVI of the attitude of the faith-less.

provide" (Gen 22:8).[42] Indeed, the Lord provides a way out of what looks like the defeat of His promises. St. Paul conveys the essence of this spirituality in the incisive phrase, "In hope he believed against hope" (Rom 4:18). That is to say, when there is no evidence that God's promise will be fulfilled, when everything indicates that His promise cannot be fulfilled, Abraham remembers Who the God of the promise is, overrides the natural interpretation of all the evidence, and places all of his hope in God. Faced with a contradiction, he believes that God cannot contradict Himself.

This is precisely what the *Catechism* says about the bold prayer of Moses at that point in the desert when God threatened to destroy the very people He had set free from slavery in Egypt.[43] Moses' faith, that is, his knowledge of God and His ways, brings him to confront the contradiction of the situation with a prayer of audacious boldness, based on his conviction that "God is love; he is therefore righteous and faithful; he cannot contradict himself; he must remember his marvelous deeds, since his glory is at stake, and he cannot forsake this people that bears his name."[44] The prophets also exhibit this kind of bold faith and hope when they proclaim that the promises of God remain in force even when His people are defeated and deported from the Promised Land. Israel lives its faith in an incorruptible hope that God's promises are fulfilled in the context of contradiction, when its vocation to be His people is most threatened.

This spirituality reaches its zenith in the death of Jesus of Nazareth, Who, on the night before His crucifixion, gives thanks to God for the victory of the resurrection *before* it happens, confident of a future in which His disciples incessantly memorialize His victory by fulfilling His command: "Do this in remembrance of me" (Lk 22:19). This is the faith and hope of the Virgin Mary who, "standing at the foot of the Cross ... is the witness, humanly speaking, of the complete negation of these words," that is, the words of Gabriel at the Annunciation regarding the kingdom without end.[45] How can a kingdom extend throughout time if the King dies? Yet Mary hopes against hope, calling to mind the marvelous works of God throughout salvation history, knowing that "with God nothing will be impossible" (Lk 1:37), and that God has the power even to raise the dead to life.[46]

Before turning to consider an event that manifests David's bold confidence in God in a situation of contradiction, it is important to recall that there will be a shift of focus in David's life. In this early stage, David experiences the contradiction between his call by God to be king and the threats to the fulfillment of his vocation principally as external threats. A primary feature of his conversion is that it leads him to redirect his vision to the internal threat of his own weakness and sin. In this, too, there is a personal recapitulation of the experience of Israel as a people.

---

42   See Gen 22:14.
43   See Ex 32:7–14.
44   *CCC*, 2577.
45   John Paul II, *Redemptoris Mater*, 18.
46   See Heb 11:19.

Understandably enough, because Israel had been enslaved in Egypt and the power of God showed itself by the mighty works that resulted in their liberation, it is engrained in the consciousness of the chosen people that the chief threat to their freedom is political and military in nature. This leads them to translate the covenant into political and military terms, and into an understanding of freedom as national sovereignty, the opposite of political subservience. It will require centuries before the divine pedagogy leads them fully to realize that His primary concern is about the interior enemy, namely, sin.

This pedagogy reaches its climax in the discernment that Israel's defeats, and ultimately the Exile, are due to sin. That there are two dimensions to slavery, one external and the other internal, is already conveyed in the experience of Moses, forty years before the Exodus.[47] On two successive days he visits the Hebrew slaves. On the first day he observes an Egyptian taskmaster mercilessly beating a Hebrew slave. True to a spirit of solidarity and justice, he intervenes and kills the Egyptian. The next day he returns, and upon seeing two Hebrews in dispute, Moses attempts to intercede, but they resent his initiative and rebuff him. These two episodes epitomize two forms of slavery, the first, Israel's domination by another nation, and the second, the exploitation of one Hebrew by another. They must have left an indelible mark on the memory of Moses, the great legislator; for, his great concern in crafting the Law was to assure both the freedom of Israel from subjugation to foreign powers and the freedom of each member of the chosen people in relation to other members.[48]

The people of Israel, then, live their vocation as God's chosen people under a sign of contradiction, always confronting a twofold threat. The early temptation will be to focus on the external threat and to neglect the internal threat of sin. Over time the people will learn that the greatest threat to its vocation is the interior reality of sin. If God is going to make it possible for Israel to be His people, in the fullest sense, sin will have to be purified. If His people are to be treated according to the dignity of being made in God's image, they will have to cooperate with God, and the necessary first step in cooperation is to arrive at seeing what God sees. Because what He sees, above all else, is man's dignity as image of God and the ruination of that dignity by sin, and His own mercy, He must lead His people to this twofold knowledge.

---

47 See Ex 2:11–15.
48 "The ten commandments, like the whole Law which is their commentary, have no other aim in view than to preserve Israel from a twofold slavery into which both ancient and modern civilizations have fallen and continue to fall. On one side there is an *exterior* slavery which would supplant the people's exclusive dependence on the Almighty. On the other side there is the whole master-slave relationship which would put each individual in danger of being no longer immediately dependent on the Almighty, since one or the other of his brothers would blot out that dependence by usurped authority" (Barthélemy, *God and His Image*, 75).

David's Confidence in God's Protection

In light of the preceding sketch of how David represents Israel's faith at the time, his reaction to Saul's persecution provides us with a profile of his spiritual mindset. The accolades of the people occasioned by David's victory over Goliath trigger another man's jealousy, and it is not just any man, but Saul, Israel's first king:

> [8] And Saul was very angry.... [9] And Saul eyed David from that day on. [10] And the next day an evil spirit from God rushed upon Saul.... [12] Saul was afraid of David, because the Lord was with him but had departed from Saul. (1 Samuel 18:8–12)

Consumed by envy, Saul sets out to destroy David. To escape his wrath, David becomes a fugitive, making a desolate region his haven. At a certain point, with Saul in pursuit, David and his followers take refuge in a cave. Unaware that they occupy it, Saul enters the cave in order, as the story narrates, "to relieve himself" (1 Sam 24:3). With the king in a most undignified and vulnerable position, David's men see this as a gift from heaven. It is obvious to them that God has delivered David's enemy into his hands and has thereby honored his covenant with David. With a quick thrust of the sword Saul would be dead, and David could assume his throne.

This is not so obvious to David. In contrast to the logic of his soldiers, David is obedient to a higher logic. David strikes at the king with his sword, but rather than to kill him, he is content simply to cut off a swath from Saul's robe. The strategy that David executes here becomes clear when, after Saul leaves the cave and is, presumably, at a safe distance, he calls after the king and holds the swath of garment to prove to Saul that he does not intend to bring the king of Israel to ruin. His argument is compelling: though he could have taken the king's life, he did not. "See, my father, the skirt of your robe in my hand;" declares David, "for by the fact that I cut off the skirt of your robe, and did not kill you, you may know and see that there is no wrong or treason in my hands. I have not sinned against you, though you hunt my life to take it" (1 Sam 24:11).

The undeniability of the combination of the swath of his robe and David's disclosure of his motive leave Saul helpless before the truth, and his heart is deeply moved.[49] From here, the narrative continues with a vivid indication of David's spiritual state at the time. He exhibits a profound respect for the office of king, and this seems to be a point that the text is at pains to make evident:

> [5] And afterward David's heart struck him, because he had cut off Saul's skirt. [6] He said to his men, "The Lord forbid that I should do this thing to my lord, the Lord's anointed, to put

---

49 See 1 Sam 24:16–22.

forth my hand against him, seeing as he is the Lord's anointed." (1 Samuel 24:5–6)

Might this be an indication of the future king's political astuteness?[50] He could be thinking that by showing such respect for the man who holds the office that will soon be his own, he is in fact laying a foundation of similar respect to be shown toward him once he is king. Or, to put it another way, were he to gain the throne by regicide he would undermine his own security as king, and encourage others to vie for it by doing to David exactly what he had done to Saul.

At a spiritually far deeper level, this attitude of respect for the office of king fits well with David's faith in the way God stands by him in the face of his persecution. It is as though he realizes that by refraining from assuring victory by his own action he is in fact gaining an overwhelming advantage over Saul. God will do battle in his behalf.[51] Believing that divine justice will have the last say in this conflict, David resolves not to take things into his own hands. As a sign of his trust in the Lord, he should be patient, and still.[52] After all, he does not want to repeat the great mistake his forefathers made in the desert, when they were derelict in remembering the great works of the Lord and failed to trust Him.[53] The lesson would be repeated, more than a millennium later, when Jesus' disciples fail to recall in faith the marvelous works of God, or even the recent miracles of Jesus, and are seized with fear during a storm on a lake.[54] In Jesus' rebuke of them for having so little faith, do we not hear an echo of God's reproach of Israel: "Today, listen to the voice of the Lord: Do not grow stubborn, as your fathers did in the wilderness, when at Meriba and Massah they challenged me and provoked me, Although they had seen all of my works" (Ps 95:8 Liturgy of the Hours)? His works are the saving power displayed in the ten plagues in Egypt, the parting of the sea, and the manna.

David's faith is strong. He does not forget this great lesson of Israel's history. Like a child desirous to please his father or mother, he does not want to receive a rebuke from the God of his fathers. His spirituality is

---

50 In his course lectures, Fr. Barthélemy probed the possibility of such a political motivation on the part of David.
51 "The Lord your God who goes before you will himself fight for you, just as he did for you in Egypt before your eyes" (Deut 1:30).
52 "The Lord will fight for you, and you have only to be still" (Ex 14:14). "You will not need to fight in this battle; take your position, stand still, and see the victory of the Lord on your behalf" (2 Chron 20:17). One might see in texts such as these, first a divine pointer to the redemption from sin that can only be accomplished by God Himself, and the way this is accomplished by the Paschal Mystery of Christ. Second, these texts stress the priority of God's action over man's action in defeating the enemy, not unlike the emphasis on God's purifying activity in the passive purifications of the spiritual life, the passive nights of the senses and of the spirit, as set forth by John of the Cross and Teresa of Avila.
53 "Our fathers, when they were in Egypt, did not consider your wonderful works; they did not remember the abundance of your mercy, but rebelled against the Most High at the Red Sea" (Ps 106:7).
54 See Mt 8:24–27.

rooted in a faith that remembers what God has done of old and draws the practical conclusion for his conduct in the present. His resolve is to rely on the Lord, knowing *in advance* that the Lord will rescue him from the hands of his enemy. It may appear that the rescue has been fulfilled when Saul is found defenseless in the cave. But what looks like a victory arranged by God is in fact, in David's view, a temptation. He calculates that his policy of not retaliating with vengeance on the man who seeks to kill him will translate into a guarantee of divine protection in the future.[55] "I know that the Lord will help his anointed;" David reasons, "he will answer him from his holy heaven with mighty victories by his right hand. Some boast of chariots, and some of horses; but we boast of the name of the Lord our God" (Ps 20:6–7).[56]

This explains the future king's willingness to rely on the judgment of God, his unshakeable confidence that divine justice will be on his side. This is reasonable enough, since God had taken the initiative to send Samuel in order to select David and to anoint him to be king of Israel. If God's purposes are not to be frustrated, if He is to be consistent with Himself, He will have to rescue David from Saul. In this light David's bold confidence is reminiscent of the audacious prayer of Moses in the desert, in which he confronts the Lord with the absurdity of exterminating the people whom He had just liberated from slavery in Egypt.[57] David has every reason to stand secure in the knowledge that God will not renege on the covenant that He established with His servant.

Among the things David says to Saul, after the latter has left the cave, and while David is dangling the corner of the king's cloak that he had cut off, the following reveals how he assesses the situation in the light of faith:

> [12] May the Lord will judge between me and you, may the Lord avenge me upon you; but my hand shall not be against you.... [15] May the Lord therefore be judge, and give sentence between me and you, and see to it, and plead my cause, and deliver me from your hand. (1 Samuel 24:12, 15)

The words of Psalm 17 correspond so perfectly to David's prayer here that memories of his encounter with Saul could have inspired it:

---

55 See Barthélemy, *God and His Image*, 133–34.
56 This text on boasting in the name of the Lord anticipates St. Paul's fully developed "theology of boasting" in God, His love, and His grace. After coming to faith in Christ, Paul no longer boasts of his relationship with God based on the law (see Rom 2:17, 23), but only of his weakness (see 2 Cor 11:30; 12:5, 9) and suffering (see Rom 5:3). This boasting in his weakness is entirely at the service of emphasizing that he boasts only in God's gifts of grace and faith (see Rom 5:2, 11; 1 Cor 4:7). In His wisdom God chooses what is lowly and despised (see 1 Cor 1:29) precisely so that all might boast in the Him (see 1 Cor 1:31; quoting Jer 9:23–26; and again in 2 Cor 10:17). Paul can boast over what God accomplishes through him (see 2 Cor 7:14; 9:2; 10:8–17) because it is evidence of God's grace at work through him (see 1 Cor 15:10; Gal 2:9; Eph 3:2, 7–8). He boasts in the source of this grace, the Cross of Christ (Gal 6:14; Phil 3:3).
57 See Ex 32:11–14.

A Prayer of David.
¹ Hear a just cause, O Lord; attend to my cry!
Give ear to my prayer from lips free of deceit!
² From you let my vindication come!
Let your eyes see the right!
³ If you try my heart, if you visit me by night,
if you test me, you will find no wickedness in me;
my mouth does not transgress.
⁴ With regard to the works of men, by the word of your lips
I have avoided the ways of the violent.
⁵ My steps have held fast to your paths,
my feet have not slipped.
⁶ I call upon you, for you will answer me, O God;
incline your ear to me, hear my words.
⁷ Wondrously show your mercies,
O savior of those who seek refuge
from their adversaries at your right hand.
⁸ Keep me as the apple of the eye;
hide me in the shadow of your wings,
⁹ from the wicked who despoil me,
my deadly enemies who surround me.
¹⁰ They close their hearts to pity;
with their mouths they speak arrogantly.
¹¹ They track me down; now they surround me;
they set their eyes to cast me to the ground.
¹² They are like a lion eager to tear,
as a young lion lurking in ambush.
¹³ Arise, O Lord! confront them, overthrow them!
Deliver my life from the wicked by your sword. (Psalm 17:1–13)

This prayer reveals an innocent heart, one with no consciousness of sin. The accusation that his enemies' hearts are closed to pity deserves special attention, since this is precisely the judgment that later he will pass on a man accused of stealing his neighbor's lamb.

> ⁵ Then David's anger was greatly kindled against the man; and he said to Nathan, "As the Lord lives, the man who has done this deserves to die; ⁶ and he shall restore the lamb fourfold, because he did this thing, and because he had no pity." (2 Samuel 12:5–6)

At the time of his persecution by Saul, however, David is eager for his day in the court of the Lord's justice. He is totally unaware of his own capacity to close his heart to pity. He is aware of sin, but it is on the part of his enemy. He cannot see that there is an enemy within.

It is important to observe that at this time David is not thinking so much of his heart but of his anointing, his vocation to be king. The terms of his righteous cause do not concern whether he measures up to this vocation. Rather, his preoccupation is another man, namely, Saul, and the threat he poses to God's plans for David. David's sense of uprightness, then, is not absolute. It is not a measure of his relation to God. Rather, it is comparative, relative, horizontal. In this there is an anticipation of the Pharisee whose self-assured righteousness is derived not only from keeping the precepts of the Law but also from comparing himself to a tax collector.[58] Eagerness to invite God's judgment can only be explained by self-assurance regarding one's innocence. The anticipated verdict is favorable because, in the mind of David, he is the one being unjustly persecuted; he is in the right.

Even when the issue is not a matter of arbitration between two parties, self-assured souls show that they consider themselves beyond reproach when they invite God's judgment. "Let me be weighed in a just balance," Job declares, "and let God know my integrity!" (Job 31:6). We know that, in the end, thoughts of the inscrutable measure of divine judgment reduce Job to silence, and he regrets his foolishness for having presumed to know the outcome of God's judgment: "Behold, I am of small account; what shall I answer you. I lay my hand on my mouth.... I have uttered what I did not understand, things too wonderful for me, which I did not know" (Job 40:4; 42:3). St. Paul will take this line of humility to its furthest logical conclusion, when he writes that the judgment of a conscience that finds nothing for which to accuse is not definitive. Only God's judgment is definitive.[59]

David will live to reverse his confident plea for God's judgment. In keeping with the tradition that attributes the psalms to him, at another point in his life the great king will renounce the possibility of any righteousness in relation to God. Rather than to invite God's judgment, a more humble and wiser David petitions: "Enter not into judgment with your servant; for no man living is righteous before you" (Ps 143:2).

The turnaround in David from inviting God's judgment to confessing in advance that the verdict of divine judgment would necessarily be a declaration of his own non-righteousness is the precise point of interest for these reflections. What could bring about such a radical change of attitude? Everything points to David's conversion and his experience of divine mercy as the explanation. The great king of Israel was humbled by his fall, and humbled still further by the grace of mercy. Humility is the first effect of God's mercy, for only the humble can receive His grace. Mercy humbles, but it does not humiliate. When God forgives, it is in order to reconcile, so that "the person who is the object of mercy does not feel humiliated, but rather found again and 'restored to value.'"[60] Humility is

---

58 See Lk 18:10–14.
59 See 1 Cor 4:3–4.
60 John Paul II, *Dives in misericordia*, 6.

rooted in the realization that the value one has in God's eyes is in its entirety a gift from above. God loves with mercy simply because He is God, because He is holy.[61] This is what David learns through his sin and conversion. The wiser David has some sense of how limited his knowledge is, even of himself. Even the fact that he cannot detect sin does not lead him to conclude that there is no sin in his heart. God has chosen David, and it is an essential aspect of this call to be refined, like gold, in the furnace of humiliation.[62] This is God's work: "Behold, I have refined you, but not like silver; I have tried you in the furnace of affliction" (Is 48:10). Only the Lord can bring about the purification of hearts: "The crucible is for silver, and the furnace is for gold, and the Lord tries hearts" (Prov 17:3).

The refined and humbled David is able to discern that there is a category of sin that is hidden from his perception, though not from God's. Aware of this, he prays, "But who can discern his errors? Clear me from hidden faults" (Ps 19:12). Truly, "The heart is our hidden center, beyond the grasp of our reason and of others; only the Spirit of God can fathom the human heart and know it fully."[63] Jeremiah is conscious of it: "The heart is deceitful above all things, and desperately corrupt; who can understand it? 'I the Lord search the mind and try the heart, to give to every man according to his ways, according to the fruit of his doings'" (Jer 17:9–10). As is St. Paul: "I do not even judge myself. I am not aware of anything against myself, but I am not thereby acquitted. It is the Lord who judges me" (1 Cor 4:3–4). And St. John: "God is greater than our hearts, and he knows everything" (1 Jn 3:20).

David's petition that God purify him of his hidden faults is all the more noteworthy once one realizes that the first step in conversion is to become aware of sin. He wants to be fully one with God, seeing all that God sees, including the sins that he senses lie yet hidden from him. God sees our sins and His own mercy, and He knows that we will take interest in and appeal to His mercy only if we are first aware of our sins. This means that the first step in conversion is the uncovering of sins. God desires that we cooperate in the process by which He restores in our hearts the love that has been voided by sin, and this requires that we be one with Him in the truth about sin and the truth regarding His mercy.

The parable of the Prodigal Son presents the opportunity to probe this mystery in greater depth, but the full knowledge of the evil of sin can be known only in light of the Cross of Christ.[64] Because this is so, David's

---

61 See Hos 11:9.
62 See Sirach 2:5.
63 *CCC*, 2563.
64 As John Paul II describes it, "... the Holy Spirit also convinces of every sin, committed in any place and at any moment in human history: *for he demonstrates its relationship with the Cross of Christ*. The 'convincing' is the demonstration of the evil of sin, of every sin, in relation to the Cross of Christ. Sin, shown in this relationship, *is recognized in the entire dimension of evil* proper to it, through the '*mysterium iniquitatis*' which is hidden within it. Man does not know this dimension—he is absolutely ignorant of it apart from the Cross of Christ. So he cannot be 'convinced' of it except by *the Holy Spirit*" (*Dominum et Vivificantem*, 32).

appeal that his hidden sins be purified is, in reality, a petition that will be definitively answered only in the Paschal Mystery of the Lamb of God, Who came to take away the sins of the world. Yet, according to the maxim that to desire something is already to possess it, at least in some initial way, the truly remarkable thing is that this prayer indicates that David is already experiencing something of the grace of the Paschal Mystery, the grace of forgiveness that comes from the sacrifice of the definitive Paschal Lamb. David will come to know, neither vaguely nor abstractly nor by logical deduction, but by experience, that God's merciful love is greater than any sin, greater than any rejection of His love. He will come to know divine mercy's sole aim is forgiveness and reconciliation for the restoration of communion with God. This is why, in the end, like St. Paul, David is not fearful of God's judgment, and can invite it. He knows that the King of kings sits upon a throne of mercy as He makes His just judgments.[65]

---

[65] See Heb 4:16.

2.
David's Sins:
A King Betrays His God, His Mission, and His People

The account of King David's sins is recounted in 2 Samuel 11. It is highly significant that David commits two sins, and that the second is a direct result of his non-repentance with respect to the first.

This first sin is adultery. One evening, while enjoying a peaceful promenade on the roof of his palace, David catches sight of a beautiful woman. He dispatches servants to bring her to him and they engaged in an adulterous act. The account is brief and straightforward, the sacred author evidently unconcerned to provide any further details. It is not, however, difficult to imagine that things begin with David surveying the grandeur of Jerusalem, the city that *he* had established as capital of *his* kingdom. Only recently he celebrated the triumphal arrival of the Ark of the Covenant. With the borders secure from his enemies, David has every reason to revel in *his* accomplishment: the peace of Jerusalem, a peace of which he is the principal human agent. Under *his* leadership, Israel achieves the status of a nation unified under a strong and charismatic king.

It is entirely possible that a sense of accomplishment caused David's heart to swell with pride. The city and his palace are so much evidence of what he has achieved. In his commentary of Psalm 51, St. Augustine is attentive to the temptations that can accompany times of prosperity. Many, he writes, fear adversity but are not sufficiently on guard against the perils of prosperity. "Prosperity is more perilous to soul than adversity to body."[1] A sign of this is that in God's Providence adversities serve to arouse people from the complacence that prosperity brings. Israel experienced this, and the prophets, like Hosea and Ezekiel, think of the time of the Exodus in the desert as an idyllic time of espousal, when Israel was so profoundly aware of its dependence on God that the people could not forget Him. How many temptations did the chosen people confront after crossing the Jordan and settling into the land of milk and honey? "Stricter watch must be kept against felicity" than against adversity, concludes Augustine, drawing a valuable lesson from David's sins in his time of well-being.

> David did not commit this sin when Saul persecuted him. When the holy David suffered the hostility of Saul, when he was tormented by his persecutions, when he fled to various places to avoid falling into his hands, he did not desire the

---

[1] Augustine, *Expositions on the Psalms*, 51, 4 (Verse 1).

woman of others, and did not kill the husband of the woman with whom he had committed adultery. In the misery of his tribulations, he was all the more intent upon God the more he seemed worthy of compassion. Tribulation is therefore useful; more useful is the scalpel of the doctor than the temptation of the devil. He became sure of himself when his enemies were vanquished, when the fear was diminished, and pride grew. The effectiveness of this example consists therefore in this, in inducing us to be afraid of good fortune.[2]

The blessing of prosperity need not be an occasion for pride. God can, and often does humble us through graces that are so manifestly beyond anything that we deserve that they produce a profound humility. Such is the humility of the Blessed Virgin Mary, and such is also the humility that David typically exhibits. Though habitually David's heart retains a strong awareness that all of his victories and successes are in reality the Lord's more than his, this particular night he closes in on himself with self-congratulatory satisfaction over his success. Such an eclipse of God could not but affect how he looks at the beautiful woman, Bathsheba. If he does not see her as belonging to God, then she can belong to him. Once pride crowds out awareness of God and the humility that accompanies it, it reigns unchecked to assess all things as subservient to itself. Pride assigns to other people the status of mere objects of possession, their value measured only in terms of the personal enrichment they can bring. This is the interior moment at which David has already become a tyrant. Samuel's warning about the tyranny of Israel's kings is already fulfilled.[3] It only remains for David to project this interior tyranny into exterior, exploitative action.

David treats Bathsheba as his property, as an entitlement, a perk that comes with the office of king. His pride produces a complete amnesia regarding the history of Israel's enslavement in Egypt, where Pharaoh justified his claim over Israel by declaring that he did not recognize the God of Abraham, Isaac, and Jacob. That is all the justification that political power requires for elevating itself beyond all limitations. By its very logic, unbridled political power cannot acknowledge any authority that precedes and would set limits to it. And this is precisely David's state of mind at this moment. Fueled by passion, pride effectively blinds David to the prerogatives of God. He is a practical atheist; that is, he does not deny God in principle but right now he acts as if God did not exist.[4] At the moment he decides to dispatch his servants, David has quite effectively set God aside; he has excluded Him from playing a role in his decision-making process. Passion has overpowered God's word, suppressing its echo in his

---

2   Ibid.
3   See 1 Sam 8:9–20.
4   On numerous occasions John Paul II makes use of the expression, "practical atheism," in this sense. See, for example, *Reconciliatio et paenitentia*, 18.

conscience. Granting his own freedom unrestricted choice, David effectively annuls the freedom of his subjects.

There is nothing accidental about David's sin. Interiorly, he purposefully suppresses his conscience, deliberately chooses to neglect to look to heaven, and consciously banishes from his awareness any thought of just judgments.[5] He has thus made truth his enemy, effectively becoming an idolater.[6] David recapitulates the primordial sin of Israel, namely, to forget God[7] and to act as if His liberating, protecting, and guiding presence meant nothing.

With God removed from his heart, David is the sovereign authority over his own freedom, and there is no appeal to a higher authority. Bathsheba's dignity is fundamentally devalued, being measured now only with reference to David's disordered desires. God is excluded, not in principle and not habitually, but in this series of acts in which the king forgets God because he has chosen to be seduced by thoughts of satisfying his disordered desires. His passions and pride bar access to the higher authority of truth and conscience.[8]

A thousand years later the true Son of David will teach His followers what to say in order to avoid becoming puffed up over their achievements—even when accomplished for God—and thereby unleashing movements of the will that can only lead to disordered desires: "We are unworthy servants; we have only done what was our duty" (Lk 17:10).

---

5 See Dan 13:9. The different translations convey these three dimensions—suppression of conscience, failure to look heavenward, and just judgments—with varying vocabulary: "And they perverted their minds and turned away their eyes from looking to Heaven or remembering righteous judgments" (Revised Standard Version [RSV]); "They suppressed their consciences; they would not allow their eyes to look to heaven, and did not keep in mind just judgments" (North American Bible [NAB]); "They threw reason aside, making no effort to turn their eyes to Heaven, and forgetting the demands of virtue" (New Jerusalem Bible [NJB]); "And they perverted their own mind and turned away their eyes that they might not look unto heaven, nor remember just judgments" (Douay-Rheims 1899 American Edition [DRA]).

6 St. Paul identifies covetousness with idolatry (see Col 3:5 and Eph 5:5). Stanislas Lyonnet comments: "According to the etymology of the Greek word, *pleonexia* [covetousness], this consists in a covetous and egocentric desire 'to possess ever more' even to the point of disregarding the rights of others. For the patristic tradition this is the vice *par excellence*, the exact antithesis of charity that defines the Christian and moves him to serve his brothers, literally 'to become a slave' (Gal 5:13) rather than to treat them as instruments of profit or pleasure" (*Le message de l'épître aux Romains* [Paris: Les Éditions du Cerf, 1971], 35).

7 See Psalm 78, especially verses 7, 11, 35, 42.

8 Aquinas teaches that in every sin there is ignorance, and underscores that ignorance is sinful when it is deliberate. The sinner becomes captivated by the object of his desire to the point that he refuses to attend to what he knows is right, realizing that if he did and if he followed the path of truth to its logical conclusion, he could not act to take possession of the object of his desire. Every sin is, then, a violation of conscience by which a person engages his freedom to override the obligation to pursue the truth to its furthest implications. Ignorance is willed "as when a man wishes not to know, that he may have an excuse for sin, or that he may not be withheld from sin; according to Job 21:14: 'We desire not the knowledge of Thy ways.' And this is called affected ignorance" (*Summa theologiae* [hereafter *ST*] I-II, Q. 6, a. 8; see also I-II Q. 88, a. 6, ad 2; II-II Q. 153, a. 5).

This wisdom would have saved David and preserved him as "a man after the Lord's own heart" (1 Sam 13:14). Such a pure heart could not even look at another man's wife, or any woman, lustfully. When the people first clamored for a king, the prophet Samuel duly warned them that they would find submitting to the prerogatives of a monarch oppressive, even when the king's dictates are necessary and just. What he failed to make explicit is that the prestige of the office of the king and the exercise of its authority depend concretely on the state of the king's heart. Even "a man after the Lord's own heart" can have a change of heart, and when this happens the throne becomes a seat of exploitation rather than service.

The Bible describes David's sin theologically, that is, in relation to God and from God's perspective. First, in relation to God, the interior reality is that David has "despised the word of the Lord," "done what is evil in his sight" (2 Sam 12:9–10), and "utterly scorned the Lord" (2 Sam 12:14). Such a verdict prescinds from consideration of mitigating circumstances and strikes the sensibilities of our own times and culture as unduly severe and extreme to the point of being intolerable. It should be kept in mind that these are the words that best correspond to a grace of insight that allows a person to pierce through all that is peripheral and accidental in order to glimpse, in a moment of truth, what it means to engage one's free will on a way that contradicts God's truth. It is not extreme to "take sides with the truth against oneself,"[9] even if this has extremely severe consequences. To do so is to see the full truth about oneself at the precise moment of deliberately overturning the order established by God, according to which human dignity consists in seeking the truth, acknowledging the truth, and conforming one's actions to the truth.[10] It is to perceive, not only one's capacity to be unfaithful to the God of purest love, but also the actual self-destructive absurdity of a creature defying his Creator[11] and thereby negating the very act by which the Creator is giving Himself to the creature at this precise moment, namely, through the voice of conscience.

To say that sin is a suicidal act is not hyperbole;[12] for, by rejecting God and His love, the sinner rejects the God Who brought him into existence and Who sustains his being. This manifests the profound irrationality of sin. The sinner rejects God's gift of Self through truth of conscience while most willingly receiving the gift of His life-sustaining love, the love by which God holds in existence all that is.[13] In this the sinner, every sinner, resembles the Prodigal Son, who refused the higher gift that his father desired to make of himself while gladly accepting the gift of his property. The property to which the sinner clings is his own

---

9 Hans Urs von Balthasar, *Prayer* (New York: Sheed and Ward, 1961), 183.
10 See Vatican II, *Dignitatis humanae*, 1–2.
11 "For without the Creator the creature would disappear" (Vatican II, *Gaudium et spes*, 36).
12 "As a rupture with God, sin is an act of disobedience by a creature who rejects, at least implicitly, the very one from whom he came and who sustains him in life. It is therefore a suicidal act" (John Paul II, *Reconciliatio et paenitentia*, 15).
13 "In him we live and move and have our being" (Acts 17:28).

freedom, desiring to make use of it outside the Father's house, that is, outside of a relationship of communion with the Father, based on His truth. Herein lies the profound contradiction of sin. It is a "No" to God in the exercise of one's freedom in a particular act. It is a defiant "I don't want the fullness of this relationship with You right here and right now because I desire something else even more." Yet, the sinner simultaneously desires, if only subconsciously and implicitly, a certain element of that relationship with God. Sin is a "No" to the divine love that would give all and a "Yes" to part of what that same love desires to give—a "Yes" to the gift of life and its continuance, which includes freedom itself, which come from God. To arrive at an undimmed realization of this is to see that one has "despised the word of the Lord" and "utterly disdained the Lord." And the fruit of such a realization is to grasp what it means for God to have loved us, for Christ to have died for us, while we were still weak and godless, while we were still sinners, and while we were His enemies.[14] For, at the moment we misuse our freedom and sin, we are truly these things.

When David finds himself transparent to the judgment of his own conscience, he knows that his capacity to be weak and godless, to be a sinner, and to be God's enemy is no merely theoretical possibility. He cannot know that a distant Son of David will be God's definitive answer to the cry of a conscience burdened by unreconciled guilt. But he does know the God of Israel's profession of faith, who revealed Himself to Moses as "a God merciful and gracious, slow to anger, and abounding in mercy and faithfulness, keeping merciful love for thousands, forgiving iniquity and transgression and sin" (Ex 34:6–7).[15] Mercy is the only hope for a sinner who has shut out God's love. For, love is a gift and cannot be gained by effort. Only if God keeps loving even after His love has been rejected is there any hope to receive His love again. And this is precisely what His mercy is: love that keeps loving in the context of having been rejected. David does not know of God's plan definitively to reveal His mercy in the paschal mystery, but this does not prevent him from believing and hoping in Christ as the definitive fulfillment of the hope of every sinner to be forgiven and to be reconciled with God. David's encounter with God's mercy is an encounter with the mystery of Christ.

Second, this passage describes the reality of David's sin from God's perspective. God asks, "Why have you spurned the Lord and done what is evil in His sight" (2 Sam 12:9) only after recounting what He, the Lord, has done for David:

> [7] I anointed you king over Israel, and I delivered you our of the hand of Saul; [8] and I gave you your master's house, and

---

[14] "While we were yet helpless, at the right time Christ died for the ungodly.... But God shows his love for us in that while we were yet sinners Christ died for us.... For if while we were enemies we were reconciled to God by the death of his Son ..." (Rom 5:6, 8, 10).

[15] In the Old Testament, this is virtually a definition of God. See Num 14:18; 2 Chron 30:9; Neh 9:17, 31; Ps 86:15; 103:8; 111:4; 116:15; 145:8; Wis 15:1; Joel 2:13; Jon 4:2.

your master's wives into your bosom, and I gave you the house of Israel and of Judah; and if this were too little, I would add to you as much more. (2 Samuel 12:7–8)

After all that God has done for him, He expects more from David. "Every one to whom much is given, of him will much be required; and of him to whom men commit much they will demand the more" (Lk 12:48). If we understand it correctly, we can see that this higher expectation is justified; God has the right to hold this expectation. The duties corresponding to this right are not arbitrarily imposed upon David, as if God could at any time act simply arbitrarily. In all of His dealings with men, God is guided by a logic of love. This is not a logic that is above Him and that could somehow constrain Him, for He is love. God's logic of love is nothing other than the emanation of His own wisdom into creation and all of His dealings with men. Having made man in His own image, man is naturally receptive to this logic of divine love. He is at home with it, finding in it the only adequate account for his existence and for his freedom. Man is made for love, and for this reason the rights of God's love, rooted in the fact that He always takes the initiative of love, do not result in any kind of forced imposition on man. God's love comes to man from the outside, from Another, but it is in no way imposed or coercive, even if does constitute a redoubtable call to man's freedom. Rather, God's love corresponds to man's deepest longings, as Jesus' miracles of healing so convincingly show. What Jesus once said to two blind men captures this logic: "What do you want me to do for you?" (Mt 20:32). God's love perfectly coincides with man's love for himself, and at the same to infinitely surpasses what is able, without faith, to ask for. And to sinful man, whose love of self is distorted because he does not know the truth about himself, God must often say, "You do not know what you are asking" (Mt 20:22).

God's right to expect David to observe His commandments simply expresses a profound truth about David in his relation to God. As image of God, David is made to receive God's love and its benefits. As a descendant of Abraham, God rightly expects David to thank and praise Him for keeping His promise by setting the twelve tribes of Israel free from slavery in Egypt, guiding them through the desert, and establishing them in the land of the promise. God rightly expects David to observe the precepts of the Law of Moses, not out of fear of punishment, but as an expression of his gratitude for God's gifts of freedom and abundance. In keeping with the logic of His love, God takes a further initiative to make David king. Thus, the most profound truth about David is that everything he has is pure gift of God's love. For him to observe God's law is the first and most fundamental way for him to love himself. For, God's law is nothing other than the wisdom He imparts to men regarding what they must do and not to do in order to preserve their enjoyment of His gifts. Religious obedience is always simultaneously fidelity to God and fidelity to oneself. This is why sin is always simultaneously an offense against God and self-destructive act of man against himself.

As the beneficiary of so many divine favors, God should be the king's constant point of reference. Yet David somehow manages to forget the Lord and act as if He and all His favors mean nothing. At this moment of shutting God out, David personally recapitulates the prophets' theme of forgetting God.[16] The great and fundamental sign of the times to which the prophets are attentive is Israel's constant temptation to act as if this people had no history with God, as if God had done nothing for them, as if they did not owe their very existence to God. They commit a sin that would be described more than two millennia later as "practical atheism."[17] Without ever denying God overtly, they engage their freedom and make choices without consulting the Lord, and thus according to criteria that come from some other source than Him. They act as if God does not exist, as if they had never experienced His redeeming and liberating love. In other words, they take for granted the freedom and abundance in the Promised Land. They cease to think in terms of gift, and at that precise moment they begin to live like the other nations, which know nothing of God's love. Rightly, then, the prophets accuse them of having forgotten their Savior. This is David's interior state.

Is this not a repetition of the sin of Adam and Eve? The essence of their sin is to have forgotten what God had done for them. He created them from nothing, and for this reason their very existence is evidence of His wisdom and power serving them out of love. They live in paradise, in a world perfectly ordered by God's wisdom, power, and love. Everything they experience is transparent evidence of God's wisdom, power, and love. And yet, precisely at the moment when God rightly expects that they recall that evidence, when their memories should be flooded with impressions of the divine benefits they enjoy, they choose to forget. They deliberately

---

[16] See Hos 8:14; Jer 2:32; 3:21; 13:25; 18:15; Is 17:10; Ezek 22:12; 23:35. When the prophets depict the people as lamenting that the Lord has forgotten them (see Is 49:14), this confirms the principle that "one is punished by the very things by which he sins" (Wis 11:16). The people sin by forgetting God, and this places them in a position of total desperation such that they think that God has forgotten them (see also Is 23:15; 49:14; Lam 5:20)! God's people perish, they cease to act as God's people, when they lack knowledge of God (see Hos 4:1, 6). This is the knowledge of faith, which is essentially the remembering of what God has done for His people. When through Hosea God makes known his preference for love and knowledge of God rather than sacrifice and holocausts (see Hos 6:6), he is simply stressing that sacrifices and holocausts are meant to be Israel's response of faith to what God has done for them, and that they cannot stand apart from this knowledge, this faith in the history of God's love for His people.

[17] This theme recurs throughout the writings of John Paul II, where it is equivalent to living "as if God did not exist." See *Christifideles laici*, 34; *Reconciliatio et paenitentia*, 18; Angelus, July 27, 2003; General Audience, April 14, 1999 (referring to *Fides et ratio*, 46–47); *Ad limina* address to bishops of the United States, November 11, 1993; *Pastores dabo vobis*, 7; Address to the Order of Friars Minor, December 10, 1997; General Audience, February 25, 1998; *Ad limina* address to the bishops of Scotland, October 29, 1992.

neglect[18] to avert to this evidence. Instead, they choose to focus on the enticing fruit, made all the more desirable by reason of serpent's allegation that God did not create them and give the commandment out of love, but out of jealousy.

Throughout the history of God's dealing with them, His people will learn the same lesson time and again. Isaiah conveys it in the great analogy with the vineyard: "What more was there to do for my vineyard, that I have not done in it? When I looked for it to yield grapes, why did it yield wild grapes?" (Is 5:4). The fruit God expects to find in His vineyard, after all His labor of tending it—after all the great works that He has accomplished to plant it—is that righteousness that consists in observing His precepts and doing so precisely because they are seen as His gift.

The commandments are His second gift, the first being liberation from slavery in Egypt and living in the freedom and abundance of the Promised Land. The second gift, the gift of the Law, is entirely at the service of preserving the first gift. The essential fruit that God rightly expects is faith. In the fullness of time, this fruit[19] is faith in the passion, death, resurrection, and ascension of Jesus Christ as the definitive revelation of God's persistent question put to human freedom: "What more was there to do to demonstrate my love?" For, in the Paschal Mystery God loves His people "to the end" (Jn 13:1), that is, to the furthest extreme of the perfection of love.[20] The one thing regarding which each man should have the greatest certitude, the certitude of faith itself, is that God loves me.[21]

At the time of committing his sins, David personifies the Lord's carefully tended vineyard in which He finds only wild grapes. At this point, David's heart is far from God and as a result he betrays the office by which the Lord established him as judge and assurer of the people's rights that are rooted in the divinely established covenant. He becomes an occasion of scandal for his neighbor,[22] the daughter of Abraham, Bathsheba, as he leads her to the spiritual death of the sin of adultery for which the punishment was also death (by stoning).[23] When he receives

---

18   See note 8, above.
19   See Jn 15:1–6.
20   The Jerusalem Bible conveys this sense of what "to the end" means in this verse by rendering it: "... but now he showed how perfect his love was."
21   "God offers us an unconditional acceptance which enables us to say: 'I am loved; I have a place in the world and in history; I am personally loved by God. If God accepts me and loves me and I am sure of this, then I know clearly and with certainty that it is a good thing that I am alive'" (Benedict XVI, Message for 27th World Youth Day, March 15, 2012). "Everything begins from the humble acceptance of faith ('knowing that one is loved by God') ..." (Benedict XVI, Message for Lent, 2013 (dated October 15, 2012).
22   "Scandal is an attitude or behavior which leads another to do evil. The person who gives scandal becomes his neighbor's tempter. He damages virtue and integrity; he may even draw his brother into spiritual death. Scandal is a grave offense if by deed or omission another is deliberately led into a grave offense. Scandal takes on a particular gravity by reason of the authority of those who cause it ..." (*CCC*, 2284–85).
23   There is an even more fundamental scandal at work here, though it is not the focus of the text. It is that the woman alone, here Bathsheba, is subject to the charge of adultery, when the initiative is entirely on the part of David. St. John Paul II addresses this in a

word from Bathsheba that she has conceived, David realizes how this threatens his office and prestige as king. All will know that she has been unfaithful to her husband, since he was away in battle. Should the king save this woman from the penalty for adultery established by Moses? But how? What can he do?

David devises a plan. He will grant a furlough to Uriah, Bathsheba's husband. When he returns home and sleeps with her, as David anticipates, then everyone will presume that her child is the legitimate fruit of their union. Only Bathsheba and David will be privy to the truth. Not only will this scheme protect Bathsheba, it will keep David's indiscretion sealed in secrecy. Unfortunately, what David expects does not happen. Uriah returns to Jerusalem, but he does not enter his own house so as faithfully to observe the discipline that soldiers do not have relations with their wives during time of war.

The irony is piquant: While Uriah risks his life as he fights for the king, the king takes his wife to himself. The scriptural account intensifies the irony of the contrast between Uriah's noble fidelity to his soldierly duties, and thus to the king, and David's reprehensible treachery. Despite David's effort to lead him to compromise his conscience by filling him with wine in the hope that, with his judgment impaired, he will go to Bathsheba, Uriah remains steadfast in observing his military discipline and spends that night sleeping at the entry to the palace. Uriah's faithful fulfillment of the duties of his vocation thwarts the king's plan to cover over his infidelity to the duties of his own vocation and serves to shine a penetrating light on David's infidelity regarding his duties as king.

This forces David to order Uriah to return to combat, sending with him sealed orders that are designed to assure that Uriah dies in battle. The orders instruct Joab, commander of the army, to place Uriah at the front of the troops and then, when the fighting is at fever pitch, suddenly to withdraw the soldiers, thus leaving Uriah without support and defenseless before the enemy. Uriah carries his own death-sentence back to camp (yet another irony), Joab obeys the order, and Uriah is slain. As it happens, an unspecified number of Uriah's comrades in arms are also killed as a result of this treacherous ruse, so that David is actually guilty of multiple homicides. In response to Joab's report of the details, the king disingenuously reassures his commander not to be discouraged by this setback, for war is unpredictable business. This is the final irony: David assures Joab that he will not hold him accountable for the deaths of Uriah and his comrades, yet there is no one who can offer to David a similar

---

meditation on the Gospel account of the woman caught in adultery. "The episode recorded in the Gospel of John [of the woman caught in adultery] is repeated in countless similar situations in every period of history. A woman is left alone, exposed to public opinion with 'her sin', while behind 'her' sin there lurks a man—a sinner, guilty 'of the other's sin', indeed equally responsible for it. And yet his sin escapes notice, it is passed over in silence: he does not appear to be responsible for 'the other's sin'! (*Mulieris dignitatem*, 14). Bathsheba's predicament is certainly among those "repeated in countless similar situations in every period of history."

declaration of not being held responsible for his own crimes. David cannot escape the truth about his sin. He cannot outrun his own conscience—an entirely futile undertaking—as the account of Adam and Eve attempting to hide themselves from the One Who is omnipresent and omniscient so graphically depicts.

While David's sin was occasioned by sexual passion, as it has been disordered by original sin, St. Augustine's analysis, discussed earlier, shows that he was not strong enough to resist the temptation because of an even deeper disorder of spiritual pride. The fact that the gratification of his lust is not immediate confirms this. He has to dispatch servants to bring Bathsheba to the palace, and for as long as it takes for her to arrive there is time for reconsideration, for repentance from his sinful intention. During that interim, how many times does David's conscience fulfill its mission, to remember God's marvelous works and to put the present moment in the perspective of the covenant, to make God's voice heard? And how many times does he disregard this call of conscience? We do not know the answer. Nevertheless, it is clear that the man entrusted to rule over God's people is himself now ruled by something other than God.

The result is a catastrophic as it is inevitable: to drown out God's voice necessarily renders one deaf to the Law that He has spoken. The only safeguard of freedom is truth: "the truth will make you free" (Jn 8:32). God is truth, and His word is truth: "your word is truth" (Jn 17:17; Ps 119:160). "This is why one can abandon oneself in full trust to the truth and faithfulness of his word in all things."[24] It is also why, "It is right and just to entrust oneself wholly to God and to believe absolutely what he says. It would be futile and false to place such faith in a creature."[25] Put negatively, "man should not submit his personal freedom in an absolute manner to any earthly power, but only to God."[26] David's lust is precisely such an earthly power. His surrender of his freedom to it brings the loss of freedom, first his own, and then that of Bathsheba and Uriah.

David transgresses the law the purpose of which is to assure the freedom of Israel and of each individual within this people. The king who is charged to serve makes Bathsheba subservient to his desires. His lust reduces her to being an object of self-gratification rather than the subject of a love that affirms her value as a person.[27] This is instructive for those

---

24 *CCC*, 215.
25 *CCC*, 150.
26 *CCC*, 450.
27 See Karol Wojtyła, *Love and Responsibility*, trans. H. T. Willets (San Francisco: Ignatius Press, 1993). Should minds habituated to twenty-first century individualism, subjectivism, and relativism react by saying that this act was a private matter between David and Bathsheba and did no harm to anyone else, two things can be observed. First, it obviously leads to life-ending harm to Uriah. Even if he had not been killed, and even if there had been no pregnancy, the adulterous act violates the exclusivity of marital self-giving. Second, every woman in Israel becomes David's property, in principle. The principle may not yet have applied concretely to the wives of Uriah's neighbors or fellow-soldiers, but so long as it is operative for one man's wife it is potentially applicable to every man's wife.

living in an age, like ours, in which law is perceived as an obstacle to personal freedom, placing limits on what one is able to do. But this betrays the presence of a disorder that causes a person to view the law as David did in the heat of his passion. For, isn't it obvious that the precept not to steal is profoundly liberating for people who otherwise could not enjoy their possessions because they would be in constant fear of having them stolen? Isn't it obvious that the precept not to commit adultery protects those who are married?

The murder of the innocent Uriah and his comrades in arms is another kind of sin. David conveniently sets aside consideration of the dignity of these men, too. His calculation regarding Uriah extends to them as well. Uriah's very existence poses a threat to David's reputation and power. Even more profoundly, his existence is witness against the interior violence that David has perpetrated against the truth, against his own conscience. In relation to David's burdened conscience, he is the righteous man, who "is inconvenient to us and opposes our actions; he reproaches us for sins against the law, and accuses us of sins against our training" (Wis 2:12). So long as Uriah lives, David cannot live with himself. The refusal to repent leads by route of the inexorable logic of sin to see others as a threat. By his sin, the king of Israel has become what the serpent accused God of being, and what Adam and Eve in their sin came to believe: that God is jealous of his prerogatives.[28] Having elevated himself above God by sinning, in reality he has lowered himself. For, God is not jealous of or threatened by his creatures. They are His glory. God is love, and the products of his love can no more threaten His transcendent perfection than a masterpiece of art can threaten the artist who produces it. But sin twists all of this around, and it is precisely the absence of love in the heart of David—the love of God and of neighbor having been evicted so that his heart could be entirely filled by love of self—that explains the logic behind his plot to do away with Uriah—and those who were in too close proximity to Uriah. So long as he reasons within his sin, as it were, taking it as a premise, there is neither truth nor freedom in either his interior kingdom or in the kingdom over which God has set him as king. In such reasoning, the sacrifice of Uriah and his comrades is a cold calculation, a means to protect the highest value of all, indeed, the only value, namely, the king's prestige and power.

Certainly, this tragic episode is instructive about how not to deal with sin. It is one thing for David to discover his weakness, and it is quite another to attempt to cover up that weakness. He might have tried to preserve his honor by less treacherous means, but the point is that David's determination to conceal his sin cannot be disentangled from his refusal to confess his sin to God. He is a man with a tortured conscience, and so long as truth is not the foundation of his relation to God, truth is absent from his

---

28 "Scripture portrays the tragic consequences of this first disobedience. Adam and Eve immediately lose the grace of original holiness. They become afraid of the God of whom they have conceived a distorted image—that of a God jealous of his prerogatives" (*CCC*, 399).

relationships with men. Without a properly functioning conscience and the fear of God that accompanies it, the king becomes the slave of another kind of fear—the fear of public opinion. Ironically, the very people he attacks hold a kind of power over him, showing that his aggression is in fact a sign of weakness. He is the precise opposite of a martyr. Rather than to refuse to yield to men who would force him to violate his conscience and to prefer to die, he refuses to yield to the voice of God in his conscience and inflicts death on others. It is the exact contrary of the apostles' bold faith: "We must obey God rather than men" (Acts 5:29)—I must obey God rather than myself! With his conscience effectively neutralized and all reference to the absolute and transcendent cut off, David's concern for prestige among the people assumes a place of importance to which it has no rightful claim. One can only imagine how hollow were the words of the psalms he sang during this time of spiritual death, if indeed he had the courage to sing them at all. If he did sing, it is clear that the state of his conscience prevented the words of the psalms from returning him to submission to the truth. For, we know that it will take an extraordinary intervention of God's word, through the prophet Nathan, to bring about David's conversion.

David's mortal disobedience makes him like his predecessor. Saul's habitual disposition is to make his decisions based on a judgment about what he thinks are the expectations of the people. Those expectations replace the truth of God as his highest value. He is unable to obey the God Whom he cannot see because he is fearful of the people whom he does see. For, surely he knows that he was selected king by people, rather than by God! In his own words: "I have sinned; for I have transgressed the commandment of the Lord and your words, because I feared the people and obeyed their voice" (1 Sam 15:24).[29] It is, perhaps, a temptation inherent in political office—an occupational hazard—to override one's conscience, where the voice of God echoes, in favor of harkening to what appears to be a more immediate and imposing voice. In reality, though, no voice is closer to us than the voice of God, and the only way to be a true servant of the people is by putting God and His truth first. Fidelity to God is the measure of fidelity to man, even as the first commandment, to love the Lord with all of one's heart, mind, soul, and strength, is the condition for loving one's neighbor.[30]

Comparing David to Saul, it is more typical of David's spiritual profile to put God first. His sins of adultery and murder constitute an exceptional moment in his life.[31] In the cave, when he has an opportunity to bring Saul to an end, David restrains himself and his men because Saul, the king who is tracking him down to kill him, is the Lord's anointed. When with joyful exuberance he dances before the Ark of the Covenant and his wife berates him for having made a fool of himself in the eyes of those observing him, David reveals his all-consuming love for God: "I was dancing before the

---

29   See also 1 Sam 13:8–13; 28:7.
30   See Mk 12:29–31.
31   The other great exception to David habitually putting God first is the sin he commits by disobeying God's injunction against taking a census. See 2 Sam 24.

Lord" (2 Sam 6:21 NAB). It is as though he did not even notice the presence of others because his heart was absorbed by the presence of God. Such is the inner life of a man with a heart after that of the Lord Himself.[32]

During the time from David's lustful look at Bathsheba to the death of Uriah and his fellow soldiers, the king's heart is far from being after the heart of God. It has swelled with passion, pride, and fear, leaving no room for God's truth to echo within it. The illusory freedom of giving unrestricted reign to his infatuation reduces him to a slave. His thinking is boxed in, limited only to what is necessary to satisfy his passion and to preserve his image among the people. The lesson here is that unrepented sin can only breed further sin. Sin, by seeking happiness independently of God and laying claim to the right to use one's freedom to do so, destroys true freedom and produces the most tyrannical enslavement. "Everyone who commits sin is a slave to sin" (Jn 8:34). A slave needs to be redeemed. The only way out is to turn to God for redemption.

The gravity of David's sins becomes all the more glaring when they are considered in light of his vocation as king of Israel. In Israel, the king is a judge charged with assuring justice. His responsibility is to preserve the twofold freedom of God's people: the freedom of the nation as a whole from domination by foreign powers, and the freedom of each individual within the chosen people from the many forms of exploitation that could occur in social and economic spheres. This freedom is God's gift to His people. Only He could establish it, but once established it is the king's responsibility to exercise the ministry of its preservation. This freedom from domination, whether external or internal, is the condition for God's people to respond to His liberating initiative by living faithfully under the covenant. As the servant of justice, then, the king's charge is to assure that order in which, to use a more modern phrase, God's people could reach their full potential by responding fully to their vocation as the people He had chosen as His own.

Murder effectively removes the very possibility of responding to God's loving initiative. Uriah and his companions, precisely in the context of risking their lives as agents of the king's office to preserve Israel's freedom from foreign powers, become victims of his abuse of power. Nothing David could have done, short of apostatizing and leading the people into idolatry, could be more opposed to his responsibilities as king.

---

[32] See 1 Sam 13:14.

3.
David's Conversion: A King Participates in God's Judgment

With the collaboration of His prophet, God treats David with a finesse that marvelously unites truth and regard for his dignity and freedom. Though David has repudiated God, God continues to love him, and this love takes the form a special intervention, the nature of which is determined by the state of David's conscience and God's wisdom for effecting his conversion. The word of God that Nathan brings to the king contains nothing that is new. It is a simple account of a heartless injustice. No doubt, the king had adjudicated any number of cases of injustice. But this case is unique because its purpose is to cause the light of truth to shine anew in David's conscience. Creating man in His image, God fashioned the conscience to reflect His own light. Man is made for truth, and his dignity is such he is the custodian of the freedom that walks purposefully and securely in the light. Nathan comes to David at a moment when his conscience is in a very dark place. By sinning, David "put darkness for light" (Is 5:20). In this he personifies Israel at the time of the Exile, when the people dwell in the darkness of their sins.[1] Nathan's mission anticipates that of Isaiah. The prophetic mission is always to bring light to those who dwell in the darkness of sin.[2]

David has exiled his own conscience to a barren place where the echoes of God's voice are too faint to be audible. In reality, through the pain of his afflicted conscience, God is shouting to him,[3] but sin has so profoundly contorted David's faculties that he remains deaf to the accusation of truth in his conscience. That accusation is already "a pledge of hope and mercy,"[4] demonstrating the irrepressible dynamism toward the truth that God plants in every soul. Nathan's mission emanates from God's fidelity to the covenant of creation that implants this dynamism. God's commitment to bring this dynamism to fulfillment will ultimately take the form of the mission of Jesus Christ, Who offers Himself in sacrifice for the purification of consciences.[5] This mission of the Son of God, to set people free with the truth about God's mercy, is already at work in the mission of Nathan.

God does not give up on David. He is The Shepherd of His people,[6] and He goes in search of His lost sheep to "rescue them from all places

---

1 See Is 9:2.
2 See Is 60:1–3.
3 "*God whispers* to us in our pleasures, speaks in our conscience, but *shouts* in our *pain*: it is His megaphone to rouse a deaf world" (C. S. Lewis, *The Problem of Pain* [San Francisco: Harper San Francisco, 2001; reprint of 1940 original], 91).
4 *CCC*, 1781.
5 See Heb 9:9, 14; 10:22; 1 Pet 3:21.
6 See Ezek 34:15.

where they have been scattered on a day of clouds and thick darkness" (Ezek 34:12). Nathan's mission falls under this heading as well. He represents the Good Shepherd, Who goes looking for David in the spiritual wilderness into which he has wondered. He is ready to speak His word anew to this lost sheep, confident that David will find His voice familiar and follow Him into the fullness of truth.[7] The Lord's confidence is grounded in that irrepressible dynamism toward the truth that has not been nor can be uprooted from David's heart. Conversion is a return to the conviction that the voice of truth in one's conscience and the voice of truth in the words of God's messengers are one and the same.

Prior to his encounter with Nathan, David's unrepentant heart is hardened against the Lord. In the Bible, hardness of heart signifies a state of the will. It is not mere ignorance, but the unwillingness to acknowledge the truth about God despite the evidence that He provides that He is acting in behalf of man. God provides sufficient signs so that a sincere seeker of the truth is responsible to assent to it. Because the signs are sufficient, perversity of the will explains why a person does not assent. Hardness of heart means that a person is not honestly seeking the truth, and is thereby betraying the most fundamental human dynamism. Obstinacy of heart, however, cannot overthrow God's sovereignty over hearts.[8] Ultimately, God cannot be dethroned. He is always the Lord of human hearts.[9] And He is always ready to speak anew to hardened hearts.

The account of David's conversion is one of the richest lessons of the divine pedagogy. God knows the human heart. David's experience of being fully exposed to the penetrating knowledge of God could very well be the source and inspiration for his inspired meditation on the Lord's inscrutable knowledge of the interior mystery of man:

> [1] O Lord, you have searched me and known me!
> [2] You know when I sit down and when I rise up;
> you discern my thoughts from afar.
> [3] You search out my path and my lying down,
> and are acquainted with all my ways.
> [4] Even before a word is on my tongue,
> behold, O Lord, you know it altogether.
> [5] You beset me behind and before,
> and lay your hand upon me.
> [6] Such knowledge is too wonderful for me;

---

7   See Jn 10:4.
8   "Since, then, the will of God is the universal cause of all things, it is impossible that the divine will should not produce its effect. Hence that which seems to depart from the divine will in one order, returns into it in another order; as does the sinner, who by sin falls away from the divine will as much as lies in him, yet falls back into the order of that will, when by its justice he is punished" (Aquinas, *ST* I, Q. 19, a. 6).
9   See 1 Sam 16:7; Jer 17:10; Act 15:8; Rom 8:27. St. John writes of Jesus: "He knew all men and needed no one to bear witness of man; for he himself knew what was in man" (Jn 2:25). "God is greater than our hearts, and he knows everything" (1 Jn 3:20).

it is high, I cannot attain it.
⁷ Where shall I go from your Spirit?
Or where shall I flee from your presence?
⁸ If I ascend to heaven, you are there!
If I make my bed in Sheol, you are there!
⁹ If I take the wings of the morning
and dwell in the uttermost parts of the sea,
¹⁰ even there your hand shall lead me,
and your right hand shall hold me.
¹¹ If I say, "Let only darkness cover me,
and the light about me be night,"
¹² even the darkness is not dark to you,
the night is bright as the day;
for darkness is as light with you.
¹³ For you formed my inward parts,
you knitted me together in my mother's womb.
¹⁴ I praise you, for I am wondrously made.
Wonderful are your works!
You know me right well;
¹⁵ my frame was not hidden from you,
when I was being made in secret,
intricately wrought in the depths of the earth.
¹⁶ Your eyes beheld my unformed substance;
in your book were written, every one of them,
the days that were formed for me,
when as yet there was none of them.
¹⁷ How precious to me are your thoughts, O God!
How vast is the sum of them!
¹⁸ If I would count them, they are more than the sand.
When I awake, I am still with you. (Psalm 139:1–18)

This song of wonder and praise is much more than the fruit of a deep philosophical insight into the perfection of God's knowledge of man. For, we know that when someone has knowledge about our deepest secrets this knowledge can be misused and exploited to harm us. We feel vulnerable when we realize that we are unable to shield ourselves from being known by others. Only when we are confident that the person who knows us in depth loves us can we relax at the thought of being so thoroughly known, at the thought of another having entered that most personal and private of spaces, our consciences. This indicates that there is an unspoken premise to Psalm 139. David (the Psalmist) must be convinced that the God Whom he celebrates for His penetrating knowledge of his soul loves him and would never act on what He knows for any reason other than to love him.

A thousand years after David, God's revelation of man to himself produces another witness to the wonder of how thoroughly God knows us. The words that a Samaritan woman uses to introduce Jesus to her neighbors condense Psalm 139 to its bare essential: "Come, see a man who told me all that I ever did" (Jn 4:29). Like David, this woman (whom Eastern Churches venerate as the martyr, St. Photina) proclaims the marvel of being known by God. It must have made a deep impression on this woman that although Jesus does not disclose that He knows about her five husbands until deep into their dialogue, He must have known about her situation from the outset. In attention-grabbing contrast to how the woman's self-knowledge causes her to isolate herself from her neighbors—going to the well at the hottest time of the day in order to avoid contact with them—Jesus' knowledge of her does not cause Him to shun her. The reality is precisely the opposite. What Jesus knows about her draws Him close to her, for His mission is to seek sinners; His mercy impels Him to make God's love known to her. And so, the Samaritan woman can stand in His presence, fully exposed before the One Who sees all things,[10] without fear because she knows that in addition to being fully known she is fully loved. The perfect love of God, fully revealed in Jesus Christ, drives out the fear of being known by Him.[11]

With Nathan's intervention and David's subsequent confession of sins, the king's time of hiding from God's penetrating gaze, as Adam and Eve did, comes to an end. His conversion is a marvelous mystery of the synchronization of two freedoms, the uncreated freedom of God and the created freedom of David. Through Nathan, God speaks His word of truth and then entrusts David to his own freedom and judgment. The great sign of this divine regard for his dignity and freedom is what David could have done in response to Nathan's intervention, but did not do. He could have hardened his heart yet further and simply ignored the prophet; he could even have ordered the prophet to be killed, as he ordered the death of Uriah. But he does not do this. Rather, he commands a different death. David regains sovereignty over his freedom by putting sin to death. He commands the execution of that part of himself that St. Paul calls the "old man,"[12] his old sinful nature, in order to become a new man[13] in the truth. With his interior kingdom restored to order, David's kingship over Israel is also restored to its proper order. Nathan is the first beneficiary of David submitting to the reign of truth within himself.

---

10 For every one who does evil hates the light, and does not come to the light, lest his deeds should be exposed" (Jn 3:20). "For it is a shame even to speak of the things that they do in secret; but when anything is exposed by the light it becomes visible, for anything that becomes visible is light" (Eph 5:12–13). "And before him no creature is hidden, but all are open and laid bare to the eyes of him with whom we have to do" (Heb 4:13). "Behold, this child is set for the fall and rising of many in Israel, and for a sign that is spoken against ... that thoughts out of many hearts may be revealed" (Lk 2:34–35).

11 "In this is love perfected with us, that we may have confidence for the day of judgment, because as he is so are we in this world. There is no fear in love, but perfect love casts out fear. For fear has to do with punishment, and he who fears is not perfected in love" (1 Jn 4:17–18).

12 See Rom 6:6; Eph 4:22; Col 3:9.

13 See Eph 4:24.

A Prophet with a Dangerous Mission

The inspired witness to David's conversion is direct and terse about the role of Nathan: "The Lord sent Nathan to David" (2 Sam 12:1). Immediately following, the text recounts what Nathan said to David. The biblical account does not inform us whether Nathan's words for David come directly from God, as if He provided a script. What it expressly attributes to God is the mission to confront David. One can well imagine how the prophet might have reacted to this commission. David has committed adultery and murder, and his heart is hardened. Is there any reason not to think that the king will continue in his obduracy? If he has refused to listen to God's word—for it is His voice that echoes in the conscience, and the seventh and tenth commandments given to Moses clearly transcribe His word about murder and adultery—then why should David heed the word of a prophet who claims to speak in the Lord's name? It is far more likely that Nathan will come to the same end as Uriah.

Given these circumstances, one can readily imagine that the potential peril of his mission moved the prophet to pray for wisdom. What words can a man speak to "cut to the heart" (Acts 4:37) of a man with a hardened heart, in order to reestablish the sovereignty of truth in his conscience? And if his words do not cut to the king's heart, if the king does not have a change of heart, from a heart of stone to a heart of flesh,[14] this will surely mean death for the prophet. Indeed, the prospect of Nathan's death, if David does not receive his message of truth in humility, points toward the fullness of revelation in Christ, which affirms the relationship between conversion and death. To turn away from sin means to die to sin.[15] St. Paul calls it a crucifixion in order to convey that this death of the old man is a participation in Christ's death.[16] In accepting the possibility of dying at the hands of King David, Nathan already participates in the Paschal Mystery of Christ. He cannot know it, but if his words are to succeed in piercing the king's heart, it will be by reason of the power of divine love at work in Christ's death, a death that He interprets in terms of the rejection of truth,[17] a death that He transformed into a sacrifice for the forgiveness of sins by His love for the Father and for all the Father's sons and daughters. For, by this sacrifice all men can know that God's merciful love is greater than sin and the condemnation of an accusing conscience.[18] Because Nathan's mission is to bring David to entrust himself to God's mercy by confessing his sins, Jesus' death on the Cross is that definitive reality that he and all the prophets longed to see.[19] And, in David's conversion, his spiritual resurrection, in reality Nathan did live to see that day![20] His own perilous

---

14 See Ezek 11:19; 36:26. Once again, we see the history of Israel personified in David.
15 See Rom 6:2, 10–11.
16 See Rom 6:6; Gal 2:20.
17 See Jn 8:37, 40.
18 See 1 Jn 3:19–20.
19 See Mt 13:17; 1 Pet 1:10–12.
20 "Your father Abraham rejoiced that he was to see my day; he saw it and was glad" (Jn 8:56).

mission is a distant participation in the mission of Christ. If David welcomes Nathan's words as truth about his sin and truth about God's mercy, it is in virtue of Jesus' sacrifice on the Cross for the renewal of his heart.

The Cross of Christ means that God never gives up on man. It means that throughout all of history God is committed to man's rehabilitation, that sin does not have the final word, and that there is hope. The very fact that God does not simply condemn David but sends Nathan to bring about his conversion reveals the divine optimism. "As I live, says the Lord God, I have no pleasure in the death of the wicked, but that the wicked turn from his way and live" (Ezek 33:11). Nathan's acceptance of his mission, and the wisdom that guides his words so that they penetrate David's conscience, shows the profound uniformity of his heart and wisdom with God's heart and wisdom. With a heart attuned to God's compassion,[21] Nathan takes his place among the great associates in the mission of mercy.[22] David's sin serves as the occasion for a new revelation of God's mercy, a revelation predestined to reach all generations through the two accounts of his conversion: the narrative account of 2 Samuel, and the interior account of Psalm 51. The heart and conscience may be encrusted and impervious to the truth for a time, but so long as a man is alive there is hope for change. God desires this change, this conversion; He delights in it.[23]

It is pure speculation to wonder whether and when David may have come to his senses without the intervention of God's prophet. The biblical account makes clear that it is the dramatic intervention of God's word through His prophet that brings about David's conversion. Conversion always "means the inmost change of heart *under the influence of the word of God* and in the perspective of the kingdom."[24] God takes the initiative in our conversion, and this initiative takes the form of an intervention of His word. Why is this so? Because God desires that we cooperate with Him in our own conversion, and this requires the engagement of our free will, and this requires that we be informed about what He desires to accomplish. This shows that between God's word and David's heart there is a marvelous harmony. His heart is ready and receptive, even if he is not aware of it. There is, in the end, a harmony, a communion in the truth, but it does not start out that way. The word of God that brings David to conversion is not of his own making. It comes to him from without, in the form of an encounter with God.[25] Once Nathan pronounces this word,

---

21　See *CCC*, 2571, 2535, 2844.
22　See *CCC*, 2575.
23　See Lk 15:7, 10, 23–24, 32.
24　John Paul II, *Reconciliatio et paenitentia*, 4 (emphasis added).
25　See the reflections of Joseph Ratzinger on the subject of encounter with Christ as an event that comes from outside the person, in *Principles of Catholic Theology: Building Stones for a Fundamental Theology* (San Francisco: Ignatius Press, 1987), 184–186. It is possible that Ratzinger's emphasis on faith as an event-encounter with Christ is the fruit of theological reaction to the Modernist reduction of faith to being the development of an interior religious dynamism. Event-encounter safeguards the historical and objective character of the divine initiative. In the post-Vatican II pontificates of John Paul II and

David can make it his own by perceiving the truth it conveys, but he could not utter it himself. For, God's mercy reveals His holiness, it is His holiness in action,[26] and His holiness is impenetrable by human understanding.

Whatever David's inner state—the work of preparatory graces being assumed—the biblical narrative leaves no doubt about the divine initiative. David does not summon the prophet, as a sick person, aware of his condition, calls for a physician. He is more like Adam, avoiding God, and God's sending Nathan is His way of saying to David, in effect, "Where are you?" (Gen 3:9). God's love always comes first,[27] and this love takes the form of a search because, deluded by sin, man is afraid of God and tries to forget Him. As we have seen, Nathan's mission is a participation in the mission of Christ. His approach to David foreshadows the definitive act of God's search for man in Jesus Christ.

John Paul II eloquently expresses this divine search as rooted in God's love and made necessary by man's sin.

> *In Jesus Christ* God not only speaks to man but also *seeks him out.* The Incarnation of the Son of God attests that God goes in search of man. Jesus speaks of this search as the finding of a lost sheep (cf. Lk 15:1–7). It is a search which *begins in the heart of God* and culminates in the Incarnation of the Word. If God goes in search of man, created in his own image and likeness, he does so because he loves him eternally in the Word, and wishes to raise him in Christ to the dignity of an adoptive son. God therefore goes in search of man who *is his special possession* in a way unlike any other creature. Man is God's possession by virtue of a choice made in love: God seeks man out, moved by his fatherly heart.
>
> *Why does God seek man out?* Because man has turned away from him, hiding himself as Adam did among the trees of the Garden of Eden (cf. Gen 3:8–10). *Man allowed himself to be led astray* by the enemy of God (cf. Gen 3:13). Satan deceived man, persuading him that he too was a god, that he, like God, was capable of knowing good and evil, ruling the world according to his own will without having to take into account the divine will (cf. Gen 3:5). Going in search of man through his Son, God wishes to persuade man to abandon the paths of evil which lead him farther and farther afield. "Making him abandon" those paths means making man understand that he is taking the wrong path; it means

---

Benedict XVI, event-encounter takes on a pastoral value of serving to convey that beyond assent to revealed truth faith is a personal relationship with Jesus Christ.

26   See Hos 11:9.
27   See 1 Jn 4:10, 19.

> *overcoming the evil* which is everywhere found in human history. *Overcoming evil: this is the meaning of the Redemption.*[28]

The intervention of God's word through Nathan is as unanticipated by David as is the Incarnation by all of Israel. That both are unanticipated (because un-anticipatable) does not mean that God did not prepare His people for them. It only means that we have to understand accurately what divine preparation is. Those whom God prepares are able to identify His intervention when it happens, not because they have received a pre-vision of the event, but because God's grace has so shaped their knowledge of His ways that they are able to recognize an event as of divine origin. They do not know precisely how, where, and when God will intervene. They know only that He will intervene, and their faith in Him and His past interventions so shapes their hierarchy of values and way of judging things that they are able to recognize His new intervention when it comes. Mature faith entails the capacity to discern the signs of the times.[29] The Church enjoys this supernatural power of discernment, for example, when she declares certain men and women as worthy of veneration. She knows the ways of the Holy Spirit, so that she is able to recognize the Spirit of holiness at work in the lives of the faithful.[30]

Mary's faith at the Annunciation displays this power to recognize God's activity. We cannot imagine anyone being more perfectly disposed to receive the gift of God, yet this did not result in Mary knowing in advance either the day or the hour. Nor could she know in advance the mystery of the Incarnation. Divine revelation is always the making known of the hidden wisdom of God.[31] Even those who live fully and unconditionally according to God's wisdom today cannot draw certain

---

28 John Paul II, *Tertio millennio adveniente*, 7. John 4:23 is a biblical foundation for this theme of God searching man: "the hour is coming, and now is, when the true worshipers will worship the Father in spirit and truth, for such the Father seeks to worship Him." If this "seeking" is taken simply as a synonym for "desire," it does not have the force of an active search. But, we know that God's desires always become action, His love becomes an initiative. So, the Father's seeking takes the form of the graces He bestows to lead men and women to faith. As we know, these graces derive from the Paschal Mystery, where Christ fully reveals what it means to worship the Father in spirit and in truth. In the Son, the Father's love is satisfied, His seeking comes to an end. Finally, in Christ, man is everything that the Father ever wanted him to be. God is at work in David's heart, searching for a heart that will adore Him in spirit and in truth. God is constructing the temple for the Lord that David desired to build, so that God is fulfilling David's desire, which is to say He is answering his prayer, in a manner that David could not have imagined. By his conversion, David's heart becomes that temple in which he worships God in spirit and in truth by offering to Him the sacrifice of a humble and contrite heart.

29 See Mt 16:1–3; Lk 12:54–56. When Jesus associates faith with His miracles of healing (see Mt 9:22; Mk 10:52; Lk 17:19; 18:42), He is not saying that faith is the cause of the miracles. Rather, the miraculous power is in Him (see Mk 5:30). He is saying that by faith those whom He has healed, and others who believe in His signs, see His signs as indications of the fulfillment of God's promises regarding the coming of the Kingdom.

30 See *CCC*, 828.

31 See 1 Cor 2:7.

conclusions from it about tomorrow. Today's fidelity to God's will is the best way to be prepared to be faithful to His will tomorrow, but it is no guarantee of knowing the details of His will for tomorrow—except that He wills our fidelity. Jesus' teaching that we can know neither the day nor the hour of His final coming[32] applies to the specific details of every manifestation of God's will. We know with certainty that He desires our response of faith. We know with certainty that He desires our fidelity to His gift of purified conscience. For, the standard way that He comes into our lives is through moments of truth in our consciences. To be alert to the truth, to be prepared to accept all the demands of the truth—this is the necessary disposition to recognize and to respond to the interventions of God in our lives. For, He is Truth, and He always come to us, and can only come to us, as Truth.

God's word is ever efficacious; it is never unfulfilled:[33]

> [10] For as the rain and the snow come down from heaven,
> and do not return there but water the earth,
>   making it bring forth and sprout,
> giving seed to the sower and bread to the eater,
> [11] so shall my word be that goes forth from my mouth;
> it shall not return to me empty,
>   but it shall accomplish that which I intend,
> and prosper in the thing for which I sent it. (Isaiah 55:10–11)

The proof that God wisely prepares men for the intervention of His word, even if those being prepared are not conscious of it, is their reception of His word. David's conversion, his acceptance of the truth of God's word pronounced by Nathan, proves that in God's plan there is a marvelous coordination between the outward, spoken word, and the disposition of the heart to whom God addresses His message of mercy.

David could not have known, in advance, the blessing of truth awaiting him the day that Nathan came to him. Entrusted by God to Nathan, the divine word of truth storms in and takes David by surprise. Perhaps the element of surprise is a key element in the strategy of divine mercy, for it leaves no room for prepared defenses. Whatever the span of time between his commission and the execution of his mission, and whatever the dynamism of interaction between the prophet's personal insights into human nature and the light of divine wisdom expanding the vision of his mind, in Nathan God finds an associate in His optimism and His mercy, a man who understands the mysterious workings of the human heart and its irrepressible openness to truth, as well as its capacity to ward it off. The tactic he adopts proves to be an effective stimulus in bringing David to conversion.

---

32   See Mt 24:36–51; 15:1–3; 25:14–31.
33   See 1 Sam 3:19.

In approaching David, with his already burdened conscience, Nathan does not play the role of accuser. That would be to stand in judgment of the king, and this would be to usurp the king's role, since the king is a judge. The prophet's tactic is to affirm and to appeal to the king's office as judge, to call upon him to exercise the authority that comes with his God-given vocation. For too long, David has been thinking in categories that do not lend themselves to conversion. He is preoccupied with saving face, with avoiding the public embarrassment that would most certainly result if people come to know about his relationship with Bathsheba. He is thinking of his prestige in the eyes of the people. These are preoccupations that leave little room for God's word to work its characteristic function of cutting to the heart. So, by bringing to the king a case of injustice, Nathan cleverly changes the venue of thought. Suddenly, David begins to think in terms of right and wrong, justice and injustice, truth and falsehood. Grace is at home with these categories. It is possible to say that the evil one and sin have home field advantage when categories of power, prestige, pleasure, and possessions fill the heart, while the Holy Spirit has home field advantage when categories of truth, justice, virtue, and goodness fill the heart.

In order to lead David to see the truth about what he has done, the first thing Nathan must accomplish is to gain home field advantage. It does not suffice that Nathan judge the king and accuse him of wrongdoing, for in that case the judgment about sin would come from the outside. If David is to "take sides with the truth against himself," he must discover the evil of sin and see it for himself, though this cannot happen without the intervention of the prophetic word. Nathan's mission teaches us the extent to which God wants the judgment about sin to come from within. God knows the truth all along, and Nathan is the first to share in His knowledge. The aim of the prophetic mission is to draw David into this communion in the truth.

Clearly, God does not want to be alone in seeing the full truth about sin, for aloneness means isolation, lack of communion, and since God is love this is contrary to His nature. As St. John of the Cross observes, "true and perfect love knows not how to keep anything hidden from the beloved."[34] In this way, Nathan's mission anticipates and participates in that of the Incarnate Son, Whose distance from the apostles as He prayed alone in the garden, and His repeated plea that they join Him in this prayer, vividly depict the divine desire for communion with those He loves. Jesus' question, "So, could you not watch with me one hour?" (Mt 26:40) reveals the pain of a heart in isolation. Jesus poses this question to every person, including David, whose conscience has wandered far from the word of God. Nathan's privilege is to alleviate the pain of the Sacred Heart of Jesus in relation to David by bringing the king to conversion, which is always a

---

[34] John of the Cross, *Spiritual Canticle*, Stanza 23, 1. In this text, John of the Cross is describing the total gift that God makes of Himself in the state of transforming union or spiritual marriage. This is the culmination of God's self-giving that begins with the first graces of conversion. David's and every sinner's communion with God in the knowledge of his sin and of God's mercy inchoately has the nature of spiritual marriage.

participation in Christ's suffering caused by sin. Conversion begins with seeing what God sees concerning the evil of sin, so that man's judgment can be a participation in God's own judgment. With Nathan's awareness of the king's sin and of its dreadful consequences, he accompanies Jesus in His agony in the garden and the entire Paschal Mystery. The prophet's mission is to draw David into this communion in the truth about sin, the truth about the price that sin exacts on God Himself, and the truth about the triumph of God's mercy. So long as there are people who are outside this communion in the drama of sin and suffering, mercy and reconciliation, the Church's prophetic mission continues: to relieve the aloneness of Jesus by bringing people to participate in His passion caused by sin so as to participate in the triumph of His love over sin.

Nathan's mission, as for all the prophets, is to be the conscience of God's people. The prophets' perspective is decidedly inward. While the people's preoccupation is with the enemies around them, the prophets' role is to forewarn them about an interior enemy. "Instead of cursing the enemy," Rabbi Heschel comments, "the prophets condemn their own nation."[35] When the conscience "is subject to fatigue, longs for comfort, lulling, soothing,"[36] the prophets' task is to break down barriers—between the people and God, and among individuals within the people—caused by weak consciences, to remain alert to every misuse of freedom, and to check moral drowsiness. Prior to the encounter with Nathan, David's conscience is in this state of dysfunction, and thus he needs a prophet. He cannot call good and evil by their proper name.[37] He cannot correct himself. He needs the intervention of God's word.

It is vital to remind ourselves that the prophets are not foreigners. God calls His prophets *from within* His chosen people. When God makes use of foreigners it is to call upon their armies to correct Israel through a humiliating defeat, to execute a judgment *from without*. The role of the prophets, in contrast, is to be a voice within the people, to remind them of their duties toward God and neighbor, which are rooted in the covenant. Too often, though, the people treat the prophets as if they are the enemy, a foreign power imposing itself upon them. In such a state the chosen people are like a man divided within himself, at war with its own conscience, and therefore at war with God's word, God's truth—God Himself. Israel's actual wars with the surrounding nations are meant to expose this interior battle, to reveal that Israel, by the misuse of its freedom, is its own worst enemy. The words of St. James capture it well: "What causes wars, and what causes fightings among you? Is it not your passions that are at war in your members?" (Jas 4:1).

So long as person relates to his own conscience as an adversary, which is to despise the word of God and to relate to it as an adversary—precisely

---

35 Abraham Joshua Heschel, *The Prophets* (New York: Harper & Row, 1962), 12.
36 Ibid., 9.
37 "A result of an upright conscience is, first of all, *to call good and evil by their proper name*" (John Paul II, *Dominum et Vivificantem*, 43).

what the serpent insinuated to Adam and Eve—he will never know a moment of peace. Restlessness will be the just punishment for sin that he has to endure, and he will remain restless until he finds rest in the forgiving and reconciling mercy of God. St. Augustine expresses it with words that are immediately intelligible for every human being:

> For where was my heart to flee from refuge from my heart? Whither was I to fly from myself? To what place should I not follow myself?[38]

One has to come to terms with oneself. The alternative is unending restlessness. And Romano Guardini lucidly comments:

> Here the self hides from its own moral gaze, taking refuge in a realm of pretense which comes into being because the will refuses to see what it should see, stubbornly ignoring facts, playing a comedy of lies.[39]

If peace is the interior tranquility of harmony among the various dynamisms of man, it simply cannot be attained so long as he attempts to evade the truth. For, truth is embedded in every being man encounters, including himself. To shun the truth is to flee from one's own heart, to fly from oneself!

The prophetic mission is to give voice to the truth of God in a situation in which a man views it with suspicion, as a threat. This is why the prophets' mission cannot fail to entail violence. The exterior violence that marks the history of the Kingdoms of Israel and of Judah is rooted in the interior violence that men do to themselves by violating their own consciences. Sent by God, the prophets are easy targets of the anguished questioning and desperate petitions that spring from the interior upheaval of consciences desecrated by sin. Job, the man reputed to be just before God, gives voice to this dire state of internal defilement and the desire to be liberated from it.

> [11] Therefore, I will not restrain my mouth;
> I will speak in the anguish of my spirit;
> I will complain in the bitterness of my soul....
> [16] I loathe my life, I would not live forever.
> Let me alone, for my days are a breath.
> [17] What is man, that you make so much of him,
> and that you set your mind upon him,
> [18] visit him every morning,
> and test him every moment?

---

38 Augustine, *Confessions*, 4.7.12 (trans. Sheed).
39 Romano Guardini, *The Conversion of St. Augustine* (Chicago: Henry Regnery Press, 1960), 20.

> ^{19} How long will you not look away from me,
> nor let me alone till I swallow my spittle?
> ^{20} If I sin, what do I do to you, you watcher of men?
> Why have you made me your mark?
> Why have I become a burden to you?
> ^{21} Why do you not pardon my transgression,
> and take away my iniquity?" (Job 7:11, 16–21)

A petition to be left alone is in effect a plea to be freed from an accusing conscience. It is a desire for a resolution with no price, basically, a superficial covering over, which Adam and Eve attempted by making loincloths. If God will not pardon, then it is better to be without Him. Without God's mercy and forgiveness, sin has the final word and there is no resolution of the internal conflict. If man is unreconciled with any one of three realities, conscience, truth, and God, he is unreconciled with all three. He is alienated from himself (conscience) and from his supreme good (God, the truth). In the most radical way he cannot live with himself. He comes to resent that he has a conscience, and this means that he resents that God and truth have access to his inner being. He resents that his very being is openness and accessibility to God and to truth. Because this is in fact what it means to be human, his very existence becomes odious. His life becomes an endless repetition of Adam and Eve's desperate futility in attempting to hide from God, Who is omnipresent.[40] There is no place to which one can withdraw in order to evade God's presence.[41] Until he recognizes that his conscience is not the invading army of a foreign power, a person wages war against himself in the vain effort to muffle a voice that cannot be silenced. Instead of taking sides with the truth against himself, such a person takes sides with himself—but this self is the "old self" of St. Paul, a false self, a pseudo-self—against the truth, and thus against his true self. The flight from conscience, the flight from truth, the flight from a prophet—anyone who bears the truth—and the flight from God are all the same. If one is perceived as an enemy then so are the others.

This is the historical drama and the anthropological reality behind Jesus' words about the rejection and persecution of the prophets[42] and His own rejection and crucifixion: "you seek to kill me, *because my word finds no place in you*. ... now you seek to kill me, a man who has told you the truth which I heard from God" (Jn 8:37, 40). Conscience is the organ of truth. It bears witness that "truth cannot impose itself except by virtue of its own truth, as it makes its entrance into the mind at once quietly and with power."[43] Jesus is the Truth, the Word of God, Who "will not cry or lift up his voice, or make it heard in the street" (Is 42:2) because He knows that if it is not heard in the heart it simply will not be heard. The death of the

---

40 See Gen 3:10.
41 See Ps 139:7.
42 See Mt 5:12; 23:29–37.
43 Vatican II, *Dignitatis humanae*, 1.

prophets and the death of Christ show that matters of truth are matters of life and death. When man sins, conscience's dynamism toward truth is meant to be a judgment against anti-truth, a condemnation of the betrayal of truth, and a new beginning of life in the truth. When the sinner resists this dynamism of conscience he redirects it outwardly, now no longer taking aim at the one who betrays the truth—himself—but the one who bears the truth in God's name. The result is still a condemnation and a death, but now it is the death of truth and the one who proclaims it.

Nowhere has this internal state of conflict and its projection outward as aggression against the truth been more vividly described than in Wisdom.

> [12] "Let us lie in wait for the righteous man,
> because he is inconvenient to us and opposes our actions;
> he reproaches us for sins against the law,
> and accuses us of sins against our training.
> [13] He professes to have knowledge of God,
> and calls himself a child of the Lord.
> [14] He became to us a reproof of our thoughts;
> [15] the very sight of him is a burden to us,
> because his manner of life is unlike that of others,
> and his ways are strange.
> [16] We are considered by him as something base,
> and he avoids our ways as unclean;
> he calls the last end of the righteous happy,
> and boasts that God is his father.
> [17] Let us see if his words are true,
> and let us test what will happen at the end of his life;
> [18] for if the righteous man is God's son, he will help him,
> and will deliver him from the hand of his adversaries.
> [19] Let us test him with insult and torture,
> that we may find out how gentle he is,
> and make trial of his forbearance.
> [20] Let us condemn him to a shameful death,
> for, according to what he says, he will be protected."
> [21] Thus they reasoned, but they were led astray,
> for their wickedness blinded them,
> [22] and they did not know the secret purposes of God.
> (Wisdom 2:12–22)

This text from Wisdom confirms the acumen of the adage: That which is received is received according to the mode of the receiver. Consider the contrast: "The Lord loves the righteous" (Ps 146:8), He delights to "bless the righteous [and] cover him with favor" (Ps 5:12). But, "the wicked plots against the righteous" (Ps 37:12; 94:21). Like the Lord Himself, the Church loves the righteous, the saints. In them, she recognizes "the power of the Spirit of holiness within her and sustains the hope of believers by proposing the saints to them as models and intercessors."⁴⁴ Saints draw us to God by drawing us to themselves. God delights in the righteous, looks approvingly on them, and says, "This is very good" (Gen 1:31), "With you I am well pleased" (Lk 3:22). What could account for others finding the righteous odious?

It is one's relation to the truth. Those who subjugate their own consciences by shutting out the truth, and who repudiate the very possibility of conversion, find the righteous man inconvenient, a reproach, an accusation, a reproof, a burden. It is a replay of the reaction of Adam, Eve, and Job to God. For, God speaks to us through His saints.⁴⁵ He is present in the righteous because the righteous live in the presence of God, and the sinner cannot abide His presence. "Depart from me, for I am a sinful man, O Lord" (Lk 5:8).

The self-inflicted violence of sin—the overthrow of truth—can only be resolved by the violence of conversion, that is, the overthrow of the lie that has usurped the reign of truth. The effect of the virtue and religious integrity of the righteous is to attract, to enamor others by the beauty of virtue, and to move them to rededicate themselves to strain forward in the pursuit of truth and virtue—in a word, to engage in conversion. The righteous man possesses precisely that which all seek: the interior harmony of a conscience at peace in the reign of God's truth within. The plot to do away with the righteous is, ironically, motivated by a search for peace of conscience. But it is based on a fundamental misunderstanding. For, in ridding the world of the righteous man a person cannot succeed in ridding himself of his own conscience. The sinner mistakes the occasion for a moment of truth, namely, the encounter with a righteous man, with the reality itself of the voice of conscience that haunts him.

With its depiction of the persecution of the righteous man, which is definitively realized in the crucifixion of Jesus Christ, the Bible reveals the ultimate playing out of the perverse logic of sin. In his penetrating analysis, St. Thomas Aquinas shows that in every sin there is a choice to disregard God's voice, to turn away from His truth by turning one's entire attention to some apparent good. In other words, in every sin there is a "canceling" of God, an overriding of the claim that God's truth has on us, its right to be heard and obeyed. And habitual sin—what Scripture calls the hardening of heart-conscience—creates a personal, interior "cancel culture," a deliberate self-exclusion from communion in the truth with God and others.⁴⁶

---

44   *CCC*, 828.
45   "In the lives of those who, sharing in our humanity, are however more perfectly transformed into the image of Christ, God vividly manifests His presence and His face to men. He speaks to us in them, and gives us a sign of His Kingdom, to which we are strongly drawn, having so great a cloud of witnesses over us and such a witness to the truth of the Gospel" (Vatican II, *Lumen gentium*, 50).
46   This anticipates the state of hell, which awaits those who die without having repented of this self-exclusion from communion in the truth. "To die in mortal sin without repenting and accepting God's merciful love means remaining separated from him for ever by our own free choice. This state of definitive self-exclusion from communion with God and the blessed is called 'hell'" (*CCC*, 1033).

Sin always begins with a choice to favor some other voice over God's voice, as is apparent in Adam and Eve acting on the word of the serpent and disregarding the words of God. Their sin entails a reversal of justice. It expels God's word, which enjoys full right of citizenship in man's conscience, and confers this very right of citizenship on the serpent's words. Nathan conveys precisely this by saying that David has "despised the word of the Lord" (2 Sam 12:9). David prefers to listen to another voice, the voice of lust, thereby trampling on the right of God's voice in order to grant this right to another voice that has no claim to it. He thereby establishes an interior "cancel culture" —an inner kingdom of injustice.[47] This is the reign of disordered love,[48] and, to satisfy his disordered desire, David misuses his royal authority and thereby becomes a king like the kings of other nations—the ironic fulfillment of the people's desire for a king in order to be like the other nations. The kingdom of injustice that David establishes within brings injustice into the kingdom Israel.

The interior "canceling" of God's word in David's conscience leads to the "cancelation" of Uriah. In words that can be seen as an elaboration of the indictment of Nathan against David, St. James expresses the same movement from an interior violence ("cancelation") perpetrated against the word of God to exterior violence: "What causes wars, and what causes fightings among you? Is it not your passions that are at war in your members? You desire and do not have; so you kill. And you covet and cannot obtain; so you fight and wage war" (Jas 4:1–2). In relation to the king's interior "cancel culture," Uriah is the righteous man whose very existence cannot fail to remind David that Bathsheba does not belong to him. By ridding the world of this righteous man, David intends to protect his personal "cancel culture," which, because it is the inculturation of a lie, is perpetually threatened by the truth. It is a futile effort to silence God Himself and the echo of His voice in his conscience.

The humble man lives in a state of constant conversion.[49] He realizes that there are any number of interior "cancel cultures" of which he is unaware until confronted by the word of God—as when Nathan confronted David. The humble man learns that in many ways he has chosen to listen to other voices. He is not surprised, then, when the truth suddenly exposes one or another of the voices that constitute his interior "cancel culture." In more

---

47 See Aquinas on the interior order of justice in man, whereby "what is highest in man is subject to God" (*ST* I-II, Q. 113, a. 1).
48 See Aquinas, *ST* II-II, Q. 29, especially article 3, where he considers the same interior order of justice (see previous note) under the heading of peace.
49 On the theme of constant conversion, see John Paul II, *Dives in misericordia*, 13: "Authentic knowledge of the God of mercy, the God of tender love, is a constant and inexhaustible source of conversion, not only as a momentary interior act but also as a permanent attitude, as a state of mind. Those who come to know God in this way, who 'see' Him in this way, can live only in a state of being continually converted to Him. They live, therefore, in *statu conversionis*; and it is this state of conversion which marks out the most profound element of the pilgrimage of every man and woman on earth in *statu viatoris*."

traditional language, this is "an unhealthy attachment to creatures"[50] resulting from disdaining God's voice and determining to avoid it in the future. The humble man expects to have his inner "cancel culture" threatened, and welcomes the moment of truth that exposes it because he loves God and His truth more than himself. He considers every victory over his interior "cancel culture" a glitter of God's glory. Now, he no longer attempts to escape God's word but seeks it wherever it may be found. He is at home with the Scriptures, in the company of saints (the righteous), because he is at home in his own conscience and the truth that he finds there.

The humble man is ever-so alert to the fact that other voices vie for attention against God's voice. A culture that "cancels" God's voice celebrates and amplifies other voices, setting them to music, enshrining them in law, inscribing them in literature, integrating them into curricula. The interior culture of the humble man, the man of conscience and conversion, who seeks and lives according to God's truth, is counter-cultural in relation to the culture that "cancels" that truth. He is the righteous man whom that culture finds inconvenient, a reproach, an accusation, a reproof, a burden.

The crucifixion of Jesus Christ is the "canceling" of the eternal Word of God, *the* Righteous Man. His judges could not imagine a fulfillment of God's promises other than as a restoration of the exterior Kingdom of Israel and the worship in the Temple of Jerusalem. This should alert anyone who thinks that he is exempt from the lingering effects of sin and projects his personal expectations regarding the fulfillment of God's promises onto His words. This is why there is a constant need for the purification of concepts, and of the virtue of hope, which can only take place if we are on guard with respect to elements of "cancel culture" that remain within us.

Universally, the crucifixion of Christ demonstrates that the drama of being human boils down to a decision about life and death. "I have set before you life and death, blessing and curse; therefore choose life, that you and your descendants may live" (Dt 30:19). There are only two possibilities. The first is an interior death, what St. Paul calls the death of the old man who is defined by sin. In this case, a person identifies with Christ and takes his place with Him on the Cross. Only from the Cross of Christ can a person "take sides with the truth against himself" and rise to new life in the truth. The second possibility is to remain an enemy of the truth and to commit oneself to its destruction. Here again it is a decision about the Cross of Christ, only with this option a person becomes an accomplice in the execution of the One Who is the truth.

All of this is present and at work in Nathan's mission to David. The entire episode is charged with the intensity of the life-or-death dynamic. Uriah and those unfortunate fellow soldiers who were with him are already dead, and David's heart is in a state of spiritual death. Nathan's life is on the line, as he approaches a man who is responsible for the death of Uriah and his comrades. Because innocent blood cries out to Him, the God of life

---

50   *CCC*, 1472.

cannot remain indifferent. Where will the death of Uriah and the spiritual death of David's sin lead? Will Nathan, and with him the truth and God Himself, be the next victim? Or will there be a death to sin, a conversion, and a resurrection of that heart after the heart of God Himself?

In the Old Testament, innocent blood cries to heaven for vengeance.[51] God says to Cain, "The voice of your brother's blood is crying out to me from the ground" (Gen 4:10). Abel is the first recorded occurrence of the persecution of the righteous man, the unrepentant sinner's violent reaction to the witness of truth in another, which the Book of Wisdom describes (quoted above). The death of the innocent Abel prefigures the death of Christ, and configures him to Christ, Whose "blood ... speaks more graciously than the blood of Abel" (Heb 12:24). From Abel to Christ a great development takes place. The justice of avenging the death of the innocent for which their blood cries is surpassed by the mercy of forgiving sins for which Christ's blood cries.[52] Through the prophet Nathan, the blood of Christ is already at work to bring David to repentance. For, God desires not the death of the sinner, but his return to life: "Have I any pleasure in the death of the wicked, says the Lord God, and not rather that he should turn from his way and live?" (Ezek 18:23).

King David's Conversion

Nathan comes to the king with a case in need of adjudication. The story that he relates accomplishes three things. First, it gets David focused on a situation that does not involve him directly. Perhaps Nathan bases his calculation on the commonly observed fact that we can often be more objective when considering the conditions and affairs of others. We are, as is said, too close to ourselves to see clearly about ourselves. Perhaps, too, in the moral sphere, we are not always immediately aware of how the truth that applies for others may also apply in our own lives. Second, Nathan's wisdom may well be to catch David with his defenses down. All along, David is unaware of the fact that the purported story of injustice is actually a parable pointing to his own sin. The prophet's strategy is to catch David off guard, as it were, with his conscience unprotected by defense mechanisms aimed at keeping the truth about his sin at a distance for which it cannot reach him. Third, though conscience properly regards judgments about one's own actions, Nathan's story of injustice leads David into a kind of outer chamber of the conscience, where the king is in a place of proximity to his own conscience without realizing it.

With the defenses around David's conscience inattentive to and unprepared for Nathan's stealthy strategy, the encounter takes place.

> [1] And the Lord sent Nathan to David. He came to him, and said to him, "There were two men in a certain city, the one

---

51   See Deut 32:43; Ps 9:12; 79:10.
52   This is how Aquinas interprets Christ's blood speaking more graciously than the blood of Abel, in Heb 12:24.

rich and the other poor. ² The rich man had very many flocks and herds; ³ but the poor man had nothing but one little ewe lamb, which he had bought. And he brought it up, and it grew up with him and with his children; it used to eat of his morsel, and drink from his cup, and lie in his bosom, and it was like a daughter to him. ⁴ Now there came a traveler to the rich man, and he was unwilling to take one of his own flock or herd to prepare for the wayfarer who had come to him, but he took the poor man's lamb, and prepared it for the man who had come to him." ⁵ Then David's anger was greatly kindled against the man; and he said to Nathan, "As the Lord lives, the man who has done this deserves to die; ⁶ and he shall restore the lamb fourfold, because he did this thing, and because he had no pity." (2 Samuel 12:1–6)

This would be a particularly moving case for David. It would no doubt call to mind myriad images from his days as a shepherd, and thereby put his homicidal act in its true perspective. For, to rule as Israel's king is to shepherd God's people,[53] and David's treatment of Uriah was anything but that of a shepherd guarding his sheep. Everything about David's life as a shepherd was the providential preparation for ruling as king. His skill with a slingshot, honed in protecting his sheep from wolves, was preordained to be decisive in the defeat of the Philistines. So too, now, Nathan's story stirs his shepherd's heart. Memories of protecting his sheep from danger suddenly flood David's consciousness, arousing sentiments of the solicitude he long ago exercised in relation to the sheep entrusted to him.

Nathan's device to play on the king's power of judgment, which had not been totally obliterated by his sinful deviation from justice, succeeds. As king of Israel, David quite naturally reaches a verdict of guilty concerning the rich man who stole and slaughtered the poor man's one and only precious lamb. For, as a psalm attributed to David's son and successor, Solomon, makes clear, the office of the king is to exercise judgment in behalf of the poor:

¹ Give the king your justice, O God,
and your righteousness to the royal son!
² May he may judge your people with righteousness,
and your poor with justice! ...
⁴ May he defend the cause of the poor of the people,
give deliverance to the needy,
and crush the oppressor. (Psalm 72:1–2, 4)

Through Nathan, God arouses David's sense of truth and justice in order to help bring the Lord's anointed, this man after God's own heart, back to God and back to his true self. The prophet's story about the stolen

---

53 See 2 Sam 5:2; Ezek 37:24.

sheep causes David to remember the applicable law: "When someone steals an ox or a sheep, and slaughters it or sells it, the thief shall pay five oxen for an ox, and four sheep for a sheep" (Ex 22:1). This is the decisive move intended by Nathan. Now the king is judging things in the light of the ordinances associated with God's covenant with His people.

It is significant that just prior to invoking the principle of fourfold restitution, David says, with the solemnity of an oath-formula: "As the Lord lives, the man who has done this deserves to die" (2 Sam 12:5). Are these words the spontaneous expression of the heart of a shepherd? It is likely so. Yet, in God's wisdom, they echo the penalty laid down for adultery: "If a man is caught lying with the wife of another man, both of them shall die, the man who lay with the woman as well as the woman. So you shall purge the evil from Israel" (Dt 22:22). David did not heed the commandment, "You shall not covet your neighbor's wife" (Ex 20:17). Let himself be seduced by the forbidden fruit of another man's wife, he incurs the penalty of death.

It is difficult to imagine that David's conscience did not catch him in the act of adultery, and then murder. If it did, he managed to circumvent its voice, both when it warned him before the act and afterward, when it convicted him of being guilty. God's plan is to jolt the king's arrested conscience with the truth about his action so that it beat again. For, God does not want to be alone in knowing the truth about David's sin. Nathan's commission is in the name of that friendship that Jesus Christ will reveal is rooted in knowing what the Father knows (Jn 15:15). To restore friendship with David, God must bring him to see the truth about his sin, which means that he must come to see it as God sees it.

All that is required now is for Nathan to say: "You are the man" (2 Sam 12:7). David stands naked, exposed, and defenseless before the tribunal of the truth seated in his own conscience. Now he sees himself as the preying wolf that, to satisfy his illicit hunger, took another man's wife. Unwittingly, in condemning the man who stole his neighbor's lamb, David implicitly passes judgment on himself and finds himself guilty. He is the one who has violated justice. He, David, is the oppressor, and Uriah is the poor man in whose favor he has judged.

The details of Nathan's story of injustice fit David's situation so exactly that there is no escape for the king's conscience. For, at the time that he sends for Bathsheba he has several wives. That night he could approach any one of these, but instead he chooses to take for himself the wife of another man. If in his first words upon learning of the man who stole his neighbor's single and precious lamb David could exclaim that such an act deserves death, how much more is death an appropriate sentence for a man who takes another man's wife! The force of the parallel is inescapable. He cannot deny the applicability of the judgment he passes on the rich man to his own case. It is too obvious. The king finds himself trapped by his own logic of justice. He stands condemned in his own eyes, by his own words, and he admits his guilt: "I have sinned against the Lord" (2 Sam 12:13).[54]

Had a relative of Uriah been privy to the words by which David avows his sin he might object that something essential is missing. Uriah is most obviously the one offended by David's actions, first by violating the exclusivity of the bond of marriage, and second by depriving him of life itself. How is it that David can state, in the psalm associated with this repentance: "Against you, you only, have I sinned, and done that which is evil in your sight" (Ps 51:4)? There are two answers. First, in the covenant with Israel God aligns Himself with the poor, especially those who suffer injustice. The evil that registers in David's conscience is defined in relation to God. Concretely, David's sin is against Uriah, but in a foundational way it is against the God Who created Uriah. The second answer makes this foundational dimension concrete. By becoming man, God identifies Himself with everyone who stands in need of justice and mercy. In Christ, God Himself says: "as you did it not to one of the least of these, you did it not to me" (Mt 25:45). By his sin, David does more than to disobey a precept. From the perspective of the One Who enjoins a precept out of love for those to whom it is given, such disobedience is necessarily also a rejection of God's love. David's transgression adds to the burden carried by the Suffering Servant: "he was wounded for our transgressions, he was bruised for our iniquities ... the Lord has laid on him the iniquity of us all" (Is 53:5–6). Thus, David's sin is an active participation in the crucifixion of the Son of God, Who "bore our sins in his body on the tree" (1 Pet 2:24). Though chronologically David is one thousand years removed from the Paschal Mystery, that mystery is present and at work in every dimension of the king's sin and conversion.[55]

The comparison between the story of the heartless man who stole his neighbor's one and only lamb and David's situation casts the light of truth

---

54 There may be more to the comparison. If the stolen lamb had been the one and only, precious lamb of the man from whom it was taken, this must mean that he was not a shepherd and that this lamb was purchased and raised in view of the celebration of the Passover. This overlays the lamb with a profound religious significance, and this reveals the owner's commitment of faith to keep the prescriptions for the celebration of the great event of liberation from slavery. The lamb represents this man's faith, his fidelity to the covenant that God established with Israel. By stealing it for his guest, the man with an abundant flock acts with disdain for the covenant and thus for the God of the covenant. In general, sins of injustice deprive people of what they have a right to, and rights derive from a person's responsibility for his life, his duty to fulfill all of the duties that are embedded in his human nature. The injustice perpetrated by the man with abundant flocks deprives his neighbor of what he needs in order to fulfill the justice of the Law by sacrificing the Passover lamb with his own family.

55 "The revelation of the mystery of the Redemption opens the way to an understanding in which *every sin* wherever and whenever committed has a reference to the Cross of Christ—and therefore indirectly also to the sin of those who 'have not believed in him,' and who condemned Jesus Christ to death on the Cross" (John Paul II, *Dominum et Vivificantem*, 29). John Paul further develops this theme of the Holy Spirit convincing the world about sin (see Jn 16:8), always in reference to the Cross of Christ, in *Dominum et Vivificantem*, 32.

on the disorder of the king's self-love, which reduces Bathsheba and Uriah to objects of his impulse. By taking Bathsheba for himself, David deprives her of the integrity of her marriage, and by ordering Uriah's death, the king deprives him of any possibility of enjoying and celebrating the freedom of Israel. As grave as this is, the prophet's primary concern is with how all of this affects David's relationship with God. It is not just a commandment that David transgresses, as if moral precepts had some kind of autonomous existence independent of the One Who is their source. David does much more than to break a rule. He scorns the One Who called him from the pasture to be king. By his sins he shows himself to be an ungrateful recipient of God's gracious initiative.

It is at this precise point that Nathan no longer speaks in his own name. With the formal prophetic introduction, he conveys to David the words received from God to disclose the Lord's perspective of unrequited love.

> [7] "Thus says the Lord, the God of Israel: 'I anointed you king over Israel, and I delivered you out of the hand of Saul; [8] and I gave you your master's house, and your master's wives into your bosom, and gave you the house of Israel and of Judah; and if this were too little, I would add to you as much more. [9] Why have you despised the word of the Lord, to do what is evil in his sight?'" (2 Samuel 12:7–9)

God thinks in terms of relationships. He is the true king of Israel, but in His plan he makes David "an associate in his compassion, his work of salvation."[56] He does not need David, as if God were not able to rule His people Himself. Rather, seeing the image of Himself in all men, God desires to call all men to take an active role in collaborating with Him in the fulfillment of His plan of love. "God is the sovereign master of his plan. But to carry it out he also makes use of his creatures' co-operation.... God grants his creatures ... the dignity of acting on their own, of being causes and principles for each other, and thus of co-operating in the accomplishment of his plan."[57] It is reserved to man, as image of God, deliberately and freely to cooperate with God and to merit the title of being God's co-worker in fulfilling His plan of love.[58]

Nathan's task is to impress upon David the asymmetry of his relationship with the Lord. God took an utterly gratuitous initiative in calling him to be king. It could be said that God fashioned him to be king and prepared him for this office, though that preparation remains entirely unknowable until God reveals to Samuel that He has selected David to be king. Here, then, is a replay of the lesson contained in the account of creation and of the sin of Adam and Eve. Out of the superabundance of His own goodness, God gives man the dignity of being fashioned in His own

---

56   *CCC*, 2575.
57   *CCC*, 306.
58   See *CCC*, 307, which refers to 1 Cor 3:9, 1 Thess 3:2, and Col 4:11.

image and likeness. He rightly expects that man will recognize in the very fact of his existence that God has loved him, for what else can explain his existence? Since the act by which God brings man into existence is an act of love, God rightly expects to be trusted, for by His gifts of life and grace He demonstrates His desire that man live and that he live fully. Yet, despite the evidence of His love, man manages, not without the assistance of the evil one, to place God in a "in a state of suspicion, indeed of accusation.... For in spite of all the witness of creation and of the salvific economy inherent in it, the spirit of darkness is capable of showing God as an enemy of his own creature, and in the first place as an enemy of man, as a source of danger and threat to man."[59] Sin is the rejection of God's love[60] in favor of relying on one's own self-love, or on someone else (another god, so-called because in the act of sin this god replaces the true God), as if God were not concerned with man's welfare and man had to watch out for himself and secure his fulfillment by himself.

The thrust of Nathan's prophetic intervention is precisely to disclose David's crimes as rejection of God's love. This leads to the king's confession of sin in relation to God: "I have sinned against the Lord" (2 Sam 12:13). Certainly, this confession is the goal of Nathan, and of God. This awareness of sin as an offense against God echoes in Psalm 51:

> Against you, you only, have I sinned,
> and done that which is evil in your sight,
> so that you are justified in your sentence
> and blameless in your judgment. (Psalm 51:4)

As previously discussed, this does not mean that David did not trespass the boundary of justice and love in relation to Bathsheba and Uriah. It simply means that sin is essentially a religious reality, entailing a reference to God. David has sinned against God by acting contrary to the demands of justice and love in relation others whom God relates to in justice and love. The confession of the prodigal son is more complete: "Father, I have sinned against heaven and against you" (Lk 15:18, 21 NJB). Obviously, David cannot acknowledge his sin to Uriah. Nevertheless, it is opportune to ask, what is the relation between sins against men and sins against God?

St. John insists on the inseparability of love of God and love of neighbor. There simply is no love of God without love of neighbor: "He who does not love his brother whom he has seen cannot love God whom he has not seen" (1 Jn 4:20). Every offence against another human being is an offence against God because it is contrary to His love for that person. Jesus

---

59 John Paul II, *Dominum et Vivificantem*, 37–38.
60 In *CCC*, 1739, the object of sin is the refusal of God's plan of love. "Sin sets itself against God's love for us and turns our hearts away from it" (*CCC*, 1850). "... the sin of the human beginning consists in untruthfulness and in the rejection of the gift and the love which determine the beginning of the world and of man" (John Paul II, *Dominum et Vivificantem*, 35).

links the second commandment—"Love your neighbor as yourself."—to the first commandment—"Love the Lord your God will all your heart, and with all your soul, and with all your mind" by saying that the second is *like* the first (Mt 22:37–40). The second is *like* the first because man is *like* God. This is why the Church Fathers base the inseparability of two commandments on the fact that God made man to be *like* Him; man is made in God's image. St. Francis de Sales incisively sums it up: "to love our neighbor in charity is to love God in man, or man in God."61 With the Incarnation, this becomes a historical reality. Every act of love for Christ is simultaneously an act of love for man and for God. "For," as Vatican II teaches, "by His incarnation the Son of God has united Himself in some fashion with every man."62 From the outset of his pontificate,63 this text figures prominently in the pontificate of St. John Paul II. From it he concludes:

> It is precisely in the "flesh" of every person that Christ continues to reveal himself and to enter into fellowship with us, so that rejection of human life, in whatever form that rejection takes, is really a rejection of Christ.64

What he said while still a Cardinal, meditating on the second Station of the Cross, applies to every thought, word, and deed—whether positive or negative—directed to another person: "Look at what you have done in this man to your God."65

David has no knowledge of this christological truth, but nothing is clearer to him than that his crime against a man is a sin against God. Once he returns to himself,66 with the help of God's word, he is exposed to himself before God. So long as he is dominated by his disordered love, David is exiled from God, from his fellow man (Uriah), and from his true self. At the summit of his passion, he loves himself to the point of contempt for God, for man, and for himself (his true self). Consumed with fulfilling his lustful desires, he banishes every other thought: of God's right to be loved and obeyed; of Uriah's and Bathsheba's rights as image of God, subjects of God's love and members of His chosen people; of his own duty to live in the truth.

In the words of St. John Paul II, David violates the right of Uriah and Bathsheba to be loved. He violates the order of justice, according to which "We are just to a person if we love him."67 He elaborates:

---

61 Francis de Sales, *Treatise on the Love of God*, Bk. 10, Ch. 11.
62 Vatican II, *Gaudium et spes*, 22.
63 See John Paul II, *Redemptor hominis*, 8, 13, 18.
64 John Paul II, *Evangelium vitae*, 104.
65 Karol Wojtyła, *Sign of Contradiction* (New York: The Seabury Press, 1979), 186.
66 "Coming or returning to oneself" is the phrase that Jesus uses to convey the conversion of the prodigal son (Lk 15:17). Conversion is always a return to God and to oneself because (1) man is made in God's image, and (2) the judgment of conscience bears upon the goodness or evil of an act, and therefore it concerns man, in relation to whom something is either good or evil, and God, Who is the source and foundation of all goodness.
67 John Paul II, *Crossing the Threshold of Hope* (New York: Alfred A. Knopf, 1994), 201.

> To be just means giving to others what is rightly due to them. A person's rightful due is to be treated as an object of love, not as an object for use. In a sense it can be said that love is a requirement of justice, just as using a person as a means to an end would conflict with justice. In fact the order of justice is more fundamental than the order of love—and in a sense the first embraces the second inasmuch as love can be a requirement of justice.... [L]ove for a person must consist in affirmation that the person has a value greater than that of an object for consumption or use. He who loves will endeavor to declare this by his whole behavior. And there can be no doubt that he will, *ipso facto*, be just toward the other person as person.[68]

This throws a new light on how we think of our relationships with others and the commandment of love of neighbor. To be the subject of a right to be loved is the result of being accredited as God's representative. Inscribed in each person's very being is a mission received from God. That mission is defined in terms of love. This has two dimensions. First, every human person, made in God's image, by that very fact elicits love from others. This is especially evident in those who are poor, needy, and suffering. Second, every human person, made in God's image, has the mission actively to love, to elicit from oneself the love-that-is-due to every person. To withhold this love or to act contrary to what it demands is to place oneself in opposition to this most fundamental mission, entrusted by God to every person.

It should be pointed out that both of these dimensions of the mission of love—the passive dimension of eliciting the love of others, and the active dimension of loving others—are united and reach their summit in the suffering and death of Jesus Christ. In the injustice, suffering, and passivity of His passion, He elicits love from us, He unleashes our love. At the same time, He actively loves us from within His suffering, which is entirely for us, and caused by our own spiritual poverty, which unleashes His love as He atones for our sins.

God takes the rejection of His representatives personally, as a rejection of Himself. When His people demand to have a king, it manifests a rejection of God as King.[69] When they do not heed the voice of His prophets, they are not listening to God Himself.[70] This theme reaches its summit when Jesus teaches that rejection of Him is rejection of the Father Who sent Him, and that rejection of His apostles is rejection of Him.[71]

---

68 Wojtyła, *Love and Responsibility*, 42. A biblical foundation for this may be seen in St. Paul's teaching: "Owe no one anything, except to love one another; for he who loves his neighbor has fulfilled the law" (Rom 13:8).
69 See 1 Sam 8:7.
70 See Jer 7:25–26.
71 See Lk 10:16.

Further, it is not just rejection and persecution of His disciples—His official representatives—that Christ takes personally. For, as indicated above, by reason of his very humanity every person receives a mission to represent Christ. This is especially true of the poor and suffering. Failure to show mercy to the poor—the hungry, the thirsty, the stranger, the naked, the sick, the imprisoned—is failure to show mercy to Christ Himself.[72]

The trigger of St. Paul's conversion is the realization that by persecuting Christ's followers he was persecuting Christ, that is, God Himself.[73] Like Paul's sin, and as is true of all sin, David's crime against Uriah makes him complicit in the persecution—the crucifixion—of Christ. And this is why it is necessary that the graces of his forgiveness, conversion, and reconciliation with God come from Christ's sacrifice for the forgiveness of sins.

We also know, however, that no sin can in any way wound or diminish God in Himself, just as no virtuous act of man can add to His perfection.[74] In the dialogues of the Book of Job, Elihu incisively enunciates the principle:

> [6] If you have sinned, what do you accomplish against him? And if your transgressions are multiplied, what do you do to him? [7] If you are righteous, what do you give to him; or what does he receive from your hand? (Job 35:6–7)

God is holy; the perfection of His divine nature precludes any diminishment or increase of His eternal beatitude. Sin diminishes man, not God. According to the logic of freedom and responsibility, sin diminishes the dignity of the sinner more fundamentally than it diminishes the dignity of those who are the victims of sin.[75] This rests on the distinction between two different orders rooted in human dignity, the moral order and the order of fundamental rights in relation to others. This is not a uniquely Christian insight, but a fundamentally human conviction. Socrates attests to it when he declares, "I would rather suffer an injustice than commit an injustice."[76]

St. John Paul II makes the point by referring to another non-Christian witness to the same primacy of the moral dimension and conscience.

The words of the Latin poet Juvenal apply to all: "Consider it

---

72   See Mt 25:31–46.
73   See Acts 9:5; 22:8; 26:15.
74   In the dialogues of the Book of Job, Elihu incisively enunciates the principle: "If you have sinned, what do you accomplish against him? And if your transgressions are multiplied, what do you do to him? If you are righteous, what do you give to him; or what does he receive from your hand?" (Job 35:6–7).
75   After listing a number of offenses against life (murder, genocide, abortion, euthanasia, or willful self-destruction), against the integrity of the human person (mutilation, torture, coercion), and against human dignity (subhuman living conditions, arbitrary imprisonment, deportation, slavery, prostitution, human trafficking, disgraceful working conditions), Vatican II states, "these do more harm to those who practice them than those who suffer from the injury" (Vatican II, *Gaudium et spes*, 27).
76   Plato, *Gorgias* (469c).

the greatest of crimes to prefer survival to honor and, out of love of physical life, to lose the very reason for living". The voice of conscience has always clearly recalled that there are truths and moral values for which one must be prepared to give up one's life. In an individual's words and above all in the sacrifice of his life for a moral value, the Church sees a single testimony to that truth which, already present in creation, shines forth in its fullness on the face of Christ.[77]

It is precisely this moral wound to conscience, the moral injury that sin inflicts upon human dignity, that unleashes God's mercy. For, while justice redresses crimes against people, and while fear of punishment has its place in constraining the proclivity of disordered self-love to violate the rights of others, especially the poor and vulnerable, the most efficacious protection of these rights and of the dignity in which they are rooted is the love that is rooted in the recognition that as images of God they are first loved by God Himself. And the most efficacious path to love of others is the experience of being loved by God—experiencing God's regard for the integrity of our conscience and for our dignity precisely when by sin one has rejected that love and thereby diminished one's integrity and dignity. The encounter with God's mercy in the context of confronting one's own moral poverty bears the fruit of a preferential love for the poor and vulnerable. Their poverty and vulnerability—whether temporal or moral—constitutes an appeal to justice and mercy even as our own sin arouses the mercy of God.

David's confession of having sinned against the Lord, then, indicates that he is aware that at the root of his injury against Uriah is his failure to put God first by reciprocating the love that God has shown to him. Bathsheba and Uriah are the victims of his sins, but the interior motive of his sins is lack of obedience to God in response to the great favor the Lord has shown to him.[78] The full measure of the inseparability of sins against neighbor and sins against God is revealed when, in the crucifixion of Jesus, God Himself becomes the victim of a sin against what His accusers think is only a man.

The preceding explains why, at the moment of his confession of sin, Nathan insists on reminding David of what God has done for him. For, David's conversion is not complete until he sees what God sees regarding the nature of his sin. God desires to re-establish communion with the repentant king, and this means that David must understand that the essence of his sin is to have disdained God's word because he failed to call to mind all of the marvelous works of God, all the evidence of God's love. He

---

77   John Paul II, *Veritatis splendor*, 94.
78   The *Catechism* brings out this connection between disobedience and the interior motivation of sin as lack of trust in God's love: "Man, tempted by the devil, let his trust in his Creator die in his heart and, abusing his freedom, disobeyed God's command. This is what man's first sin consisted of. All subsequent sin would be disobedience toward God and lack of trust in his goodness" (*CCC*, 397).

deliberately and thus culpably neglected to consider the history of God's love for him.

Nathan's words to David following his sin is not the first time that he schools the king regarding all that the Lord has done for him, as well as what He will do for him. Neither God's choice of David to be king nor His promise that David's house will have no end is based on David's worthiness. They are entirely rooted in God's sovereign will. David's sin certainly did not take God by surprise. Foreseeing it already at the time of the famous messianic promise in Chapter Seven of 2 Samuel, God's intention is to drive home the lesson that His interventions are predicated uniquely on His own love and wisdom rather than on any worthiness of David. For, by sinning David proves himself unworthy. This is why it is so important to read about David's sin in Chapter Twelve in light of the messianic promise in Chapter Seven of 2 Samuel.

The first personal history lesson of God's love for David occurs when the king discloses to the prophet his desire to build a temple for the Lord.[79] While the construction of a temple for God's glory is good and praiseworthy, David is troubled in conscience and seeks confirmation and consolation from the Lord's prophet. His unease is rooted in the realization that he has inverted his priorities by first building for himself, and for his posterity, an elegant palace, a symbol of his authority as king, while having neglected to build a temple for the Lord, a dwelling place for Ark of the Covenant. David is, after all, at heart a liturgist. Liturgy is his first and fundamental vocation, whether this takes the form of his many psalms, a dance of praise and thanksgiving,[80] or the spontaneous sacrifice of a broken and contrite heart.[81] What could be more natural for a heart so attuned to the service of God than to desire to provide an appropriate dwelling for Him?

David's desire seems so manifestly right that even the prophet is taken in by the logic and affirms the king's intention: "And Nathan said to the king, 'Go, do all that is in your heart; for the Lord is with you'" (2 Sam 7:3). The Lord, however, reasons according to a higher logic.[82] "But that same night the word of the Lord came to Nathan, 'Go and tell my servant David,' "Thus says the Lord: Would you build me a house to dwell in?" (2 Sam 7:4–5). In God's plan, David is not the one to build a temple. If there is an explanation as to why, it must be found in the following litany of all that the Lord has done for David and will do for him.[83] God called him to be king,

---

79 See 2 Sam 7:1–29.
80 See 2 Sam 6:13–15.
81 See Ps 51:17.
82 Aquinas makes this distinction by contrasting when prophets speak from their own spirit to when the speak from the Spirit of God: "... even the prophets spoke at times from their own spirit, and at other times from the Spirit of God. For example, we read that the prophet Nathan (2 Sam 7:3), speaking out of his own spirit, advised David to build a temple, but that later, under the influence of the Spirit of God, he retracted this" (Aquinas, *Commentary on the Gospel of St. John*, Ch. 3, Lect. 6 [Marietti, 541]).
83 See 2 Sam 7:8–16.

remained with him and assured victory over his enemies. Looking to the future, God will make David famous, guarantee peace and prosperity for His people, and assure for David's progeny an unending dynastic lineage.

In Israel's pilgrimage of faith, the future-looking part of Nathan's discourse will take on an importance that far outlasts the immediate context and purpose of his interaction with David. It will become a focal point of Israel's messianic hope, a renewal of God's fidelity to His covenant that was first established with Abraham. There is no small irony in the fact that precisely at the moment that David conceives the idea of building a house for God, God declares that He will build a house for David.[84] David's desire to build a temple for the Lord did not come from the Lord but from David himself. God makes this clear when, through His prophet, He asks: "In all places where I have moved with all the sons of Israel, did I speak a word with any of the judges of Israel, whom I commanded to shepherd my people Israel, saying, 'Why have you not built me a house of cedar?'" (2 Sam 7:7). Though building a temple is clearly not in itself evil, it is simply not God's will for David to build one. God has called David, not just to do good in general, but to do the particular good that God wills and that corresponds to his vocation. Within the parameter of the duties of his vocation David is obviously free to exercise the virtue of prudence in order to give direction to his freedom with regard to concrete actions concerning God's will. The erection of a temple, apparently, falls outside that sphere of prudential determination.

It could well be that God's knowledge of David's heart governs the divine veto of David's intention. Perhaps building a temple would have become a point of pride for David and swell his heart with self-satisfaction. In this passage, then, God appears to give David a forceful reminder that what we do for Him must always be a response to what He does for us. Our relationship with God is based on the humble recognition that all we have has been received as a gift of God's love. Only when our initiatives to serve Him and to express our love for Him are rooted in this humility are they immune from becoming points of pride. One thinks of Jesus' words about those who prophesy, cast out demons, and perform might works in His name—all good things in themselves—are, nevertheless, not doing not doing the Father's will.[85]

David's desire to build a temple for the Lord does correspond to God's will in the sense that God clearly desired that His people have a central place for sacrificial worship. It will be David's son, Solomon, who builds the stone Temple of Jerusalem. But it will be another son of David, Jesus Christ, who definitively fulfills the desire of David and of every human being to worship God in spirit and in truth by succeeding in making the entirety of life a sacrifice of obedience. Jesus thus definitively reveals that the outward sacrifices of the exterior kingdom are meaningful only to the extent that they

---

84   See Joseph Ratzinger, *A New Song for the Lord. Faith in Christ and Liturgy Today* (New York: Crossroad Publishing Company, 1997), 80–81.
85   See Mt 7:21–23.

point to and are accompanied by the interior sacrifices of the inner kingdom. "Behold, to obey is better than sacrifice" (1 Sam 15:22). Jesus is himself the true temple (Jn 2:19–21), where the true sacrifice of being "obedient unto death" (Phil 2:8) is offered to God. David may not be aware of it, but in God's plan of love, his desire to build a temple for the Lord will be purified by his experience of God's mercy, so that he is able to arrive at understanding that true worship of God is the praise of God for his mercy, and only a humble, contrite heart is capable of this praise.

> [15] O Lord, open my lips,
> and my mouth shall show forth your praise.
> [16] For you take no delight in sacrifice;
> if I were to give a burnt offering,
> you would not be pleased.
> [17] The sacrifice acceptable to God is a broken spirit;
> a broken and contrite heart, O God,
> you will not despise. (Psalm 51:15–17)

The king's desire to build a temple for the Lord will be fulfilled in the interior sacrifice of his own heart, which anticipates and is an actual participation in the perfect sacrifice of Jesus Christ.

When he sinned, not only did David fail to consider God's previous loving interventions in his behalf and His promise. David has to relearn the fundamental lesson that man's relation to God is always based on God's utterly gratuitous choice. It is always a question of grace. David has to relearn that he did not choose God, but God chose him. Jesus' words to the apostles hold a truth that is valid in every age of the economy of salvation: "You did not choose me, but I chose you and appointed you that you should go and bear fruit" (Jn 15:16). God's initiative is always first: "In this is love, not that we loved God but that he loved us" (1 Jn 4:10). "We love because He loved us first" (1 Jn 4:19). The reversal of this relationship is a constant risk. God seems resigned to taking this risk, for He desires to associate men and women with Himself for the accomplishment of His plan. Therein lies a potential conflict that only divine wisdom is sufficient to resolve. On the one hand, sinful men prone to pride will be tempted to overvalue their accomplishments and begin to measure their relation to God on that basis. To be convinced of this, one need only think of the accusation St. Paul makes of his former way of thinking of justification, that is, his relationship with God, on the basis of his works,[86] or the story Jesus tells of the Pharisee and the tax collector in the temple.[87] On the other hand, the dignity with which God endows the creature made in His image and likeness is fulfilled only in a free

---

86   See Phil 3:3–11.
87   See Lk 18:9–14.

collaboration with God, by taking his place in God's plan and producing fruit.[88] The entire history of salvation bears witness to this.

Perhaps this is why the most fruitful missions and apostolates are inseparable from those of the great saints who have gone through the purification of the dark nights. How many saints were granted fruit for their labors only after early setbacks, prolonged exercise of patient fidelity, perseverance despite no prospect of success, and a deepened understanding of their dependence on God, of their sin, and of the absolutely gratuitous mercy of God? God does desire that we collaborate with Him in the fulfillment of His plan, but lest the fruit of this collaboration become an occasion for pride and thus threaten communion with God, humility is absolutely indispensable. The most convincing evidence for this is the vocation of the Blessed Virgin Mary to be the mother of God.

In his mission to David, Nathan's aim is precisely to construct this foundation of humility. He achieves it by confronting David with the full truth about his sins. By defining the king's sins as a failure to return God's love, Nathan's goal might be to arouse in David memories of his friendship, with Jonathan, son of Saul, so as to make it possible for David to see his sins from God's perspective. The two friends lived faithfully the covenant into which they entered with one another,[89] until Jonathan's death, which was devastating for David: "I am distressed for you, my brother Jonathan; very pleasant have you been to me; your love to me was wonderful, passing the love of women" (2 Sam 1:26). David could draw from the experience of losing this friend in order to formulate some idea of how his own spiritual death deprived God of the joy of friendship with him. God could very well say of David: "I am distressed for you, my servant, David; very pleasant have you been to me. Your love to me was wonderful."

God's distress is over David's spiritual death. The distress of Christ in the paschal mystery definitively reveals how the separation caused by the death of sin affects God. The distress of His paschal charity is already evident as He weeps over the death of His friend, Lazarus,[90] and as He weeps over Jerusalem.[91] He selects three of His closest friends to witness when He "began to be greatly distressed and troubled" (Mk 14:33), "even unto death" (Mt 26:37–38), in the Garden of Gethsemane. Why, in God's plan, is it important that there be witnesses to these three revelations of the distress of the Sacred Heart of Jesus, and in particular of the distress in Gethsemane, which is the Gospels' last explicit statement about Jesus' interior state? Because God wants us to know how our sins wound His love. And why does God desire this? Because He desires that penitent hearts respond to sin as He does. He wants penitents whose consciences are in a state of distress to believe that distress over sin is properly divine and human, and that the distress of a penitent heart is a grace of participation in God's

---

88 See Jn 15:1–8, 16.
89 See 1 Sam 18:3; 24:18.
90 See Jn 11:36.
91 See Lk 18:41.

own distress over lost friendship with man. Perfect contrition is participation in the distress of the Sacred Heart of Jesus over sin.

God wants man to know the distress that sin causes Him to experience because only in this way can man know just how much God loves him. David, of course, does not know the mystery of Christ, but he does not know the inconsolable distress that results from the loss of a friend. A friend is another self, according to Aristotle,[92] so that to lose a friend is to lose happiness itself. For, man is made to make a gift of himself, to live in the joy of mutual self-giving.[93] A friend knows in advance that what he says and does will be understood, received, and affirmed by his friend because truth and virtue constitute the bond of friendship. To lose a friend is to lose that enfleshment of transcendent truth that friends love more than they love themselves and for the sake of which they love one another. To lose a friend is to find oneself isolated in a happiness that by its very nature demands to be shared. Because friendship is the highest good, there is no distress that can equal that of losing a friend.

The distress of Jesus over the death of Lazarus, over Jerusalem, in Gethsemane, and throughout the paschal mystery—His distress over all evil and suffering and sin—reveals the intensity of the love that makes Him desire to call men His friends: "You are my friends ... I have called you friends" (Jn 15:14–15). Jesus recapitulates, that is, He fulfills and brings to perfection, all of the distress of all time of those who, like David, suffer the loss of a friend. For Jesus, it is the death of sin that causes His distress: "Is it not a grief to the death when a companion and friend turns to enmity?" (Sir 37:2). David's conversion entails the realization that by his sin he has been the cause of God to be distressed over His friend refusing to receive His love and to love Him in return.

For David, Nathan's words are truth and light. The encounter with God's word is a moment of great anguish, but also of great grace! It is anguish-filled because David sees the full truth about the evil of his actions. His own words reveal that he understands that sin is inseparable from death: "The man who has done this deserves to die" (2 Sam 12:5). Is this not an echo, in the image of God, of God's own declaration that sin brings death? "Of the tree of the knowledge of good and evil you shall not eat, for in the day that you eat of it you shall die" (Gen 2:17).[94] Yet, it is also grace-filled, because this intervention of God's word is decisive in bringing David to the truth that leads to conversion. This is a magnificent example of how grace builds on nature and raises it to the height of its dignity in the truth. David's conscience (nature) is working but by itself it cannot reach to the depth of truth needed to produce conversion. The prophet brings God's word (grace) in order to instruct (heal and elevate) the king's conscience. His own acute sense of justice not having been

---

92 See Aristotle, *Nicomachean Ethics*, IX, 4.
93 See Vatican II, *Gaudium et spes*, 24.
94 With these words, the God Who becomes a man in order to take upon Himself the punishment for the sins of the world condemns Himself to death.

totally corrupted by sin, David can, so to speak, cooperate with God in passing judgment on himself. If the Lord is to respect His creature's liberty it is difficult to imagine how things could be otherwise. To say that God does not want to be alone in seeing the fullness of the truth about sin and mercy is to say that He does not desire to leave unfulfilled man's capacity to see what He sees and to participate in His reaction to sin.

Because the word of God enlightens man's conscience in the line of truth for which it is made, David's judgment about his sin is entirely God's and entirely his, but it is his only by reason of being healed and elevated by grace to participate in God's judgment. It comes to him from the outside, from God through His prophet. It is God's first. But it does not remain a totally external pronouncement; it does not remain only God's. Rather, it causes an illumination. David does not confess, "The Lord has told me that I have sinned," but simply, "I have sinned." He cannot know what Jesus will reveal about the Holy Spirit's mission to convince the world about sin.[95] But this does not prevent him from experiencing the joint witness of the Holy Spirit and his own spirit[96] regarding the truth about his sin and about God's love. Without the prophetic intervention, David's conscience would not arrive at this judgment regarding himself. But, by the working of grace, a supernatural light transforms the judgment he makes about the injustice that Nathan brought before him into a judgment of himself. In this way, David offers a dramatic case of our Lord's teaching:

> For with the judgment you pronounce you will be judged,
> and the measure you give will be the measure you get.
> (Matthew 7:2)

This version of the Golden Rule, now expressed in terms of judging, rests upon the natural exigency in human beings to be consistent in the application of moral principles. The Golden Rule contains an inner logic the denial of which places a person in a state of contradiction. What we consider good and what we desire for ourselves demands to be considered good and desired for those we love. The inverted Golden Rule—love yourself as you would love your neighbor—also gets at this demand for consistency, and it is precisely here that the judgment elicited from David by Nathan's parable of injustice becomes a judgment against David for the injustices that he committed. If the Golden Rule is the answer to the tendency of fallen nature to judge others as somehow less worthy of the good things we desire for ourselves, its inverted form is the remedy to the tendency to exempt oneself from the demands of justice. Together, the Golden Rule and its inverted form uproot hypocrisy in our dealings with others and with ourselves.[97] The just judgment that David pronounces as

---

95 See Jn 16:7–9.
96 See Rom 8:16.
97 Jesus sets forth the Golden Rule in Mt 7:12. He addresses the hypocrisy of failing to live up to the inverted Golden Rule in His teaching about the concern to remove a speck

the king whose office is to assure justice in the exterior kingdom is called to life by that same judgment regarding the kingdom within.

There is impenetrable mystery in conversion, because it entails the mystery of freedom. Prior to his conversion, David repudiates the claim that truth has on him, first when he sleeps with Bathsheba, and again when he obstinately refuses to repent of that sin. He repudiates the claim of truth another time when he orders the death of Uriah, and yet again for so long as he obstinately refuses to repent of that sin. We cannot know how many moments of truth occurred in his conscience and how many times he beat back the gnawing of his nature, which is made for the truth. We do know that compliance with the demands of truth is not to be taken for granted, presumed. David clearly hardened his heart against the truth to override the natural dynamism to conform his actions to the truth. Why doesn't he continue in his obstinacy? Why does he finally humble himself before the truth? Is it because of the authority of God's prophet? What are the interior movements that lead to taking sides with the truth against himself? What explains the fact that the same freedom that earlier resists the claim of truth now acquiesces to it?

Anyone who has raised children has had occasion to observe the dynamic that occurs when a child stubbornly refuses to obey his parent and then obeys that same parent by accepting the punishment that the parent imposes. A four-year-old disobeys her mother's instruction not to stand on her chair, yet she dutifully accepts and complies with the time-out by going to her room for five minutes. This inconsistency appears contradictory if we think that the issue is always a direct and principled confrontation with parental authority itself. In reality, such a confrontation is only implicit. The rejection of authority involved in a particular act of disobedience is a means to the end of obtaining something or doing something that the child desires. The child is blinded by her desire, which is all she can see at the moment. Once the fascination with the forbidden reality passes, the child naturally returns to the established order of submission to her mother's authority.

As the child matures morally, that is, with respect to mastery over her own freedom, the exterior consequence of a time-out will become an interior consequence of remorse and the development of the capacity for more consistent obedience and, when disobedience occurs, for self-correction. Along the path of moral maturation, children become more aware of the relationship, we could say, the covenant, that is at stake whenever they are tempted to disobey. They discover that parents do not exercise their authority arbitrarily but out of love for their children. They come to realize that their relationship with their parents is a higher good than the fleeting enjoyment of something that their parents forbid. And with this discovery and this realization, in their relation to their parents and

---

from someone else's eye while neglecting the log in one's own eye (see Mt 7:3–5). If it truly is out of love that a person desires to remove a speck from a brother's eye, then that same love impels a person to love himself as he loves his neighbor by removing a speck, and for even great reason, a log, from his own eye.

to God,[98] they become more responsible and more capable of perfect contrition,[99] that is, a remorse that corresponds to the loss or attenuation of their relationships with their parents and with God.

There is all the difference in the world between the disobedience of a five-year-old boy and a man like David. When a mother instructs her son to stay close to her while she is shopping in a department store, she is probably asking too much of him. When he gets separated from her, it is not because he deliberately disobeyed but because he got distracted. A five-year-old has a limited attention span. He starts out keeping his mother's directive in mind, but the eye-catching displays so captivate him that he simply loses track of his mother. Certainly, the sin of a man like David has something in common with the distraction of the small boy. Catching sight of Bathsheba, David loses custody of his own heart and he thereby loses track of God. This is only the occasion of sin, the moment of temptation when a man must weigh the relative value of two goods that are in competition with one another: on the one hand, the prospect of sexual gratification, and on the other hand, his relationship with God. Unlike the mother who misjudges her son's capacity to remain focused on her instruction, God does not misjudge David's capacity to rule over his own freedom. He rightly expects him to prefer fidelity to God above everything else.

No matter how deliberate the sin, there is always hope for conversion—unless a sinner obstinately sets himself against graces of conversion by repudiating the truth of God's mercy, the truth of God's readiness to forgive on the condition that the sinner acknowledge and reject his sin. This resistance is called the blasphemy against the Holy Spirit,[100] which is the only sin that cannot be forgiven.[101] In the words of Benedict XVI, this means that, "God, by creating free creatures, giving them freedom, has renounced a part of his power, empowering our freedom. In this way He loves and respects our free response of love to his call."[102]

Pope Benedict expounds on how we should understand that God's setting a limit to His own power is actually the definitive proof of the perfection of His power:

> Like a Father, God wants us to be his children and to live as such in his Son, in communion, in full intimacy with Him. His omnipotence is not expressed in violence, it is not expressed in the destruction of every adverse power as we would like, but is expressed in love, in mercy, in forgiveness, in accepting our freedom and in the *untiring call to conversion of heart*, in an attitude that is only apparently weak—God seems weak, if we think of Jesus Christ who

---

98 In God's plan for children, the relation with parents and with God are inseparable because parents "are in a way the first representatives of God" for their children (*CCC*, 239).
99 See *CCC*, 1451–53.
100 See John Paul II, *Dominum et Vivificantem*, 46–47.
101 See Mt 12:31–32.
102 Benedict XVI, General Audience, January 30, 2013.

prays, who lets himself be killed. An apparently weak attitude, consisting of patience, gentleness and love, shows that this is the true way of being powerful! This is the power of God! And this power will win! The wise man of the *Book of Wisdom* addresses God in this way: "You are merciful to all, for you can do all things; you overlook people's sins, *so that they may repent.* For you love all things that exist.... You spare all things, for they are yours, O Lord, you who love the living" (Wis 11:23–24a, 26).

Only one who is truly powerful can endure evil and show compassion; only one who is truly powerful can fully exercise the power of love. And God, to whom all things belong because all things were made by Him, reveals his strength by loving everyone and everything, in a *patient waiting for the conversion* of us men, whom he wants to have as children. *God awaits our conversion.* God's all-powerful love knows no bounds, so much so that "he did not withhold his own Son, but gave him up for all of us" *(Rom* 8:32). The omnipotence of love is not that of the power of the world, but that of total gift, and Jesus, the Son of God, reveals to the world the true omnipotence of the Father, giving his life for us sinners. This is the real, authentic and perfect divine power: to respond to evil with good, to insults with forgiveness, to murderous hatred with the love that gives life. Then evil is really defeated, because washed by the love of God; then death is finally defeated, because transformed into the gift of life. God the Father raises the Son: death, the great enemy (cf. 1 *Cor* 15:26), is swallowed up and deprived of its poison (cf. 1 *Cor* 15:54–55), and we, freed from sin, can access our reality of being God's children.

So when we say "I believe in God the Father Almighty," we express our faith in the power of the love of God who in his Son dead and risen defeats hatred, evil, sin and opens us to eternal life, that of children who want to be always in the "Father's House." To say, "I believe in God the Father Almighty," in his power, in his way of being Father, is always an act of faith, of *conversion,* of *transformation of our mind,* of all our affection, of our entire way of life.[103]

Pope Francis echoes this same insight when he says, "God's 'patience,' shown in his mercy towards sinners, is a sign of his real

---

103 Ibid., emphasis added.

power."[104] God's love, patience, mercy, and power are revealed and thus defined in relation to man's conversion from sin.

God's omnipotence is the perfection of His love, and His love is perfect because He is patient until the surpassing power of His own goodness and beauty to move man's freedom from within wins its victory in man's conversion. We are so accustomed to hearing St. Paul's hymn to love that we take the patience of love for granted. Anyone who has really loved knows that, in reality, patience is compatible with only the most perfect love. Waiting is a crucifixion for love, for love desires union and is wounded by any distance between lover and beloved, and time is a kind of distance. The tension between love's desire for union now and the perfection of love that yields to the wisdom of patience are detectable in the words of the weeping Jesus over Jerusalem: "O Jerusalem, Jerusalem, killing the prophets and stoning those who are sent to you! How often would I have gathered your children together as a hen gathers her brood under her wings, and you would not!" (Mt 23:37). One might also see in the weariness of Jesus, as He waits for the Samaritan woman to come to the well,[105] a revelation of the weariness that accompanies God's love because it must be patient. To say that God is patient means that His love for man is so great that His love submits to His wisdom—the divine logic of love—for the sake of respecting man's freedom and the eventual reconciliation that comes when he finally opens himself to receive His mercy.[106]

The murder of Uriah demonstrates that death is the final consequence of the refusal to repent. When men disregard God's voice in their consciences, there is no ultimate foundation for determining right and wrong. In such a situation, men have no rights and there is no Supreme Court to which to appeal because there is no Supreme Judge that men recognize. Hauntingly, by shutting God out, David makes himself a tyrant, one who "rules his subjects as though they were his slaves."[107] In this way, he makes himself like Pharaoh. Though the chosen people reside in the Promised Land, Uriah's death at the order of their king means that, at this moment, they are still in Egypt. Pharaoh's defense for the preservation of unlimited control over his slaves seems to have penetrated the heart of David: "Who is the Lord, that I should heed His voice…? I do not know the Lord" (Ex 5:2). Apt words to convey David's despising of the word of the Lord! Pharaoh does not recognize God's authority, and as a consequence there will be widespread death in Egypt. So long as David fails to acknowledge God's authority in the kingdom within, the exterior kingdom is subject to violence. He, David, not God, has "power over life

---

104 Francis, *Amoris laetitia*, 91.
105 See Jn 4:6.
106 For Aquinas, patience is the virtue which endures the sorrow that accompanies the delay in the fulfillment of a desire. It especially concerns the "sorrows inflicted by other persons" (*ST* II-II, Q. 136, a. 4, ad 2). Patience assures that a person act according to the dictates of reason in the context of dealing with the sorrow of being separated from someone whom he loves.
107 Aquinas, *ST* I-II, Q. 105, a. 1, ad 5.

and death" (Wis 16:13). The mere possession of the Promised Land cannot effectively shield Israel from slavery. If political authority does not recognize that it is established under God then there is no limit to its authority. While it is true that David does not claim limitless authority over the entire people, it is also true that if one man has no rights then in principle the entire people has fallen into slavery again. In his sins, David chooses tyranny over the just judgment that is the *raison d'être* of his office as king. The path he chooses inexorably leads to another kind of death, because it leads to the unpardonable sin of the blasphemy against the Holy Spirit. If he should persist in this state it is definitive spiritual death that awaits him.

Created Anew by God's Mercy

By the power of God's word and grace, David does not remain in the state of spiritual death. God's mercy raises him to new life. He acknowledges his sin: "I have sinned against the Lord." Now that David comes to see what God sees regarding the truth about sin, he can also come to know what God knows about His mercy: "And Nathan said to David, 'The Lord also has put away your sin; you shall not die'" (2 Sam 12:13). David will not die, but there will be more death because of his sin. The son born to Bathsheba will die in his infancy, and many years later another son of David, Absalom, will also die. Most importantly, David's own words will be fulfilled: "The man who did this deserves to die." Indeed, the David who committed the terrible crimes against man and against God deserves to die. And he does die, or rather, he has died the death of a hardened heart.

Now, in order to bring David back to life, another death is necessary. In the language of St. Paul, David's old self must be executed.[108] This is precisely what conversion is—"a death-event."[109] Through this "death-event," that is, through his conversion, David is re-created. So that this is truly a co-creation in keeping with David's dignity as image of God, God places within David the desire to be re-created: "Create in me a clean heart, O God, and put a new and right spirit within me" (Ps 51:10). David's conversion is the fulfillment of two desires, God's and the king's, the latter's being a participation in the former's. David becomes a new creation by the power of God's word and the baptism of tears of repentance.[110]

---

[108] See Rom 6:6.
[109] Joseph Ratzinger, Address at St. Michael's College in Toronto, April 15, 1986. See also *Principles of Catholic Theology*, 55–67.
[110] Tears of repentance constitute an outward sign of the interior disposition that corresponds to Baptism. See John Paul II, *Orientale Lumen*, 12. On tears of repentance see Gregory Nazianzen, *Oration on the Holy Lights*, 17; John of Damascus, *Exposition of the Orthodox Faith*, IV, 9; John Cassian, *Conferences* III, XX, viii: "by the affection of love is the weight of our sins overwhelmed: for 'charity covers a multitude of sins' (Prov 10:12; 1 Pet 4:8). In the same way also by the fruits of almsgiving a remedy is provided for our wounds, because 'As water extinguishes fire, so does almsgiving extinguish sin' (Sir 3:30). So also by the shedding of tears is gained the washing away of offences, for 'Every night I will wash my bed: I will water my couch with tears.'

Finally to show that they are not shed in vain, he adds: 'Depart from me all ye that work iniquity, for the Lord hath heard the voice of my weeping' (Ps 6:9). Moreover by means of confession of sins, their absolution is granted: for 'I said: I will confess against myself my sin to the Lord: and Thou forgavest the iniquity of my heart'; and again: 'Declare thine iniquities first, that thou mayest be justified' (Ps 31:5). By afflicting the heart and body also is forgiveness of sins committed in like manner obtained, for he says: 'Look on my humility and my labor, and forgive me all my sins'."

4.
David After His Sin and Conversion: The Kingdom Within

David's conversion makes him a new creation, a new man who has been raised from the death of the old man. The stark contrast between the two becomes clear when the bold confidence in God that characterized his earlier relationship with God is placed alongside a set of traits that emerge during the period that follows his sin and conversion. It becomes clear that the king's trust in God in an earlier stage had left his spiritual imperfection unnoticed. Too great a focus on the exterior kingdom leaves the interior kingdom unattended. The new David displays a profound humility rooted in a new awareness of God's grace and mercy.

The portrait of David from the period of his reign over Israel entails a severe trial. Once again, he is subjected to persecution, only this time it is at the hands of his own son, Absalom. The precise point of contrast with the first phase is the king's new way of reacting to this persecution. The former display of bold assurance that the Divine Judge will find in his favor and acquit him disappears and is replaced by a new assurance regarding the place of suffering in God's plan. No longer presuming upon God's favor, and no longer inviting God's judgment, he senses that there is a mysterious place for affliction in God's plan, and he rises to the height of love for his enemy. David shows the fruits of a profound transformation, and in this second segment of his life he is, more than ever, a man whose heart is fashioned after the heart of God Himself.[1]

Three short discourses of David after his sin and conversion reveal a radical change in his understanding of divine favor. Earlier in his life, persecution was the occasion for David to call upon God to protect him and to vindicate his just cause. After his conversion, in the same circumstance of persecution, David's disposition is completely different. Now he is fully aware of the totally gratuitous nature of God's favor and call. There can be no question of justice and vindication of rights, only of mercy and forgiveness. This new way of relating to God also affects his way of relating to others.

Absalom's Revolt and David's Self-Entrustment to God's Mercy

The transformation of David's thinking first appears when the king is forced to flee his capital city. David's own son, Absalom, leads a revolt against his father. With support for Absalom among the people so great,

---

[1] See 1 Sam 13:14.

David realizes that his loyalists cannot defend Jerusalem. This forces David to flee for safety, and as he leaves the city an entourage of loyal subjects—his family, servants, and soldiers—accompanies him. At this the priests responsible for ministries associated with the Ark of God take the initiative to escort the Ark in the march of defeat. As the sign of God's presence among His people, it is only natural for them to assume that the Ark should accompany the one whom the Lord anointed as king of His people. David, however, does not subscribe to this logic; he sees things in a different light. He remains the one God has chosen, the Lord's anointed, but, perhaps mindful of what had befallen his predecessor as a result of his sins, David realizes that his infidelity to God is such that he can make no claim to divine protection. And so he says:

> [25] "Carry the ark of God back into the city. If I find favor in the eyes of the Lord, he will bring me back and let me see both it and his habitation; [26] but if he says, 'I have no pleasure in you,' behold, here I am, let him do to me what seems good to him." (2 Samuel 15:25–26)

What is consistent about David before and after his sin is that he refers his cause to God. The Lord is his primary point of reference for understanding the events of his life, the Source of the meaning of all that happens to him. Yet there is this most significant difference, that after his conversion David no longer presumes the outcome of this appeal to God. The experience of the total gratuitousness of divine mercy has taught him that there is no right that he can invoke for a favorable judgment. His trust is in the Lord alone, in the disposition of His mercy, and he is ready to accept a judgment of persecution rather than one of victory. If it should be God's decision, he is prepared to accept being cut off from the presence of God in the Ark of the Covenant.

Particularly telling is David's expression of hope. His exodus does not necessarily mean that he will never see the Ark or inhabit Jerusalem again. He envisions a possible future, but it is clearly beyond his power to assure. So he remits that future to the Lord. Moreover, David has good reason not to be presumptuous regarding the fulfillment of his hope. For, he had humbled himself in acts of penance when he pleaded with the Lord to spare the life of the infant who was the fruit of his indiscretion with Bathsheba, and the Lord did not relent of this punishment (2 Sam 12:14–18). David's dread is to live with the knowledge that his sin was the cause of this infant's death.

David also knows that if God has spared his own life it is because He has a plan for his future. For, he knows that the just punishment for adultery is death: "If a man commits adultery with the wife of his neighbor, both the adulterer and the adulteress shall be put to death" (Lev 20:10). David's situation is much like that of the woman caught in adultery. She, too, faced the prospect of death for her sin, and Jesus knows that for this reason her conversion is authentic. The same principle is evident in the conversion of the prodigal son, whose father does not need to lecture him or threaten him with punishment because he has already confronted the prospect of death as a consequence of his sin. If, then, God suspends the precept of Leviticus 20:10 by assuring that knowledge of David's sin remain known only to Nathan, it must be because He intends to bring about the king's conversion and the further good that will come in the rest of his life.

David does not question God's mysterious wisdom, which includes an unknown future for the king. David's preference might well have been to be the one to die for his sin, rather than the infant. For, as we will see, this way of thinking comes to light when his son, Absalom, is killed. Another son, another untimely death, all to assure that David's dread over his sin and its consequences produce a fruit that lasts longer than a momentary act of repentance. Death might actually seem preferable to David, rather than living with the dread of the "knowledge of good and evil" (Gen 2:17) and being "bowed down" because, in his own words: "my iniquities ... weigh like a burden too heavy for me" (Ps 38:4).

Just as He had foreseen David's sin, God foresees a future for him, a mission to bear witness to the Lord's mercy. Even more demanding on his hope than that this future is unknown to him is that there should be any future at all. For, as we have seen, he knows that he deserves death. With this awareness, any future seems to be something that should not be enjoyed because it is, in keeping with the logic of sin, in a fundamental way illicit. Is it possible simply to move on from sin? Can the memory of sin be somehow erased, so that a person may be allowed to experience at least some fleeting joys in life? To confront the true measure of the evil of sin as an offense against God, who is infinite in goodness, is to take on a burden that far exceeds man's capacity to endure: "My punishment is greater than I can bear!" (Gen 4:13); "For my iniquities ... weigh like a burden too heavy for me" (Ps 38:4). "A man's spirit will endure sickness; but a broken spirit who can bear?" (Prov 18:14).

The only path forward is to believe that God is "merciful and gracious, slow to anger, and abounding in steadfast love and faithfulness ... forgiving iniquity and transgression and sin," even if He "will by no means clear the guilty," that is, leaving them unpunished (Ex 34:6–7). God's plan of mercy that forgives sins includes the punishment of a broken heart. The repentant and forgiven sinner can only bear the memory of his sin when he believes that his broken heart is pleasing to God. It them becomes an acceptable sacrifice. How heroic, then, the hope, based on this faith in God's mercy, that receives an undeserved future as a precious gift with which to atone for past sins and thereby to bear witness to God's greatest attribute, His mercy! Sin, it is true, does cancel our relationship with God, and therefore life itself, since God is the source of life. But because God is merciful, this cancellation lasts only for so long as we delay in turning to God in humble repentance. The authenticity of David's conversion is manifested by the way that he accepts God's forgiveness and embraces His plan for a new mission, namely, to collaborate with God in the revelation of mystery of the inner kingdom. In David, God is preparing His people to grasp and to live in the hope that will be fully revealed in Jesus Christ, that "whenever our hearts condemn us" and there appears to be no hope for the future, "God is greater than our hearts" (1 Jn 3:20) and, by forgiving us, grants us new life. But this new life of the inner kingdom is not like the former life of measuring God's fidelity by way of the exterior kingdom. In his enduring dread over his sin, David anticipates the mission of the Suffering Servant, who "was wounded for our transgressions, crushed for our iniquities; upon him was the punishment that made us whole, and by his bruises we are healed" (Is 53:5). The essence of the inner kingdom is the reign of faith in the mercy of God and the place of enduring dread over sin in His plan of love in the human heart. This is also the reign of hope that my heart broken by dread over my sins will be received by God as an acceptable sacrifice. The inner kingdom is, finally, the unleashing of healing love by participating in God's own mercy, fully revealed in Jesus Christ, the Suffering Servant, for all who are crushed by the burden of knowing the true depths of the evil of sin.

David, then, is consigned to a future in which his "conversion of heart [will be] accompanied by a salutary pain and sadness which the Fathers called *animi cruciatus* (affliction of spirit) and *compunctio cordis* (repentance of heart)."[2] Whatever hope he has to be faithful to his vocation as the king of God's people is rooted in his embrace of the unknown future that the God of mercy has designed for him. And so he hopes to return to Jerusalem in order to see the Ark of the covenant, since this would correspond to his best understanding of a future for the king of Israel. At the same time, the fulfillment of this hope rests entirely on the favor of God.

For God to look on someone with favor is for Him to take a totally gratuitous initiative of beneficence.[3] David now personifies "the People of the 'poor'—those who, humble and meek, rely solely on their God's mysterious plans, who await the justice, not of men but of the Messiah."[4] When He instructs His disciples to do good to those from whom nothing is expected in return,[5] Jesus stresses that acts of gracious favor are done for their own sake and are not based on a calculation of some derived benefit, which would make them a means to some end. He is not thereby precluding that the one showing gracious favor should expect that the favored one manifest his awareness of having been favored. God rightly expects those to whom He shows favor to make a return of thanksgiving and praise,[6] and that they in turn treat others graciously, as they have been

---

2   *CCC*, 1431.
3   On the Hebrew word translated as "favor" see Jacques Guillet, *Themes of the Bible* (Notre Dame, IN: Fides Publishers, Association, 1960), 20–24.
4   *CCC*, 716.
5   See Lk 6:30–34; 14:12.
6   Jesus graciously receives the thanks and veneration of Mary Magdalene (see Lk 7:36–50), and of the leper He healed (see Lk 17:11–19).

treated.[7] The point about David's sin and conversion is that in God's plan these are ordered to the revelation of the inner kingdom and the reign of divine mercy in the hearts of men. The psalms, attributed to David, are his return to the Lord for the gracious favor the Lord showed him, his sacrifice of thanksgiving.[8] They are the liturgy of the inner kingdom.

David's hope is based on his intuition of a mysterious relation between his acceptance of the just punishment for his sin and God's favor. The king's insight is that his defeat and exodus have a place in God's plan for him. God intends them to be medicinal. By accepting this punishment as God's verdict, His just judgment, God will look on him with favor. By his acceptance, then, David aligns his will to God's will; he is in communion with God. He corresponds to what God desires him to be in the context of his having sinned. This suffering regarding the exterior kingdom is meant to correspond to the suffering of remorse of conscience, the suffering that concerns the interior kingdom. David's twofold repentance—exterior and interior—elicits from God a look of approval, a look of favor, that reflects the way God first looked at creation: "And God saw that it was good" (Gen 1:10, 12, 18, 21, 25). David's humility and self-entrustment to God's good pleasure elicits that same look of approval of the Creator.

In fact, the penitent king is aware that his repentant heart is a gift of grace. It is not his own work, for it began only with the word of God that came to him through the prophet Nathan. And God's word is as efficacious on that occasion as it was when God created everything. David's clean heart is a new creation on God's part. The grace by which God gives sinners a new, clean heart is greater than His act of creation:[9] "O God, you reveal your almighty power above all by showing mercy and forgiveness...."[10] For this reason, it gives Him greater glory. Nevertheless, creation "is, in a way, the model and basis for all of God's further acts."[11] This is why in Psalm 51 David petitions the Lord, "Create in me a clean heart, O God" (Ps 51:10). In the Bible, the verb, "to create," conveys God's work of bringing something into existence that previously did not exist: the work of creation itself; the freedom of Israel after being liberated from slavery in Egypt; His kingdom of justice in Christ, the "new creation" (2 Cor 5:17).[12] The essence of this final work of creation is the renewal of humanity through the gift of a clean heart, which comes with the gift of a

---

7   See the conclusion to the parable of the unforgiving debtor: "You wicked servant! I forgave you all that debt because you pleaded with me; and should not you have had mercy on your fellow servant, as I had mercy on you?" (Mt 18:32–33). More generally, God expects those who have benefited from His gracious favor to produce fruit. See Is 5:1–7; Jn 15:1–8.
8   See Ps 116:12, 17.
9   See *CCC*, 349.
10 Prayer for the 26th Sunday of Ordinary Time.
11 Christoph Schönborn, *Living the Catechism of the Catholic Church. A Brief Commentary on the Catechism for Every Week of the Year*, Vol. I: *The Creed* (San Francisco: Ignatius Press, 1995), 45.
12 See Jacques Guillet, "Le Psaume *Miserere*," *La Maison-Dieu* No 23 (1953): 68–69.

"new and right spirit" (Ps 51:10). David knows that this spirit is holy,[13] that is, that it comes from the God Who alone is holy, and that this spirit makes it possible for him to be steadfast in fidelity to the Lord. By this power of this spirit, David can become what he is called to be. He can correspond to God's will in the way that other creatures seem to do so effortlessly, as Jeremiah so vividly contrasts other creatures' steadfastness to the deviation from God's will of His people: "Even the stork in the heavens knows her times; and the turtledove, swallow, and crane keep the time of their coming; but my people know not the ordinance of the Lord" (Jer 8:7). It is to be expected, then, that God would react to this new creation as He did to the first, that is, seeing the goodness that He has produced, that He would see that it is good or look upon it with favor and love, as Jesus looked upon the rich young man when he professed having observed all of God's commandments.[14]

The definitive act of God looking with favor upon creation takes the form of the heavenly Father expressing His love to His eternal Son, "You are my beloved Son; with you I am well pleased" (Lk 3:22). Jesus is the new creation. In Him the Father's love is fully satisfied because He is everything that God ever wanted man to be.[15] Jesus is the eternal Son of God. He is pure receptivity to the Father's love. He is the clean heart that places no obstacles to what God desires to give, a heart in which the fullness of justice resides. Here, justice is not just one of the moral virtues. Rather, it must be understood in the biblical sense as the effect in man of God's fidelity to Himself by fulfilling His promises.[16] For man to be just means that he corresponds in every way to God's vision of what he should be. Christ has received the fullness of justice "in order that it may become justice in the hearts of many human beings, predestined from eternity in the Firstborn Son to be children of God."[17]

Through the grace of conversion, David's heart becomes renewed. He becomes just again, and this is a grace of participating in the fullness of justice in the heart of Christ. David becomes a new creation through, with, and in Him: "Therefore, if anyone is in Christ, he is a new creation" (2 Cor 5:17).[18] Though he does know it, David's prayer that God might look with favor on him is, in reality, a petition that God Himself become a man and offer Himself in sacrifice. For, by the decree of Eternal Wisdom, that is, the divine logic of love, this is the means by Eternal human hearts can be justified by faith and thereby participate in Christ's fullness of justice. And

---

13 "Do not cast me away from your presence, and do not take your holy spirit from me" (Ps 51:11). ESV and NAS capitalize Holy Spirit, while NAB and NJB do not. Certainly, with the benefit of Christ's revelation of the Holy Spirit, Christians can see a reference to the Holy Spirit in this verse. David does not know this spirit as a divine person, but as a participation in the power of God.
14 See Mk 10:20–21.
15 See John Paul II, *Redemptor hominis*, 9.
16 On the biblical notion of justice, see Stanislas Lyonnet, *Les étapes du mystère du salut selon l'épître aux Romains* (Paris: Les Éditions du Cerf, 1969).
17 John Paul II, *Redemptor hominis*, 9.
18 See also Gal 6:15; Rev 21:5.

this means that they participate in His experience of the Father's look of favor upon His Son. This is the very meaning of Christian Baptism:

> With Baptism we become *children of God in his only-begotten Son, Jesus Christ.* Rising from the waters of the Baptismal font, every Christian hears again the voice that was once heard on the banks of the Jordan River: "You are my beloved Son; with you I am well pleased" (Lk 3:22). From this comes the understanding that one has been brought into association with the beloved Son, becoming a child of adoption (cf. Gal 4:4–7) and a brother or sister of Christ. In this way the eternal plan of the Father for each person is realized in history: "For those whom he foreknew he also predestined to be conformed to the image of his Son, in order that he might be the first-born among many brethren" (Rom 8:29).[19]

This is simply an application of the christological principle set forth in the *Catechism*: "Christ enables us to live in Him all that He Himself lived, and He lives it in us."[20]

David, of course, was never baptized with water in the name of the Trinity. But it is nonetheless baptismal graces in which God's mercy causes him to participate. Mercy, John Paul II tells us, is love's second name.[21] As God's first love of creation delights in His creatures and looks upon them with the approval of His favor—"And God saw that it was good" (Gen 1:10)—so His re-creative merciful love makes a gift of a clean heart so that He can once again look with favor on man and say, "And God saw ... that ... it was very good" (Gen 1:31).

By his faith in God's mercy and his emerging grasp of the mysterious relation between that mercy and man's embrace of the consequences of sin, David becomes a participant in the mystery of Christ. It is a great grace, a gift from God, that David is able to see things this way and thereby anticipate the paschal mystery. What Jesus says of Abraham is equally applicable to David: "Your father Abraham rejoiced that he was to see my day; he saw it and was glad" (Jn 8:56). David's faith, like that of Abraham, is in the God Whose plan of redemptive love culminates in Jesus Christ. His Yes to God in conversion is, therefore, an implicit Yes to the totality of God's plan. And this is the source of the joy for which David has the temerity to pray even in the midst of his conversion: "Make me hear joy and gladness; let the bones which you have broken rejoice" (Ps 51:8). This is "the joy of conversion,"[22] for with God the hope is sure that today's mourning will bring tomorrow's rejoicing: "You have turned my mourning into dancing; you have loosed my sackcloth and girded me with gladness"

---

19   John Paul II, *Christifideles laici*, 11.
20   *CCC*, 521.
21   See John Paul II, *Dives in misericordia*, 7.
22   John Paul II, *Tertio millennio adveniente*, 32.

(Ps 30:11).[23] This is a participatory joy, for God Himself rejoices over the conversion of sinners, as Jesus reveals in the Parable of the Prodigal Son. The joy of the one who converts is a borrowed joy. Already in the Old Covenant, God rejoices over the conversion of His people, depicted as the rebuilding of Jerusalem:

> [4] You shall no more be termed Forsaken, and your land shall no more be termed Desolate; but you shall be called My delight is in her, and your land Married; for the Lord delights in you, and your land shall be married. [5] For ... as the bridegroom rejoices over the bride, so shall your God rejoice over you. (Isaiah 62:4–5)
>
> I will rejoice in Jerusalem, and be glad in my people. (Isaiah 65:19)
>
> The Lord, your God, is in your midst, a warrior who gives victory; he will rejoice over you with gladness, he will renew you in his love; he will exult over you with loud singing. (Zephaniah 3:17)

No one rejoices more perfectly over the conversion of sinners than God Himself, because His love is perfect. "Do I not rejoice when they turn from their evil way and live?" (Ezek 18:23 NAB). Man's joy in conversion is a participation in the joy of God Himself when sinners return to Him.[24]

At the point of leaving Jerusalem, king David is placed in the position of his forefather, Abraham. Like Abraham, David leaves the security of a predictable future. He sets out for a future that he cannot know. His future now is entirely in the hands of God. He can only entrust himself to God's plan. He has to proceed in a "cloud of unknowing" or darkness. But this is precisely the remedy for his having taken his future into his own hands, for having failed to consult the Lord about his desire for Bathsheba. David's kingship and his entire future is placed on the altar of Isaac. If he finds favor with the Lord, if his sacrifice of faith is found acceptable to the Lord, he can hope to receive his kingship back, even as Abraham received Isaac anew. The exterior circumstances of David's defeat and exodus point to the interior testing and purification of faith.

After David flees Jerusalem with his entourage another incident occurs. A man named Shimei, of the House of Benjamin, like Saul, and therefore a man who is predisposed to believe the worst about David, hurls

---

23 For other texts on joy following sorrow, see: Jer 31:13; Is 35:10; 51:11.
24 This is the meaning of Jesus' conclusion to the parables of the lost sheep and the lost coin. Teaching in a culture that does not pronounce the holy Name of God, Jesus uses the expressions "joy in heaven" and "joy among the angels of God" (Lk 15:7, 10) to communicate that God Himself rejoices over the conversion of sinners. In the Parable of the Prodigal Son, the explanation for the father's exuberant joy over his son's return is repeated three times (Lk 15:24, 27, 32).

stones in the direction of the king and his men. It is only a symbolic action, though, since with his soldiers surrounding him, the king is secure against the threat of just one man. At the same time, Shimei curses the king, blaming him for the demise of the family of Saul (2 Sam 16:5–8). When one of David's men requests permission to put an end to Shimei's disrespect, the king's reply reveals his new way of understanding suffering and persecution.

> [10] "What have I to do with you, you sons of Zeruiah? If he is cursing because the Lord has said to him, 'Curse David,' who then shall say, 'Why have you done so?'" [11] And David said to Abishai and to all his servants, "Behold, my own son seeks my life; how much more now may this Benjaminite! Let him alone, and let him curse; for the Lord has bidden him. [12] It may be that the Lord will look upon my affliction, and that the Lord will repay me with good for this cursing of me today." (2 Samuel 16:10–12)

God's love will not permit its rejection to be the last word. David's sin has already been pardoned, but now he seems to grasp the mysterious way in which God's mercy works. He perceives that God draws close to those who suffer the torment of knowing that they are responsible for evil in the world. This conviction about how God responds to the distress of conscience is the foundation of the bold prayer: "Consider my affliction and my trouble, and forgive all my sins" (Ps 25:18).

We may very well be at the origin of one of the most famous verses of the Bible: "a broken and contrite heart, O God, you will not despise" (Ps 51:17). St. Augustine sees in David's words evidence of penance: "Acknowledging his guilt he embraced his penance."[25] It is as though David has a groping intuition that persecution is a sign of divine favor.[26] God's deliverance of David into the hands of his enemy is in reality the sign of a future victory, and in this we have a remarkable prefiguring of Christ being delivered into the hands of sinful men, only to bring the definitive victory over sin by loving "to the end" and by rising on the third day.

The promise made to David about an unending reign is fulfilled in Jesus, the true "son of David,"[27] the long-awaited heir to David's throne. David's kingship prefigures that of Christ in more than one way. A dimension of that prefiguration that is often overlooked concerns the way that Christ takes upon Himself all the affliction of all of the sins of all time. Though Christ's kingdom is not of this world[28] because He is not of this world,[29] nevertheless its inauguration takes place in this world. In Him, the

---

25 Augustine, *Expositions on the Psalms*, 51, 15 (Verse 10).
26 Cf. Barthélemy, *God and His Image*, 141–142.
27 See Mt 1:1, 20; 9:27; 12:23; 15:22; 20:30f; 21:9, 15; 22:42; Mk 10:47f; 12:35; Lk 3:31; 18:38f.
28 See Jn 18:36.
29 See Jn 8:23.

Kingdom of God is already at hand,[30] it has come upon Jesus' contemporaries,[31] its secret has been made known,[32] and its keys have been entrusted to Peter.[33] It is a Kingdom subject to violence,[34] that is, the violence of conversion,[35] and the violence that Christ Himself must endure in order to merit the graces of conversion for all. Just as David's affliction over his own sin is the cause of the unleashing of divine mercy, Christ's suffering over all the sins of all times seals the "covenant of mercy"[36] promised to every sinner who repents and turns to Him.

Here we find ourselves at the very heart of the Gospel of Jesus Christ, as Job anticipates it. "I know that my Redeemer lives" (Job 19:25). Through Job's suffering, God brought him to a certain realization that his very suffering is a source of hope. Fr. Barthélemy incisively describes this:

> He knows then that his groaning, which is his advocate, will abide. And one day the Almighty will be touched and will change his expression toward him who was unjustly put to death. Even though he died in despair, outside his flesh he will see God. He will see Him as one who is on his side and not against him, someone who is no stranger to him, although all his life Job has suffered from this stranger of a God. Such is Job's hope.[37]

It is clearer in the case of David than it is for Job that the intuition about God's favorable reaction to his suffering is based on a realization of the justness of the affliction, because it is manifestly related to his sin.[38] In

---

30   See Mt 10:7.
31   See Mt 12:28.
32   See Mt 13:11.
33   See Mt 16:19.
34   See Mt 11:12.
35   See Paul VI, *Evangelii nuntiandi*, 10.
36   The endurance of the covenant depends so greatly on God's mercy that some translations render the copulative "covenant and mercy" as "covenant of mercy" (see the NAB and NJB translations of Neh 1:5). Consistent with this, the NAB also renders a phrase of Neh 9:32 as "covenant of mercy." Is 54:10 and Lk 1:72 also link God's mercy to the covenant in such a way that His mercy guarantees the perpetuation and fulfillment of the covenant.
37   Barthélemy, *God and His Image*, 16.
38   Barthélemy makes a strong case that Job is wrestling with unreconciled guilt, with the intuition that no one is righteous or just before God (see Ps 143:2; Rom 3:20). The NJB links this verse of Psalm 143 to Job 9:2 and 14:3–4, indicating a similarity of subject. Barthélemy's view depends on interpreting Job's righteousness as the representation of Israel's own presumed righteousness resulting from the zealous reform of King Josiah. In Job, Israel is engaging in a profound theological reflection on the upheaval done to its understanding of God's ways when Josiah was killed in battle and the people eventually deported. This was not the expected response from God to the people's conversion to embrace the precepts of the Law with zeal. In Job, then, Israel is purifying its concept of righteousness or justification, and coming to realize, ever so slowly according to the divine pedagogy, that justification cannot be accomplished by man's own efforts to keep

Job and David and every unsettled conscience, that groaning in travail of all creation[39] is as it were most intensely focused and realized. It is man's dignity to carry responsibility for the disorder that he has brought into the world by sin. This is his just punishment, but precisely because it has its place in the supreme order established by God, an order so surpassing that it even takes disorder into account, this just punishment becomes a source of hope. "The verdict of the judgment of conscience remains a pledge of hope and mercy."[40]

Job's living Redeemer, his hope, is the God of divinely perfect freedom and love. This perfection reveals itself by imparting a created freedom and love to those He creates in His own image, and especially in the way that God turns even the misuse of created freedom and the rejection of Love into a fuller revelation of His own freedom and love. In Jesus Christ, God definitively reveals the perfection of His love as mercy that brings out of the evil of sin the good of a renewed and reconstituted freedom and a new and purified love for God on man's part. "Christ had become for these people the discovery of creative love; the rational principle of the universe had revealed itself as love—as that greater reason which accepts into itself even darkness and irrationality and heals them."[41] This greater reason is the logic of love called mercy—love's second name, a love that keeps loving in the context of its having been rejected—that Jesus Christ reveals in and through His own suffering out of love.

By the graces of conversion David becomes a participant in this order of Superior Rationality that the irrationality of creatures cannot annul. He becomes an associate in God's saving love, a cooperator in the divine logic of mercy that draws the supreme good out of the worst evil, that of sin. It is for this reason that it can truly be said that at the moment of confessing one's sins, that is, at the moment of consciously placing even the disorder and irrationality of sin into the all-embracing and transcendent Rationality of the Logic of Mercy fully revealed in Jesus Christ, "at that very moment [a man] adds to his own dignity as a man. No matter how heavily his sins weigh on his conscience, no matter how seriously they have diminished his dignity, the very act of truthful confession, the act of turning again to God, is a manifestation of the special dignity of man, his spiritual grandeur."[42]

---

the Law, that sin goes deeper and that in the end, no matter how just a man may be in his behavior, sin remains. "Who can say, 'I have made my heart clean; I am pure from my sin'?" (Prov 20:9). Job, then, is wrestling with an unsettled conscience, and stands in salvation history as yet another pointer to the mission of Jesus Christ, Whose blood alone purifies consciences (see Heb 9:14).

39 See Rom 8:22.
40 *CCC*, 1781.
41 Joseph Ratzinger, *Truth and Tolerance* (San Francisco: Ignatius Press, 2004), 155–56.
42 Karol Wojtyła, *Sources of Renewal: The Implementation of Vatican II* (San Francisco: Harper and Row, 1979), 142. It is possible that was inspired by Aquinas in *ST* III, Q. 89, a. 3. "When we pray, we enter into the workings of divine providence by placing the secondary conditional cause from which certain effects will follow, according to the divine decrees. Lastly, when we are on our knees before God, we are thereby raised to a

Man alone, who is responsible for all of the disorder in creation resulting from his sins, possesses the capacity, and thus the dignity, to insert this very disorder into the higher order of God's merciful and forgiving love, and by that very act to cooperate with God in the realization of the higher order of divine mercy.

The Fruit of Love of Enemies

By experiencing the depths of the misery of sin within himself, David comes to understand the rebellion that infects the hearts of all men and the desolation of being separated from God. In the context of the collapse of the king's exterior kingdom, God is at work building the foundations of the kingdom within. The historical desolations that he experiences—defeat at the hands of his own son, the (apparent) end of his reign, the death of his infant son—point to the interior desolation that comes with the realization that one has been unfaithful to Fidelity itself, that one has cut oneself off from the source of life, and, most importantly, that if strict justice were the foundation of man's relation to God there would be no hope.

At the same time, David has experienced the Lord's power in victory over his enemies. His defeat of Goliath is paradigmatic. From a human perspective, David was outmatched. Yet, like Abraham, relying on God rather than himself, David hoped against hope and defeated him. For, like God Himself, David does not regard appearances: "You come to me with a sword and with a spear and with a javelin; but I come to you in the name of the Lord of hosts, the God of the armies of Israel" (1 Sam 17:45). The victory that David anticipates is the Lord's victory, so "that all this assembly may know that the Lord saves not with sword and spear" (1 Sam 17:47). The future king's triumph over the threat to the exterior kingdom contains the lesson that will be relearned with regard to the sin that threatens the inner kingdom. Here, too, the battle is the Lord's, and his weapon is above all the word of the Lord that his prophet will bring onto the battlefield.

In his transparency to himself, David realizes what he truly deserves, and this is precisely why he is able to arrive at the heights of love's perfection, where love becomes mercy. His interior state echoes the words of the prodigal son and the centurion: "Father, I have sinned against heaven and before you; *I am no longer worthy* to be called your son" (Lk 15:21); "Lord, *I am not worthy* to have you come under my roof ..." (Mt 8:8). To declare oneself *unworthy to be loved* is to renounce any claim, and right to be loved. One can only appeal to and rely solely on God's mercy. But this implies that a person knows that there is a divine attribute that is greater than justice. We ask God, then, not to look on our sins with justice in mind, but to look to Himself, to the perfection of His love and mercy. The Church's liturgy puts it this way: "Look not upon on our sins but on

---

greater dignity, for the proper use of prayer will conform our will to God's" (Jordan Aumann, *Spiritual Theology* [Westminster, MD: Christian Classics, 1987], 170).

the faith of your Church."[43] Our faith rests solely in the mercy that Christ has revealed in His teachings on forgiving seven times seventy times, in the parable of the prodigal son, in the parable of the unforgiving debtor. He has revealed divine mercy above all in His own sacrifice for the forgiveness of sins. Look, O God, at the unleashing of mercy in Your own Son's heart. Remember His sacrifice and hear His prayer for mercy when You think of our sins.

God showed mercy to David when Nathan announced that he would not die on account of his sin. Now, as the fruit of his conversion, it is David's privilege to make mercy present to others, to make God's mercy known to other men.

The sublime perfection of David's mercy is seen above all in his attitude toward his rebellious son, Absalom. While the king's soldiers treat his son like any enemy, desiring only to rid the king of his threat, David himself is anxious that his son not be killed in the ensuing battle, and commands his generals, "Deal gently for my sake with the young Absalom" (2 Sam 18:5). Do these words not correspond to the essentials of Jesus' priestly prayer? Can we not easily picture Jesus saying, "Be gentle with sinners, Father, for my sake"?

In the end, Absalom is killed, and this death, rather than to relieve the king, produces the cry: "O my son Absalom, my son, my son Absalom! Would I had died instead of you, O Absalom, my son, my son!" (2 Sam 18:33). Can there be any doubt that these words are rooted in a father's profound sense of personal responsibility for death of his son? Nathan had linked the death of the child born of Bathsheba to David's sins, and David seems to take this as a principle by which he can interpret all evil that befalls him. Shimei's curses are all the more readily understood in light of the fact that David's own son turns against him. By sinning, David contributes to the great disorder of creation and thus to its "groaning with labor pains" (Rom 8:22), and so it is only just that he appropriate this groaning. Because his sin is so close to him, because it has been granted to him to see in himself the mystery of iniquity,[44] he is forever changed.

Heretofore, David had thought that the default setting of human experience is peace and blessing, and that evil and suffering simply punctuate our lives. Now he arrives at the higher wisdom of knowing that if a default setting of human experience is to be identified, it must be on the side of the evil and suffering that are a consequence of sin. Is this not, in the end, the lesson contained in the very origins of God's chosen people? Slavery was their condition in Egypt, and were it not for God's merciful love and powerful act of liberation, slavery would remain their condition. The fact that Israel's first understanding was that this slavery was due entirely to the sinful state of the Egyptians should not be allowed to obscure the clear fact that over nearly six centuries the divine pedagogy

---

43   Roman Missal, Communion Rite.
44   See the profound reflections on the mystery of iniquity in John Paul II: *Dominum et Vivificantem*, 39, 48; *Reconciliatio et paenitentia*, 14–19.

would lead Israel to come to see that its defeat and loss of the Promised Land and temple were in fact God's just judgments in response to His people's sins.[45] At this point, Israel could grasp something of the mystery of cooperation with God in its own purification through conversion by receiving its chastisements as just punishment and grace.[46] David personifies this great lesson of the divine pedagogy. His interior state of taking personal responsibility for the death of Absalom and desiring to have died in his place anticipates the theology and spirituality of the suffering servant, the "man of sorrows ... acquainted with grief [who] has borne our griefs and carried our sorrows ... [and] was wounded for our transgressions ... bruised for our iniquities; upon him was the chastisement that made us whole, and with his stripes we are healed." It is the Lord's doing to have "laid on him the iniquity of us all;" "it was the will of the Lord to bruise him." And so it is indeed a great grace to cooperate with God by being "stricken for the transgression of my people ... when he makes himself an offering for sin" (Is 53:3–10).

Jesus Christ definitively reveals what God's pedagogy only sketches in David's desire to die in place of Absalom and in the suffering servant. In Him, God becomes man in order to bring to perfection such experiences of suffering that are vicarious and salvific. With these we see just how carefully God prepares for the revelation in Jesus Christ. In David and the suffering servant, the kingdom within is gradually developing as Israel is internalizing the lesson that will culminate in the disclosure of why it was "necessary that the Christ should suffer" (Lk 24:26; Acts 17:3; 26:23). For David and the suffering servant, this revelation fulfills and completes the partial yet already profound understanding that God permits the evil and suffering in order to "unleash love."[47] Man's misuse of the gift of his freedom by sinning becomes, in keeping with the divine logic of love,[48] the occasion for God to exercise His freedom for an unleashing of the depths of His own love. This is at the very heart of Christian faith, formulated by St. Paul: "where sin increased, grace abounded all the more, so that, as sin reigned in death, grace also might reign through righteousness to eternal life through Jesus Christ our Lord" (Rom 5:20–21). Only in the light of the Cross and Resurrection of Christ does the logic of David's love for his enemy become revealed as God's own logic of

---

45 See Dan 9:7, 8, 11.
46 "While patiently bearing sufferings and trials of all kinds and, when the day comes, serenely facing death, the Christian must strive to accept this temporal punishment of sin as a grace" (*CCC*, 1473).
47 "... suffering, which is present under so many different forms in our human world, is also present in order *to unleash love in the human person,* that unselfish gift of one's 'I' on behalf of other people, especially those who suffer" (John Paul II, *Salvifici doloris*, 29).
48 "Logic of love" is a phrase often used by John Paul II and Joseph Ratzinger to convey something of the mystery of the revelation of God's love in Jesus Christ. God's love is in keeping with His wisdom, His logic, while at the same time His wisdom is at the service of fully revealing His love. This "logic of love" culminates in the Paschal Mystery of Jesus Christ. It is from the Cross of Christ that one must begin in order to define love as God does.

love, so that it becomes logical to proclaim, regarding the sin of Adam and Eve: "O happy fault, O necessary sin of Adam, which gained for us so great a Redeemer!"[49] Through his spiritual resurrection, David arrives at a degree of love that could not have been attained in any way other than as the fruit of God's forgiving and reconciling mercy. David's love for Absalom in his rebellion is the fruit of the great king having experienced God's love for him in his own rebellion.

Absalom dies without knowing anything of his father's wish to die in his place. Thus, it is pure speculation to wonder how this knowledge might have changed his heart and led him to look at things in a new perspective and to a conversion. For Christian faith, in contrast, the matter is settled. Every believer can say, with St. Paul, that Christ "loved me and gave himself for me" (Gal 2:20).[50] Is it not this mystery in which David has become a participant, first by receiving God's forgiving love, and then by loving his rebellious son as he has been loved? In this way, the new commandment that Christ enjoins on those who believe in Him is realized in David: "A new commandment I give to you, that you love one another; even *as I have loved you*, that you also love one another" (Jn 13:34). Having seen himself as God's enemy and having received mercy, David is placed at very the heart of the Gospel, that "while we were enemies we were reconciled to God by the death of his Son" (Rom 8:10). His knowledge of God's ways anticipates the profession of faith that "God shows his love for us in that while we were yet sinners Christ died for us" (Rom 5:8). David's conversion produces in him that poverty of spirit that is "the great achievement of the Holy Spirit's hidden mission during the time of the promises that prepare for Christ's coming."[51] With this humility he is "not far from the kingdom of God" (Mk 12:34). Indeed, he stands on the threshold of the definitive revelation of that kingdom by the divine wisdom and logic of love, as the power of God's love is made

---

49   John Paul II, *Redemptor hominis*, 1.
50   Commenting on this text, Ratzinger writes: "Each one of us can and may apply to himself the dramatic personalization that Paul accomplishes in these words [of Gal 2:20]. Every man may say: The Son of God loved *me* and gave himself up for *me*. Only with this statement does christological catechesis become gospel in the full sense of the word.... In all truth Christ walked his path for me.... When we have learned to believe this again, when we are able to announce it to others as the message of truth, evangelization takes place" (*Gospel, Catechesis, Catechism, Sidelights on the Catechism of the Catholic Church* [San Francisco: Ignatius Press, 1997], 71). There is all the difference between an intellectual assent to a revealed truth that receives the truth as mere data or information, and the reception of truth as Good News corresponding to a person's existential search for the meaning of life. When that search takes place in the context of awareness of personal sin, then the discovery of God's merciful love in the Paschal Mystery cannot remain data to be memorized and retained merely by memory. It becomes light for one's living, an answer that quenches the thirst to resolve the question whether sin has the last word and if there is any hope to which one can cling for meaning and purpose in life. When the content of faith is received in this way, it transforms one's life so that the believer's life itself is a radiation of this Good News and the meaning it brings. This is the vital source of the New Evangelization.
51   *CCC*, 716.

perfect in weakness[52] and Christ Himself made perfect in His mission as Mediator through suffering.[53]

By accusing David of having shamed his servants precisely by showing this kind of mercy toward his son, by accusing him of having "loved those who hate you," (2 Sam 19:7), the king's general, Joab, does nothing other than to accuse David of carrying out Christ's commandment to love one's enemy.[54] In this David proves that he is indeed a "man after the heart of God Himself" (1 Sam 13:14), that he is truly "a son of his heavenly Father" (Mt 5:45).

This is a fitting juncture at which to return to the question about the legitimacy of the boldness of David's earlier confidence in God as Vindicator of the rights he acquired by reason of being anointed king. In light of the preceding it should be clear that the issue is not so much about the quality of his assurance as it is about the object or content upon which his assurance bears. Early in his life, David sees the Lord's protection as assurance of victory over external threats to his reign. After his conversion, and because of it, his attention is refocused; now it is on the internal threat to his kingship, namely, his own sin. This is the key point for these reflections on conversion, and it is reinforced by realizing that the place assigned to David in salvation history is to prefigure Jesus, the Messiah-King, the one through Whom the Lord fulfills His promise to David that his "throne shall be established forever" (2 Sam 7:16).

Jesus establishes His Kingdom through fidelity to the Father by suffering and dying for the reconciliation of sinners. He accomplishes this by perfecting the consciences of worshippers, and He does this by purifying them with His own blood, that is, the love with which He offers His life as a sacrifice for sin.[55] His sacrifice and its fruit of purifying consciences fulfill Jeremiah's prophecy of the New Covenant.[56] While Jeremiah foresees that the New Covenant will entail God writing His law on people's *hearts* so that it is within them, the Letter to the Hebrews conveys the same thing in terms of *conscience*. Jesus' kingdom and His reign are the only ones that respect, preserve, enrich, and perfect human dignity and freedom because He rules as Truth and thus as King of consciences. His single law is the law of love of God and love of neighbor, and this law is actually the Third Person of the Blessed Trinity, the Holy Spirit, Who is the Person-Love, the Person-Gift of the Trinity,[57] Who dwells within those believe in Christ. The result is that the law no longer comes to man from the outside, as though it were foreign to him and only the promise of reward and the fear of punishment are able to assure compliance. Rather, by the gift of the Holy Spirit, a person identifies with the law, seeing it as the most exact expression of his very being. Justified

---

52 See 2 Cor 12:9.
53 See Heb 2:10; 5:8–9.
54 See Mt 5:44.
55 See Heb 9:9, 14; 10:22.
56 See Jer 31:31–34; Heb 8:8–12.
57 See John Paul II, *Dominum et Vivificantem*, 10, 22, 23.

by faith and enjoying the gift of a purified conscience, those who believe in Christ become a law unto themselves.[58] This is why St. Thomas attributes submission to law as a sign of the influence of the Holy Spirit.[59] In the end, to obey God's law is to fulfill the God-given dynamism to love oneself.

With the conversion brought about by the merciful love of God fully revealed in Christ, man becomes a new creation and he experiences that original harmony between the law in his mind and God's law that typified the state of Adam and Eve prior to their fall. No longer is man condemned to delighting in God's law and knowing that it is just and good and holy, only to find that there is a contrary law at work within him.[60] The law of the Spirit of Christ now dwells in those who have faith in Christ,[61] constituting His disciples as God's children who are dead to sin, thereby establishing within them the Kingdom of God, which is "righteousness and peace and joy in the Holy Spirit" (Rom 14:17). The capacity of the repentant King David to love his enemy is an incontrovertible sign of the God's rule in his heart, of the kingdom within.

Covenant, kingdom, temple, and sacrifice are inseparable. As the temple is the sacred place of the presence of God and of sacrifice within the Kingdom of Israel, so Christians become the temple of His kingdom.[62] The sacrifice is no longer an exterior rite but a personal participation in the sacrifice of Christ, so that a Christian can offer himself, through, with, and in Christ, as a "living sacrifice, holy and acceptable to God, which is your spiritual worship" (Rom 12:1). This is the sacrifice that Christ makes possible by purifying consciences, which is to write His law on His people's hearts and to rule them through the dictates of their consciences, which echo His voice. Christ exercises His messianic reign through consciences that freely submit to Him because He has purified their consciences by His blood.[63] This is to say that those who turn to Him for forgiveness and reconciliation with God become participants in the logic of love according to which the Cross is the throne of the King of Glory. Christ rules through the consciences of those who believe that his Cross is the throne of grace and mercy.[64]

---

58   See Rom 2:14.
59   See Aquinas, *ST* I-II Q. 96, a.5 ad 2.
60   See Rom 7:12–23.
61   See Rom 8:11.
62   See 1 Cor 6:19.
63   "Christ governs by means of the conscience. Christ is therefore able to exercise his government over the Church more effectively the more open and pure are above all the consciences of those to whom is entrusted the care of their flocks" (Joseph Ratzinger, *Church, Ecumenism, and Politics. New Essays in Ecclesiology* [New York: Crossroad, 1988], 60). "But our Divine Savior governs and guides the Society which He founded directly and personally also. For it is He who reigns within the minds and hearts of men, and bends and subjects their wills to His good pleasure" (Pius XII, *Mystici Corporis Christi*, 39).
64   "Let us then with confidence draw near to the throne of grace, that we may receive mercy and find grace to help in time of need" (Heb 4:16).

If David's place in salvation history is to point to the kingship of Christ, it is highly fitting that he learn what it truly means to be a king after the heart of God Himself. It means to be subject to the love of the Eternal King, even to the point of loving one's enemies. To arrive at this degree of love, it was necessary for David to realize that by sinning he had become God's enemy, and to experience God's mercy and forgiveness.[65]

The Third Psalm

Psalm 3 preserves for us a glimpse into the heart of David at the time of his flight from Jerusalem: "A Psalm of David, when he fled from Absalom his son" (Ps 3:1). As in many psalms, it begins with David making his situation known to the Lord: "O Lord, how many are my foes! Many are rising against me" (v. 1). He immediately adds: "many are saying of me, there is no help for him in God" (v. 2). Did others actually say this, or are these words expressive of his interior struggle to persevere in hope? Jesus was similarly taunted as He hung on the Cross: "He trusts in God; let God deliver him now, if he desires him; for he said, 'I am the Son of God'" (Mt 27:43). Two kings, David and Jesus, confront what appears to be the complete negation of the promises of God.[66] It is the only way for God to establish His kingdom in a world marked by sin. For, sin is itself the fundamental negation and, as we have seen, it is in keeping with God's wisdom that people are punished by that by which they sin.

David's presentation of his situation to God echoes the cry of Israel under the oppression of slavery in Egypt. If there is no God Who hears and takes interest, there is no hope. It is important to note that neither Israel nor David complains that if God is God, if He is all-powerful and all-loving, then He would not have allowed the oppression to occur in the first place. That would effectively destroy the very foundation of prayer in a situation of disaster. Why God does not intervene to preempt suffering is certainly a vexing question. Would it require any greater display of power on His part to remove it altogether? Why does He seem powerless in preventing suffering, only to extricate His people from suffering after it has overtaken them? Why does He always seem a day late? Where is the wisdom in this?

Certainly, the moment of suffering is not the time to entertain such questions. Suffering imposes a kind of pragmatism, an undistracted focus on removing the cause of the suffering. In such moments, God's track record of coming to the aid of the oppressed is all that counts.

> [1] My son, if you come forward to serve the Lord,
> prepare yourself for temptation.

---

65   John Paul II richly develops what it means for Christ to reign in hearts through consciences in his reflections on the Christian's participation in the kingly office of Christ. See, for example, Wojtyła, *Sign of Contradiction*, 137–143 and John Paul II, *Redemptor hominis*, 21.
66   See John Paul II, *Redemptoris Mater*, 18.

² Set your heart right and be steadfast,
and do not be hasty in time of calamity.
³ Cleave to him and do not depart,
that you may be honored at the end of your life.
⁴ Accept whatever is brought upon you,
and in changes that humble you be patient.
⁵ For gold is tested in the fire,
and acceptable men in the furnace of humiliation.
⁶ Trust in him, and he will help you;
make your ways straight, and hope in him.
⁷ You who fear the Lord, wait for his mercy;
and turn not aside, lest you fall.
⁸ You who fear the Lord, trust in him,
and your reward will not fail;
⁹ you who fear the Lord, hope for good things,
for everlasting joy and mercy.
¹⁰ Consider the ancient generations and see:
who ever trusted in the Lord and was put to shame?
   Or who ever persevered in the fear of the Lord and was forsaken?
Or who ever called upon him and was overlooked?
¹¹ For the Lord is compassionate and merciful;
he forgives sins and saves in time of affliction. (Sirach 2:1–11)

By presenting the theme of forgiveness of sins, the final line in this passage introduces the consciousness of the moral dimension involved in misfortune and calamity. How could David fail to recall Nathan's words: "'Now therefore the sword shall never depart from your house, because you have despised me, and have taken the wife of Uriah the Hittite to be your wife.' Thus says the Lord, 'Behold, I will raise up evil against you out of your own house'" (2 Sam 12:10–11). The prophet directly links Absalom's rebellion to David's sin. It is not always the case that a particular suffering is the direct effect of one's own misuse of freedom. But this matters little. We know that all disorder in the world is a result of sin, and we know that all have sinned. For this reason, any instance of suffering can and should be the occasion to become conscious of one's own sin and complicity in the vengeance that chaos inflicts upon mankind. This is true even when the suffering concerns others rather than oneself. A conscience enlightened by faith knows how to turn every form of suffering into an acknowledgement of sin and an act of repentance. This moral dimension entirely changes the perspective. God cannot intervene to prevent the misuse of freedom without destroying that very freedom. But He can intervene to make man's sin the occasion for a greater revelation of His love, wisdom, and power in mercy. A sense of personal responsibility for the misuse of freedom (Could there be any other explanation for its misuse?) is required to perceive something of the rightness in the way God is at work in suffering. The distinction between outward enemies and the inward enemy remains, but with a deepening sense of sin one perceives that they are mysteriously related. While unbelievers take misfortune and calamity as indicators that there is no God, faith sees them as indicators of the wisdom of His pedagogy and hope anticipates His victory. In and through suffering, God is testing and purifying faith and hope. This conviction is the foundation of prayer in time of trouble.

The alternative to this faith and hope becomes inescapably clear at such times: "Many are saying of me, there is no help for him in God" (v. 2). In the purification of faith and hope, nothing is more obvious than that the one who has misused his freedom does not deserve the help of God. Indeed, in this situation God delivers His chosen ones over to their enemies, that is, the enemies opposed to confiding in His mercy, the enemies set against remembering that the Lord is "merciful and gracious, slow to anger, and abounding in mercy and faithfulness, keeping merciful love for thousands, forgiving iniquity and transgression and sin" (Ex 34:6–7). This is the truth about God that is the foundation for an appeal to Him in time of distress.[67] The prayer of desperation is based solely on the truth that God is merciful. Only if God does not allow the rejection of His love (which is the essence of sin) to stop Him from loving us is there any hope.

The haunting suggestion that God remains indifferent to David's plight and will not involve Himself in this situation becomes the occasion for a profession of faith: "But you, O Lord, are a shield about me, my glory, and the lifter of my head" (v. 3). This verse shows that by faith David appropriates the truth about God's love and power. The metaphor of a shield conveys that God's strength comes to David's protection; God's glory becomes David's glory, and he is no longer downcast. In humility, he credits God with the lifting of his head, because God is His hope: "Why are you cast down, O my soul, and why are you disquieted within me? Hope in God; for I shall again praise him, my help and my God" (Ps 42:5). If there is hope for withstanding the attack of the outward enemy, the hope is even greater for the vanquishing of the enemy within, sin. Only supernatural hope can save us from becoming despondent. For David, faith is more than assenting to the truth of a number of assertions about the Lord. It is also to believe that these truths about God assure him of a hopeful future. The truth about God makes it possible for him to find meaning even in his suffering, even if this serves to remind him of his sin. In this confidence of faith and hope David can cry out to the Lord, knowing that He answers (v. 4). He can entrust himself to the Lord and sleep, knowing that he will be sustained (v. 5). An army of ten thousand cannot shake his hope in the God Who delivers those who are faithful from their enemies (vv. 6–8).

On the other hand, the allegation that "There is no help for him in God" (v. 2) echoes the great lie of the serpent, that God is not love. To make the

---

67 See Ps 88:15; 103:8; 145:8.

case that God gave Adam and Eve the commandment out of jealousy and not out of love is to say that God is of no help to man in his pursuit of living a fully human life. This lie about God's love gives rise to the greatest fear man can know, for if God is not love, then He is indeed man's enemy. It would be preferable if there were no God at all! The devil sees in man's becoming aware of sin a particular vulnerability to the suggestion that "there is no help from God." And the reason is that this is the premise that gives rise to sin in the first place: God did not love by giving the commandment, why should He love you now? Having seduced Adam and Eve into doubting God's love so that they strike out on their own in the quest for fulfillment, now, for even greater reason, there is no reason to expect any help from a jealous God who has been offended by man's rebellion. This is an absolutely coherent and closed system, so long as the premise that God is jealous of His prerogatives remains unchallenged.

The divine logic for dismantling this diabolical canard is not a lesson in logic. It is not even a lesson in love, if by "lesson" one understands a process of re-examining the available data, clarifying definitions, and assuring the accuracy of deductions. No, God's answer is to provide new data, new demonstrations of His love. The history of salvation is nothing other than the record of His ever-new demonstrations of love. All of biblical revelation is the account of what God has done to provide man with the data that forces him to challenge the diabolical premise and to come to believe in His merciful love. The operative distinction is between what sinners deserve (justice) and what they are in fact offered (mercy). It is true that awareness of sin entails awareness of being undeserving of God's love, for by its nature sin is rejection of God's love. The ever-new data is that man's rejection of God's love not only cannot stop Him from continuing to love, but in reality it unleashes greater and greater demonstrations of His love, with Christ's death and resurrection being the definitive demonstration. Nothing short of the boldness (*parrhesía*) of faith in this revelation of God's love makes it possible to live "in the certainty of being loved"[68]—precisely when we need it most, that is, in the context of having rejected his love—and in that certainty to profess our faith that "if we are faithless, He remains faithful—for He cannot deny himself" (2 Tim 2:13). Such faith is our victory over the "ruler of this world" (Jn 14:30; 16:11),[69] for it is from the world that does not know of God's witness to His merciful love that the fear that He is not love arises. In this state of faithless fear, our hearts can only condemn us when we become cognizant of sin. Christ's testimony to God's merciful love alone has the power to reassure our hearts in this condition, for God's love "is greater than our hearts" (1 Jn 3:20).

---

68 *CCC*, 2778.
69 See 1 Jn 5:4.

The Sacrifice of a Broken and Contrite Heart

Enlightened by God's word, David consents to the dynamism of the truth and confesses his sin. In the memory of Israel, which is also the Church's memory, Psalm 51 remains "a psalm of David, when Nathan the prophet came to him, after he had gone in to Bathsheba" (Ps 51:1–2). It expresses in unequaled fashion the sentiments of a sorrowful and repentant sinner.

> [1] Have mercy on me, O God, according to your merciful love;
> according to your abundant mercy blot out my transgressions.
> [2] Wash me thoroughly from my iniquity,
> and cleanse me from my sin!
> [3] For I know my transgressions,
> and my sin is ever before me.
> [4] Against you, you only, have I sinned, and done that which is evil in your sight,
> so that you are justified in your sentence and blameless in your judgment....
> [6] Behold, you desire truth in the inward being;
> therefore teach me wisdom in my secret heart....
> [7] Purge me with hyssop, and I shall be clean;
> wash me, and I shall be whiter than snow.
> [8] Make me hear joy and gladness;
> let the bones which you have broken rejoice.
> [10] Create in me a clean heart, O God,
> and put a new and right spirit within me....
> [17] The sacrifice acceptable to God is a broken spirit;
> a broken and contrite heart, O God, you will not despise.
> (Psalm 51:1–17)

Verse four is especially important because it indicates the success of Nathan's mission. By faith, David has come to see things from God's perspective. He acknowledges that God's sentence and judgment are true. But what, precisely, is the content of His sentence and judgment? What exactly is it that, by faith, David is able to see from God's perspective?

The answer to this question requires that we put aside what seems to be the obvious meaning, namely, that David is acknowledging that God is right to punish him for his sin. As we have seen, David's punishment, beginning with the guilt of conscience, is medicinal, rehabilitative. So, punishment is not an end in itself; it is a means to the goal of conversion, which puts an end to sin. As the Psalm continues, David amply expresses various aspects and fruits of conversion. Thus, it would seem that these fruits of conversion are related to the sentence of punishment as proof of the justness of God's judgment. David is bearing witness to that mercy by which God is faithful to the promises He made by forgiving him and restoring him as king of Israel.

The New Jerusalem Bible points us in the direction of another way to understand the judgment of God, by qualifying God's justice as salvific and indicating that His judgment brings about a victory.

> Against you, you alone, I have sinned,
> I have done what you see to be wrong,
>   that you may show your saving justice when you pass sentence,
>   and your victory may appear when you give judgment.
> (Psalm 51:4 NJB)

A note accompanying this verse reinforces this translation: "God is wholly pure and upright, and by pardoning demonstrates his power over evil and his victory over sin." David is singing the praises of God, not for the justness of His sentence, but for the victory of His fidelity over David's infidelity.

St. Paul quotes this same verse, and it is highly significant that he takes his quotation from the Greek version of the Old Testament, in which God is the one who is being judged: "That you may be justified in your words, and prevail when you are judged" (Rom 3:4). The "words" to which the Psalm refers here are the promises that God made to David. God shows Himself to be faithful to His promises precisely in the context of David's infidelity. This sense of the text fits into the point that Paul is making in this section of Romans. Man's infidelity does not nullify the fidelity of God, and God is true even when man is false (vv. 3–4), so that human "wickedness serves to show the justice of God" (Rom 4:5). Stanislas Lyonnet summarizes St. Paul's thought here:

> It is not without good reason that in Romans 3:4 St. Paul, perhaps influenced by the Septuagint, saw in verse four of the same Psalm 51 a reference to God's saving justice rather than His vindictive justice. In Paul's mind, then, when David says that "God is just" he does not intend only or chiefly to acknowledge that his punishment was deserved, as is generally thought, but rather that despite the infidelity of man God remains faithful to Himself by upholding His promises of salvation. This is not only an act of humility similar to that of the good thief, it is a genuine act of faith in the unshakeable fidelity of the God of the covenant. It has been said quite rightly that David's humble confession is less a statement about "an exacting judge" than it is a resplendent illustration of "the fidelity of the God of love in the

fulfillment of His promises of salvation" (A. Feuillet).[70]

David confessed God's fidelity to His promises of salvation, promises that man's infidelity, far from canceling, serves "to manifest" (Rom 3:5).[71]

The last phrase of Psalm 51:4, as quoted by St. Paul, refers to God prevailing when He is judged. The question is, judged by whom? It is a trait of Israel's faith to be conscious that the other nations are watching God's chosen people. And as they watch they are making judgments about Israel's God, how He conducts His affairs with this people whom He has chosen and with whom He has entered into a covenant. Moses expresses this awareness regarding Egypt. Having witnessed the ten plagues and the parting of the sea at the beginning of the liberation of the tribes of Jacob, Israel's God would appear unable to complete what He has begun. It would be strange indeed if God set this people free only to exterminate them Himself. Who could believe in such a God?[72] In line with this, Joshua realizes that God's reputation is at stake in the outcome of the battles fought by His people.[73] And in the psalms, when the Lord seems slow to intervene and it might appear that He has abandoned His people, Israel expresses this dimension of its faith with the question, "Why should the nations say, 'Where is their God?'" (Ps 79:10; 115:2). In every dark night in its history, when Israel endures the just punishment for its own sins, while it awaits the day of God's mercy, this chosen people is haunted by the question, "Where is your God?" (Ps 42:3, 10). It is the question that all of salvation history insists be asked, definitively, eschatologically, when the Messiah of God is crucified and dies. At this time, the question is phrased as mocking taunts: "If you are the Son of God, come down from the cross." "He trusts in God; let God deliver him now" (Mt 27:40, 43). It is *the* question that sinful man cannot avoid asking, the question that alone captures the meaning of the death and burial of God's anointed, and the entire breadth of Holy Saturday. It is the question that has only one possible answer: mercy, new life, resurrection.

No one can escape the question, "Where is God?" This is especially intense in times of suffering, when there is not hope unless there is a God, and unless this God is both benevolent and all-powerful. Faith answers this question, but mysteriously it does not leave the question behind, as if it could be answered once and for all. Rather, faith "keeps the question alive"[74] and, as it develops, even magnifies the intensity with which it is asked. This is why the saints' participation in the paschal mystery deepens as they undergo the purifications of the dark nights. The spiritual anguish

---

70 Stanislas Lyonnet, *Le message de l'épître aux Romains* (Paris: Les Éditions du Cerf, 1971), 27–28.
71 Lyonnet, *Les étapes du mystère du salut selon l'épître aux Romains*, 48.
72 See Ex 32:12; Num 14:15–16; Deut 9:28.
73 See Josh 7:9.
74 Joseph Ratzinger, *The Nature and Mission of Theology* (San Francisco: Ignatius, 1995), 23.

of the saints is the fulfillment of the Church's vocation—including David and all the just within Israel, which is the Church in preparation for the coming of Christ—to participate more and more perfectly in the paschal mystery of Christ. To live in faith is to live a constant purification or testing in order to learn that the question, "Where is your God?" is in reality the way that the image of God formulates the question first asked by God, "Where are you?" (Gen 3:9). Prior to the sin of Adam and Eve, these questions could never be asked. In Jesus Christ, true God and true man, they attain their existential and eschatological concentration, as the Son of God asks on behalf of both God and man, "Why have you forsaken me?" (Mt 27:46). So long as the question remains unanswered, death and the fear it engenders reign,[75] which means that sin remains an impenetrable problem with no solution. The only answer is called Resurrection, in other words, grace and mercy.[76]

The fundamental vocation of the Church in every age—including David and Israel—is to be light to the nations. Israel becomes fully aware of this vocation in the context of the captives' return from Exile.[77] When the nations see that God has returned His people to rebuild Jerusalem, they will believe in Him and glorify Him.[78] But the restoration of Jerusalem is much more than a reconstitution of a nation among other nations. For, Israel understood its captivity in Babylon as punishment for its sins,[79] and for this reason the restoration of Jerusalem is a sign pointing to the purification of Israel's faith and the people's reconciliation with God. Israel's faith, then, is inseparable from God's work, is its effect, and enters into what it means to be light to the nations. The vocation of God's people is to bear witness to Him by singing of the wondrous works He has performed for them.[80] Even their captors will one day acknowledge: "The Lord has done great things for them" (Ps 126:2).

Psalm 51 and David's conversion need to be read in light of the preceding. The Psalm is a confession of sins that takes the form of a profession of faith. It is a hymn that extols the triumph of God's faithfulness over man's unfaithfulness, the victory of divine mercy over man's sin. God's greatest work, the work that gives Him the greatest glory, is the transformation or the renewal of man's heart. In this way, it is a bright light for all who follow the life of David and who are ready to make judgments about his God based on how He treats the king of Israel. In other words, anyone who has confronted his own sins and who searches through the history of religions will discover in David and in Israel the

---

75 See Heb 2:15.
76 See Rom 5:14, 17, 21.
77 See Is 42:6; 49:6; 51:4; 60:3; Lk 2:32; Jn 8:12; 9:5.
78 See Tob 13:11; Is 3:2–3; 49:6; 60:3; Jer 3:17; Bar 4:24; Ezek 5:5; Mic 4:2; Zech 8:22.
79 See Daniel 9. The prophets variously refer to it as the "time of their suffering" (Neh 9:27), the "time of bereavement" (Is 49:20), the "time of trouble" (Jer 2:27, 28; 11:12, 14), the "time of final punishment" (Ezek 21:25, 29).
80 See Ex 15:10; Judg 6:13; Ps 77:8–20; 98:1; Isa 12:5; 44:23. See also: Deut 32; 1 Sam 12:24; Ps 40:5; 71:17; 89:1; 145:6; Is 12:4; 48:20; 60:6; 61:1; Jer 31:7.

light of truth regarding God's response to man's sin. The vocation to be light to the nations is fulfilled by bearing witness to God's mercy, both through the change in one's behavior—on display especially in the worship of God and showing mercy to others and being ready to forgive them—and in the words that explain this behavior by showing that it is the fruit of experiencing God's mercy.

Through the witness of God's mercy to His people, the marvels of God become known among the nations. As indicated above, Israel is always aware that the nations are watching. This means that Israel's God is always on trial; He is always pleading His case, not only to Israel, but through Israel to the nations.[81]

> Before the nations, Yahweh thus stands as one perpetually accused. Yet, Israel's vocation is to assure that He leave the legal hearing against Him as the victor: "that You prevail when You are judged." God's people accomplish this by confessing "the justice of God," that is, His fidelity to His promises of salvation, despite the infidelity of a stiff-necked people.[82]

St. Paul understands his own vocation in these terms, as is evident in what he writes to Timothy:

> [15] The saying is sure and worthy of full acceptance, that Christ Jesus came into the world to save sinners. And I am the foremost of sinners; [16] but I received mercy for this reason, that in me, as the foremost, Jesus Christ might display his perfect patience for an example to those who were to believe in him for eternal life. (1 Timothy 1:15–16)

Like David, and like St. Augustine and all the saints, Paul speaks of himself only to extol the mercy of God. If Paul has received mercy, and if he is the limit case, then for even greater reason can all others—all the nations—hope in God's mercy and forgiveness.

The vocation of the apostolic Church is to sing God's praises. Since He should be praised above all for His greatest work, and since His greatest work is the justification of sinners,[83] then it is above all for His

---

[81] "This verse [Ps 51:4] evokes one of the great themes of the Old Testament, that of a trial. Yahweh has a lawsuit against His people (Hos 2:4; 4:1; 12:3; Jer 2:9; 29:25, 31; Is 1:18; 3:14; 5:3). This case dates from the day that God elected Israel. The first stage, in the desert at Meribah, perpetuates the memory of the moment when the Hebrews, shortly after being liberated from Egypt, level an accusation against the Lord (Ex 17:7). Quite incredibly, in this trial Yahweh is not first of all a judge, but a plaintiff. Doubtless, He is always the one who pronounces a sentence, but he begins by making his case. His case is so clear that anyone can render the verdict" (Jacques Guillet, "Le Psaume Miserere," *La Maison Dieu*, No 23 [1953]: 62–63).

[82] Lyonnet, *Les étapes du mystère du salut selon l'épître aux Romains*, 48.

[83] See Aquinas, *ST* I-II, Q. 113, a. 9.

mercy, by which He accomplishes this greatest of His works, that we should praise Him before the world. Thus, St. Augustine writes: "Let him praise You not who does not realize your mercies, which my soul's depths confess to you."[84] And since it is by His mercy that God forgives man's sins, profession of faith in His mercy is necessarily also a confession of sins. Thus, St. Augustine enters his own conversion as evidence of the truth about God:

> With thanksgiving let me remember, O my God, all your mercies to me and let me confess them to you. Let my bones be filled with your love, and let them say to you: "Lord, who is like unto you?" (Ex 15:11). "You have broken my bonds. I will sacrifice to you the sacrifice of praise" (Heb 13:15). I will narrate how you broke them asunder. And when they hear these things, let all who adore you say: "Blessed be the Lord, in heaven and on earth. Great and wonderful is his name." (Psalm 148:13)[85]

Like David and Israel of old, St. Augustine is aware that the nations are watching.

> But do You, my inmost Physician, make clear to me what fruit I gain by [so confessing]. When the confessions of my past sins,—which You have forgiven and covered up [Ps 32:1], giving me joy in You, changing my life by faith and Your sacrament—are read and heard, they stir up the heart. It no longer lies in the lethargy of despair and says "I cannot," but keeps wakeful in the love of Your mercy and the loveliness of Your grace, by which every weak man is made strong [2 Cor 12:10], since by it he is made conscious of his weakness. As for the good, it rejoiced them of sins committed in the past by men now free from them: not because these things are sins, but because they were and no longer are.[86]

It could be that this vocation to be light to the world regarding God's mercy, shared by David, Israel, Paul, and Augustine, is what David has in mind when he writes, in the same Psalm 51: "Then I will teach transgressors your ways, and sinners will return to you" (v. 13). David and Paul and Augustine are eye-witnesses to the doctrine of God's mercy, which is no abstract doctrine but Good News for all who suffer under the indignation of an accusing conscience. Only heaven knows how many people the witness of David and Paul and Augustine has saved from despair.

---

84 Augustine, *Confessions*, 6.7.12 (trans. Sheed).
85 Augustine, *Confessions*, 8.1.1 (trans. Ryan).
86 Augustine, *Confessions*, 10.3.4 (trans. Sheed).

David, Israel, and the Church are sacramental signs of God's mercy. While the primacy falls on the interior dimension of faith, purification of conscience, and the acceptable sacrifice of a humble and contrite heart, this by no means eliminates the exterior dimension of the temporal consequences of sin. With keen insight into just how profoundly sin distorts our hierarchy of values, St. Thomas observes that the divine wisdom is on display in the temporal punishment for sin. If, he notes, in addition to the remission of sins and the imparting of grace, Baptism entailed liberation from the temporal punishment for sin, then people would seek Baptism for the wrong reason; they would seek to alleviate the temporal punishment of sin and neglect the restoration of communion with God.[87] The exterior kingdom seems to command more attention than the kingdom within—until the encounter with sin and with God's mercy.

David's restored communion with God in the kingdom within entails his understanding of God's hierarchy of values and the role of suffering in His plan of love. He lives "patiently bearing sufferings and trials of all kinds" and "strive[s] to accept this temporal punishment of sin as a grace."[88] The perception of the relation between the two is the foundation of David's hope that in His mercy God will restore him to his kingship. David, then, not only endures the humiliation of his defeat and retreat from Jerusalem. To face the possibility of never seeing the ark of the covenant again is the external reality that corresponds to his acceptance of the internal sentence of divine judgment, namely, that he live with a broken and contrite heart, with that "salutary pain and sadness which the Fathers called *animi cruciatus* (affliction of spirit) and *compunctio cordis* (repentance of heart)."[89] Such affliction of spirit is a participation in God's own sorrow and upheaval of heart over man's sin. God sees in David's humble and contrite heart, in his remorseful conscience, a participation in His own Son's suffering caused by sin.[90]

David's affliction and contrition express his awareness that by God's grace he has returned to the truth of the kingdom within: "Behold, you desire truth in the inward being; therefore teach me wisdom in my secret heart" (Ps 51:6). Truth resides again in his heart because he has taken sides with the truth against himself, which means that he has sided with God. David is aware that God is drawn to those who embrace the truth at the cost of self-condemnation, even as Christ accepted to be condemned and embraced the Cross as a result of his testimony to the truth about God's love for sinners and the truth about His oneness with the Father. David, then, has a prophetic intuition of the reality that will become fully revealed when the Father's love is fully satisfied by His Son become man. David has received the graces of a baptism of tears, and this can only meet with

---

[87] See Aquinas, *ST* III, Q. 69, a. 3.
[88] *CCC*, 1473.
[89] *CCC*, 1431.
[90] "When the Spirit of truth permits the human conscience to share in that suffering [the suffering of Christ], the suffering of the conscience becomes particularly profound, but also particularly salvific" (John Paul II, *Dominum et Vivificantem*, 45).

the same response that was heard on the bank of the Jordan River: "You are my beloved Son; with you I am well pleased" (Lk 3:22).

In conversion, man's humility and God's mercy are correlative. In fact, as a response to sin, a contrite heart is already a gift of grace, an effect of God's mercy. God's grace is necessary even to identify sin: "to do its work grace must uncover sin so as to convert our hearts."[91] This conversion of the heart, St. John Paul II explains, "requires convincing of sin; it includes the interior judgment of conscience, and this, being a *proof of the action of the Spirit of truth* in man's inmost being, becomes at the same time the start of a new grant of grace and love."[92] One of the great fruits of experiencing God's mercy is to be liberated from the anxiety and labor of keeping sin hidden, as Adam and Eve tried to cover themselves and to hide from God in the garden, or as the Pharisees wanted to cover themselves in good works, or as the Samaritan woman avoided her neighbors by coming to the well at the hottest time of day. It is a bold prayer of faith in God's mercy to ask Him to make known one's hidden faults: "But who can discern his errors? Clear me from hidden faults" (Ps 19:12). Similarly, Sirach petitions that his sins not go unchecked, lest they multiply.[93] It is a tremendous grace to reach this level of humility, to realize that God knows us more penetratingly than we can know ourselves,[94] and to come to love Him so ardently as to desire to cooperate with Him in uncovering sin.

Sin places an obstacle to God's love, and a contrite heart is the first effect of His love after a person has sinned.[95] St. Thomas repeatedly quotes verse 19 of Psalm 51 in order to distinguish between the interior, spiritual sacrifice, and the ritual act of offering a sacrifice. The ritual sacrifice is meant to be a sign of the interior sacrifice and it has no efficacy if it is not accompanied by the interior sacrifice. Psalm 51 expresses David's awareness that God's grace of mercy has produced in him a disposition of humility and contrition that normally is stirred up and expressed by ritual sacrifice. The awareness of his sin and God's mercy is so keen that he perceives with acute insight the distance between the outward sign and the interior reality. The ritual sacrifice is not without value, but it becomes empty and inefficacious if it is not accompanied by the interior sacrifice of contrition.

The lesson in this is valid for all times. In an early stage of the spiritual journey, a person committed to giving himself totally to God experiences the distance between exterior sign and interior reality as personal

---

91 *CCC*, 1848.
92 John Paul II, *Dominum et Vivificantem*, 31.
93 See Sir 23:1–3.
94 "The heart is our hidden center, beyond the grasp of our reason and of others; only the Spirit of God can fathom the human heart and know it fully" (*CCC*, 2563). See also Augustine, *Confessions*, 10.1–2.
95 In the *Catechism*, conversion is "the first work of the Holy Spirit's grace" (*CCC*, 1989), and "the first effect of the gift of love is the forgiveness of our sins" (*CCC*, 734). "This endeavor of conversion is not just a human work. It is the movement of a 'contrite heart,' drawn and moved by grace to respond to the merciful love of God who loved us first (Ps 51:17; cf. Jn 6:44; 12:32; 1 Jn 4:10)" (*CCC*, 1428).

shortcoming. When God withdraws His consolations, dismay sets in, caused by the realization that his sentiments, attitudes, and states do not adequately correspond to the realities signified in the liturgy. Whether the cause be inattention, distraction, or routine, the discrepancy between the rite that is celebrated and one's inner state is in reality an opportunity for grace to fortify the foundation of humility. What advice, spiritual exercise, or discipline can empower a person seeking holiness to conform inwardly to what the liturgy makes present? While there is a bank of wisdom in the writings of saints and spiritual masters on methods upon which one can draw, the conformity of one's soul with the soul of Christ cannot be acquired by our efforts alone. It is above all a gift of grace, and this grace comes in a form that is at first extremely disconcerting because it does not match our expectations. Our expectation is that progress means moving ever closer to God through ever increasing virtue. Yet, because of sin, grace must make known the true distance that sin creates between God and man. This perfects the humility by which man cooperates with God in his own conversion, by receiving the graces of his mercy.

To come face-to-face with one's own sin, to confront one's own capacity to become hard-hearted—not just theoretically but in the concrete situation of having actually having done so—is an event that gives rise to only two alternatives. A person must either open up to the God Who opens to him in love and recommit himself to return fidelity for fidelity and love for love, or cling to a self-fabricated claim to a "'right' to persist in evil"[96] and to isolate his freedom from the truth for which it is made. It is the inevitable choice between renewal of the covenant with God, that is, conversion, or the blasphemy against the Holy Spirit. To acknowledge anew the primacy of truth makes one humble, for humility is essentially the recognition of truth's claim to guide, to inform my freedom. It is acknowledgement that I am not the absolute master of my life, that my life's meaning and fulfillment have been predetermined by my Creator and reconfirmed by my Redeemer. Conversion entails measuring myself against this truth and accusing myself of non-submission to it. But this, by itself, would be nothing but condemnation, for "no living man is righteous before" God (Ps 143:2), since "all have sinned" (Rom 3:23). Conversion also entails a further measurement, the need to measure my measurement of sin against the truth about God's mercy, to break out of the gravitational pull that would isolate sin from its relation to God. For, sin is an offense against God, and the truth about God is revealed in the historical record of His fidelity in the face of man's infidelity—a record that culminates in the paschal mystery of Jesus Christ, God's final word, after which the Defense rests.

The humble acceptance of the truth about sin and the truth about divine mercy produces a sense of the disproportion between sign and inner reality. What sign could possibly be adequate to express the spiritual dread entailed in confronting my deliberate rejection of the God Who created and redeemed me, when I clearly see that the concept of hell as "definitive self-

---

96 John Paul II, *Domininum et Vivificantem*, 47.

exclusion from communion with God"[97] rightly corresponds to what I have done? At this moment I realize how all the cries for justice around which I have previously rallied, good as justice is, would leave me without hope. For, if justice is the final word in relation to sin, I realize that hell is the just punishment for my sin. In light of all of this, every sacrifice that is only an outward expression of the state of my soul is pitifully inadequate. This does not mean that there is anything lacking in the wisdom by which God instituted ritual sacrifice. It only means that He intended His chosen people to come to that point of spiritual maturity at which they recognize the deficiencies of the sacrifices of the Old Covenant and come to long for a definitive sacrifice that is. Finally, an adequate expression of the perfect contrition to which His mercy and grace lead them. King David's perfect contrition entails a longing for a definitive sacrifice that obliterates the distinction between the ritual sign and the reality it signifies. His contrition *is* that perfect sacrifice, in anticipation, because is already a participation in the sacrifice of Christ, Who "brings to perfection all human attempts to offer sacrifices."[98] For, Christ is the High Priest who was made perfect in His priestly office by His suffering.[99] Because His suffering is directly proportionate to His love, this means that Christ's sacrifice is perfect because of the perfection of His love.[100] As in the case of the penitent woman,[101] David's great, sorrowful love for God indicates that his sacrifice has been found acceptable and his sins have been forgiven because the Father sees the sorrow-unto-death of His Son in his sorrow.

Cut Off from the Father's Love

Only the sacrifice of Christ fulfills this longing for a perfect sacrifice. His is the ultimate and definitive reference point for every sacrifice of a broken and contrite heart. Hanging on the Cross, His body—wracked, tortured, broken, and exhausted—is the sacrament of a love that loves "to the end" of what love can endure in a world marked by sin. "My soul is very sorrowful, even to death" (Mk 14:34). Jesus experiences the most intense and consuming grief possible because suffering is a function of the intensity and perfection of knowledge and love. The ocean of His love becomes a tidal wave of grief, unleashed when His very being is on the verge of collapse (the perfect realization of David's bones wasting away) by the awareness of God's Love being rejected. Because He *is* that Love, because there is a perfect identification of His being with this Love, His

---

97   *CCC*, 1033.
98   *CCC*, 1350.
99   See Heb 2:10; 5:9.
100 "And this grief in Christ surpassed all grief of every contrite heart, both because it flowed from a greater wisdom and charity, by which the pang of contrition is intensified, and because He grieved at the one time for all sins" (Aquinas, *ST* III, Q. 46, a. 6, ad 4).
101 "Therefore I tell you, her sins, which are many, are forgiven, for she loved much; but he who is forgiven little, loves little" (Lk 7:47).

whole being is caught up in the event of sin. God is love, and "in him the whole fulness of deity dwells bodily" (Col 2:9).

Only He can comprehend what it is like for man to be cut off from the Father's love, for He is the only begotten Son. He *is* Son. That is everything He is; that is all He is. This has to be kept in mind when reading the Parable of the Prodigal Son, which comes from the human imagination of the Eternal Son. To imagine a son's rejection of his father means to imagine the cancellation of life itself, a void that would be complete nothingness but for the now haunting and terrorizing memory of what it was like to live as the father's son. For, father and son are correlative. Being father and being son come into existence at the same time. While earthly fathers are men before becoming father, the Eternal Father *is* Father. That is everything He is; that is all He is. For the Son to imagine being without the Father is for Him to imagine such an absolute void, pure nothingness, the total and complete negation of being. To be the Son or not to be at all, these are the stark terms of the issue. If it is difficult for us to grasp this, if we are tempted to see it as exaggeration, it is precisely because we can imagine the continuance of life apart from the Father. This means that there is something in us, something about us, that is not yet contained in our relation to Him, something that we mistakenly think could subsist apart from Him. For Jesus, that is impossible. His whole identity and being are relatedness to the Father.

Thus, His knowledge of hell is perfect, and it is this perfect knowledge of sin and of hell that is at the root of His incomparable suffering. The words of Scripture are fulfilled in His suffering: "Look and see if there is any sorrow like my sorrow which was brought upon me" (Lam 1:12). Christ's interior anguish over sin "surpassed all grief of every contrite heart," St. Thomas concludes, because His knowledge of the evil of sin exceeds what anyone else could know and His love is the greatest love a man can have. In addition, the magnitude of His sorrow for sin is unrivaled because He "grieved at the one time for all sins."[102]

In Christ the heart of man afflicted by the dread of sin is also the anguish of God over sin. Is it possible that God Himself, the Creator Who is infinite perfection, which excludes all suffering, be in some way affected interiorly by the sins of man? Based on various Old Testament texts, St. John Paul II and Benedict XVI draw our attention to the Bible's disclosure of the inner dimension of God's reaction to sin. For John Paul, the text is from the account of the flood sent to purify the earth of sin. The flood is an action rooted in God's reaction to man's sin: "I am sorry that I have made them" (Gen 6:7). This is, of course, anthropomorphic language, and the "concept of God as the necessarily most perfect being certainly excludes from God any pain deriving from deficiencies or wounds." Nevertheless, "in the 'depths of God' there is a Father's love that, faced with man's sin, in the language of the Bible reacts so deeply as to say: 'I am sorry that I have made him.'" We know that in the end "this inscrutable and indescribable fatherly 'pain' will

---

[102] Aquinas, *ST* III, Q. 46, a. 6, ad 4.

bring about above all the wonderful economy of redemptive love in Jesus Christ."[103] Because He knows what it means to be the object of God's supreme delight and to be able to elicit from the Father the words that He heard at the time of His baptism in the Jordan River, "You are my beloved Son, with you I am well pleased" (Lk 3:22), Jesus knows the opposite as no other can know it. He knows what it is like to be the object of God's displeasure and to elicit from Him the words, "I am sorry that I have made him." For the eternally begotten Son Who becomes man, nothing could more accurately depict hell. This is what it means for Him take on the punishment for our sins. He endures the full force of the deluge, as if the earth were flooded by the tears of the heavenly host. This expression of God's sorrow over man's sin at the same time calls out to the depths of his heart: "Deep calls to deep at the thunder of your cataracts; all your waves and your billows have gone over me" (Ps 42:7). In the sorrow of heart of Jesus, God's will is done on earth as it is in heaven!

In reality, these waves are the "surging waves of our indignation,"[104] the accusations of our "troubled conscience."[105] The text of Genesis may appear to be a naïve projection onto God (anthropomorphism) of man's abhorrence for his own sin and disgust with himself. In the light of the history of God's dealings with His people, and especially in the full light of the mystery of Christ, the disclosure of God's regret at having made man is a profession of faith in a God Who does not withdraw from being involved in man's history, a God Who accompanies man as he grapples with his troubled conscience, a God Whose love cannot be impeded by sin. The mystery of Christ is no mere projection of man's experiences on to God. It is, rather, God's assumption of man's experiences. Man's experience of interior suffering or remorse for sin is the image's way of reacting to sin as God does. It is "a distant echo of that 'repentance of having created man' which in anthropomorphic language the Sacred Book attributes to God ... an echo of that 'reprobation' which is interiorized in the 'heart' of the Trinity and by virtue of the eternal love is translated into the suffering of the Cross, into Christ's obedience unto death."[106] Suffering over sin with a broken and contrite heart is man's participation in God's own response to sin that is definitively revealed in the sorrow, even to death, of Jesus Christ.

For Benedict XVI, the text of Hosea 11:8–9 is the occasion for a remarkably similar teaching. Hosea describes God's heart as recoiling within Him as He considers how to respond to the rejection of His love. Because of man's sin, God's heart is in turmoil, overturned, in a state of

---

103 John Paul II, *Dominum et Vivificantem*, 39.
104 Liturgy of the Hours, Psalm-Prayer accompanying Psalm 42 for Morning Prayer, Monday, Week II.
105 Liturgy of the Hours, Psalm-Prayer accompanying Psalm 51 for Morning Prayer, Friday, Week I.
106 John Paul II, *Dominum et Vivificantem*, 45.

upheaval.[107] Hosea's examination of his own conflicted heart becomes revelation of God's love for His people. Hosea's prophetic mission is to reveal that God's love for His people is a spousal love. The prophet himself falls in love with a woman who is unfaithful to him, giving herself to other men. He could invoke the law, repudiate her for adultery, and, in appeal to penalty for adultery in the code of justice, have her stoned. Even if, like Joseph, the husband of the Virgin Mary, he were "unwilling to put her to shame [and] resolved to divorce her quietly" (Mt 1:19), the outcome would be the same. Either way, she would be dead to him. The problem is that he truly loves her, and for his love justice is no consolation. He cannot imagine living happily without her. And so, the demands of justice conflict with the demands of his love. Hosea portrays God as in the same situation. His insight is that in God, saving and forgiving love triumphs over the justice of repudiation and punishment. The perfection of divine love makes it impossible for God to give up on His people and to resign Himself to their rejection of His love. His calculation is divine, not human: "for I am God and not man, the Holy One in your midst" (Hos 11:9). God's love "is so great that it turns God against himself, his love against his justice."[108] If God were to grow angry with His people and to punish them with a definitive repudiation, this would wound the love by which He created them, liberated them from slavery, and fashioned them to be His most precious possession. In this sense, then, such a chastisement would be "simultaneously directed against Himself.... He cannot repudiate her without rendering judgment against Himself."[109]

What the Old Testament reveals about divine love in the anthropomorphic language of God's interior remorse (John Paul II) and a heart in turmoil (Benedict XVI) is definitively realized in Jesus Christ. In Him, God Himself suffers and dies because of men's sins. In the end, God is not content to reveal His love through metaphors.[110] His definitive revelation is not, "My love for you is like ..." Rather, it is the supreme act of love, which is so important for man to know that Christ discloses the state of His heart as He confronts the conclusive logic of sin: "My soul is very sorrowful, even to death" (Mt 26:38). "Greater love has no man than this, that a man lay down his life for his friends" (Jn 15:13). "God proves His love for us" (Rom 5:8 NAB)[111] by suffering and dying for us, so that we are able to say: "the life I now live in the flesh I live by faith in the Son of God, who loved me and gave himself for me" (Gal 2:20). This demonstration of God's love is the undoing of the doubt about His love, which is at the root of sin, and this is why it is necessary that God reveal

---

107 See Joseph Ratzinger, *Behold the Pierced One* (San Francisco: Ignatius Press, 1983), 62–64. Ratzinger returns to Hos 11:8f again in *Jesus of Nazareth: From the Baptism in the Jordan to the Transfiguration* (San Francisco: Ignatius Press, 2008), 206–07.
108 Benedict XVI, *Deus caritas est*, 10.
109 Joseph Ratzinger, *Daughter Zion* (San Francisco: Ignatius Press, 1983), 22.
110 "The pierced Heart of the crucified Son is the literal fulfillment of the prophecy of the Heart of God [in Hosea 11:8-9]...." (Ratzinger, *Behold the Pierced One*, 64).
111 See 1 Jn 3:16: "This is the proof of love, that he laid down his life for us" (1 Jn 3:16 NJB).

it—the mysterious necessity that Christ should suffer and die—[112] so that we might "know the love of Christ" (Eph 3:19); or, as Jesus Himself put it: "so that the world may know that you have sent me and have loved them even as you have loved me" (Jn 17:23). Moreover, it is precisely our faith in God's love that constitutes that joy for the sake of which Christ—God Himself—endured suffering and death.[113]

We know that Christ's suffering and death are not the final word about God's love. They constitute the sacrifice of His supreme act of love for His Father and for men, and the resurrection reveals that this sacrifice is supremely pleasing to the Father and accepted by Him. This movement from the darkness of death and suffering to the light of new life is the definitive fulfillment and paradigm of the prophetic pattern of devastation preceding restoration. St. Paul presents it in terms of humble self-abasement being followed by exaltation. Christ "did not count equality with God a thing to be grasped, but emptied himself, taking the form of a servant." He "humbled himself and became obedient unto death," and because of this "God has highly exalted him" (Phil 2:6–9). By humbly lowering Himself in His suffering and death on the Cross, Jesus fulfills His own teaching. If His disciples are to live as He lived, they must live by the law, "whoever humbles himself will be exalted" (Mt 23:12). But this is only an application of the universal law regarding the relation of sinful men to God: "for every one who exalts himself will be humbled, but he who humbles himself will be exalted" (Lk 18:14).

Of course, the humility of Christ and the humility of the sinner have two different origins. The humility of sinners corresponds to the reality of their state, whereas the humility of Christ corresponds only to His mission to save sinners. It is precisely in this mission, more precisely, in the love that both animates the mission and that constitutes its essential content, where the two humilities meet, so that one can rightly speak of a "mutual abasement" of Christ and sinners.[114] For the sake of sinners, Jesus accepted to be counted among sinners.[115] The humility of sinners is laced with hope for being exalted through God's mercy because God highly exalted Jesus in response to His humility. Humility is the interior reality that corresponds to the calamity of the true prophets, while exaltation corresponds to their prophecies of restoration and peace. Definitively fulfilled in the mystery of Christ's exaltation following His self-abasement, sinners participate in His humility by confessing their sins and in His exaltation through the healing power of God's mercy. In this way, the revelation of God's mercy in the paschal mystery promulgates the law that "the secret of ascending is to descend," as St. Augustine puts it: "Consider, O Brethren, this great marvel.

---

112 See Lk 24:26, 46; Acts 3:18; 17:3; 26:23.
113 See Heb 12:2.
114 "The mystery of the union of God with the soul takes place in the depths of the abyss, in the mutual self-abasement of God and the creature" (Luis M. Martinez, *Secrets of the Interior Life* [St. Louis, MO: Herder & Herder, 1949], 13).
115 See Is 53:12.

God is on high: reach up to Him, and He flees from you; lower yourself before Him, and He comes down to you."[116]

Returning now to David's insight in Psalm 51 about the sacrifice of a broken and contrite heart, when he identifies such an afflicted heart with the sacrifice acceptable to God, he anticipates the definitive sacrifice of Christ's pierced heart, which sin causes to be sorrowful even to death. It is the sacrifice of accepting the just punishment for sin, which is to place oneself in that zone of the nothingness of sin, the zone that can only be described as the absence of God's love and the corresponding obliteration of human dignity—that unique and absolute indignation produced by an accusing conscience. Beyond not clinging to His prerogatives as God the Son, Christ abases Himself in the despoilment of everything pertaining to human dignity. This is what David has in common with Christ. Sin has its apparent triumph; it seems to have thwarted God's will. The vocation and mission of both kings appear to have failed—which implies that God's plan has failed. And this thought, that God has withdrawn or given up or failed is the real source of grief unto death: "It is my grief that the right hand of the Most High has changed" (Ps 77:10). To face sin for what it truly is is to confront a world without God, since sin is rejection of His love. That is the state of a humble and contrite heart—clinging to God with nothing to offer Him except a broken and contrite heart. Since the heart symbolizes the very mystery of what it means to be human,[117] this means that the totality of Christ's being is sacrifice. There is no part of His being that is spared, as if there were another path for His life, another possibility for fulfilling His mission, another way for Him to give Himself totally to His Father and to man—another way to *be* Son. Immolation is not just an action; it is what He is.

Thus, Christ's sacrifice is of supreme value in God's eyes because it is a participation in God's own reaction to sin, His fatherly pain and His heart that recoils within itself. These remain anthropomorphisms only until God becomes a man and has a heart that can be pierced by the rejection of His love and can reveal God's own fatherly pain: "He who has seen me has seen the Father" (Jn 14:9). On the Cross, this all-consuming anguish is what Jesus offers His Father. On the Cross, the Son of God hangs deprived of the possibility of offering a ritual sacrifice, and this is no doubt why He celebrated the Last Supper prior to His betrayal and arrest. The doctrine of the substantial presence of Christ in the Eucharist assures that there is no distinction between the outward sacrifice and the interior sacrifice, since the Priest Who offers and the Victim offered are one and the same. If there is anything exterior in this sacrifice it is the Lord's lacerated body. This is why it is important to look beyond the physical aspect of Calvary in order to see the interior, spiritual sacrifice of obedient love.[118]

---

116 Martinez, *Secrets of the Interior Life*, 6–7.
117 See John Paul II, *Redemptor hominis*, 8.
118 See Rom 12:1–2; 5:19.

Love is the only sacrifice that is pleasing to God because love is the total gift of oneself to Him, and this is all that He desires. In reality, it is in order to make this sacrifice of love possible that God has loved us first. For, "We love, because he first loved us" (1 Jn 4:19). "Our love for God," St. Thomas comments, "presupposes that God has loved us first." Consequently, "The fact that we love him is a sign that he loves us."[119] For, "Nothing so induces us to love someone as the experience of His love for us."[120] Love is the only fully adequate return to God for the love that He shows us. It is the only gift that is capable of satisfying God's love for us. This is why love is the true sacrifice.

> What then does sacrifice consist of? Not in destruction, not in this or that thing, but in the transformation of man. In the fact that he becomes himself conformed to God. He becomes conformed to God when he becomes love. "That is why true sacrifice is every work which allows us to unite ourselves to God in a holy fellowship," as Augustine puts it.[121]

Only the love that unites us to God can overcome the sin for which sacrifice is offered, because the very nature of sin is the rejection of God's love.

The sacrifice that is pleasing and acceptable to God is man's transformation from doubting His love to faith in His love that is pure openness, pure receptivity to being loved. This is why Christ alone can satisfy the Father's love: "You are my beloved Son; with you I am well pleased" (Lk 3:22). God's love is satisfied when man becomes what He envisions him to be, when man receives from Him all that He has to give.[122] Christ's sacrifice is the acceptable sacrifice to God because despite all the evidence of having been abandoned by the Father, He never ceased entrusting Him to and receiving the Father's love. This is the meaning of the passivity of His death on the Cross, where all He could do is simply to *be* the Son and to receive from the Father. Faith is our participation in Christ's unflinching confidence in His Father's love and in His uninterrupted reception of that love. "Faith, in its deepest essence, is the *openness* of the human heart to the gift: *to God's self-communication in the*

---

119 Aquinas, *Commentary on St. Paul's Letter to the Romans*, Ch. 5, Lect. 1 (Marietti 392).
120 Aquinas, *Summa contra gentiles*, IV, 54, 5.
121 See Joseph Ratzinger, Address for Journées liturgiques de Fontgombault, July 22–24, 2001. See also Augustine, *Exposition on the Psalms*, 118 (27), 5–6.
122 "He it was, and he alone, who satisfied the Father's eternal love, that fatherhood that from the beginning found expression in creating the world, giving man all the riches of creation, and making him "little less than God" (Ps 8:6), in that he was created "in the image and after the likeness of God" (cf. Gen 1:26), He and he alone also satisfied that fatherhood of God and that love which man in a way rejected by breaking the first Covenant (cf. Gen 3:3–16) and the later covenants that God "again and again offered to man" (Eucharistic Prayer IV) (John Paul II, *Redemptor hominis*, 9).

Holy Spirit."[123] This faith is the renewal of our minds that makes our entire life a spiritual sacrifice that is acceptable to God.[124]

The Logical Worship of a Broken Heart

At the outset of Psalm 51, David implores the Lord: "Have mercy on me, O God, according to your merciful love" (Ps 51:1). Later, he expresses the conviction of faith that gives him the hope that his petition will be answered: "The sacrifice acceptable to God is a broken spirit; a broken and contrite heart, O God, you will not despise" (Ps 51:17).[125] God will not despise, that is, He will not overlook or think lightly of a broken and contrite heart. The reason is that He is pure, merciful love and desires only to forgive, and a humble heart is one that is open to receiving this gift. For this reason, "God opposes the proud, but gives grace to the humble" (Jas 4:6). By his repentance and conversion, the humble David no longer despises God's word but fully adheres to His word regarding his mercy: He is "a God ready to forgive, gracious and merciful, slow to anger and abounding in steadfast love" (Neh 9:17).

God is constant in His mercy, the "God of forgiveness" (Neh 9:17 NAS), the God Who reveals Himself, Who virtually defines Himself, as the God Who forgives. He is "the God of those who repent."[126] The only question concerns man. Is man ready to receive His forgiveness? Is this what he desires? We do not know precisely how long David remained hardhearted and resisted the truth. It had to be at least nine months, since the child that Bathsheba conceived by David had been born at the time of Nathan's confrontation. The precise duration of David's impenitence is less important than the interior reality. Throughout that time, David could not receive God's mercy because the very condition for receiving it, the desire for it, was absent. During that period, David acts as one "who claims to have a *'right' to persist in evil*."[127] Conversion brings an end to this claim. It entails denouncing that so-called right and acknowledging the right of the truth—about sin and about God's mercy—to reign in man's conscience. David's broken and contrite heart entails a return to this reign of truth, accompanied by admission of and sorrow for having deliberately

---

[123] John Paul II, *Dominum et Vivificantem*, 51. In *Redemptoris Mater*, 8 and 13, John Paul describes Mary's faith as openness to God's gift, that is, to His love.

[124] See Rom 12:1–2.

[125] There is a parallel or symmetry between David's hope that God will not despise his sacrifice and his own having despised God's word, and thus God Himself. The Hebrew verb for "to despise" here is the same verb that Nathan uses to describe David's disregard for God's word (2 Sam 12:9). To despise means "to look down upon," not sufficiently to value something or someone. Though David has sinned by thinking too little of God, he hopes that God will think well of his repentance from despising God's word, which means that now David greatly values His word. How could God refuse to accept his adherence to His word?

[126] Prayer of Manasseh 1:13.

[127] John Paul II, *Dominum et Vivificantem*, 46.

withdrawn from that reign and a recognition that God's mercy is the only foundation for hope to be received anew by God.

This is why the sacrifice of a broken and contrite heart is acceptable to God. Indeed, in a broken and contrite heart God sees a reflection of the heart of His own Son: a desire for communion with man; suffering caused by sin; the mission to submit Himself to and definitively to reveal the Father's mercy. For, God is "ready to forgive, gracious and merciful, slow to anger and abounding in mercy" (Neh 9:17). A broken and contrite heart is already the work of God's mercy, transforming a sinner into one who seeks precisely what God desires to give. God's mercy is the water that sinners seek, and God desires nothing other than to give that water. "God thirsts that we may thirst for Him."[128]

Because of God's regard for man's dignity—his freedom and responsibility for his life— patience accompanies His mercy: "The Lord is patient with men and pours out his mercy upon them" (Sir 18:11), and "with great forbearance" does He "govern us" (Wis 12:18). God's patience is entirely ordered to man's conversion. St. Peter assures us, "The Lord is not being slow in carrying out his promises...; rather is he being patient with you, wanting nobody to be lost and everybody to be brought to repentance" (2 Pet 3:9 NJB).[129] Thus, we should "consider the patience of our Lord as salvation" (2 Pet 3:15 NAB).

In the Bible, God and men ask the same question of one another: "How long?" For man, it is the anguished question of those who await His saving intervention, "How long, O Lord? Will you forget me for ever? How long will you hide your face from me?" (Ps 13:1).[130] In His turn, God asks, "How long will this people despise me? And how long will they not believe in me, in spite of all the signs which I have wrought among them?" (Num 14:11).[131] The answer to both questions is: For so long as it takes the sinner to offer God the sacrifice of a broken and contrite heart. This is the meaning of Israel's seventy-year long purification during the Exile: "Speak to the heart of Jerusalem, and proclaim to her that her service has ended, that her guilt is expiated" (Is 40:2 NAB). God returns His people to Jerusalem once their faith has been renewed so that they can possess the Promised Land anew, as pure gift, and as a fruit of this renewed faith adhere to the Lord's commandments.

David's period of purification leading to repentance is much shorter, but it serves the same purpose. After his conversion, David could possess his kingship anew, as pure gift, and so long as he keeps in mind the relation between this gift and God's commandments, he remains a good steward of the gift by adhering to the commandments. His conversion reverses the sin by which he despised God's word, a despising that God

---

128 *CCC*, 2560.
129 See also Rom 2:4.
130 See also: Ps 6:3; 35:17; 74:10; 79:5; 80:4; 89:46; 90:13; 94:3; Is 6:11; Hab 1:2; Zech 1:2.
131 See also: Ex 16:28; Num 14:27; 1 Kings 18:21; Jer 4:14; 13:27; 23:26; 31:22; Hos 8:5. In Jesus, God does not ask the question through a prophet but directly asks, "O faithless generation, how long am I to be with you? How long am I to bear with you?" (Mk 9:19).

takes personally. Through Nathan, God asks, "Why have you *despised the word of the Lord*, to do what is evil in his sight?" Then follows the just punishment and the reason for it, "Now therefore the sword shall never depart from your house," and the reason is: "because you have *despised me*, and have taken the wife of Uriah the Hittite to be your wife" (2 Sam 12:9–10).[132] David sinned by taking no account of God's word, setting it aside because—and this is critical—because it conflicted with what he desired even more. The point is that David ought to value God's word more than any desire that conflicts with it because God loves David more than David is able to love himself. God has proved this by all that He has done for the people of whom David is a member, and for David himself. Thus, the essence of his sin is to disregard all that God had done for him. It is to say, in effect, "Right here and right now, my definition of what is best for me trumps Yours." For David to despise God's word, and thus God Himself, is the result of valuing something else much more, namely, Uriah's wife. It is to harden his heart against the impact that God's marvelous works *for him* are meant to have. They are meant to have an abiding place in his memory, and thereby to inform his conscience in every action. After all that God has done for David, how is it that David could fail to cherish His word and to observe what He commands?

By rejecting the word of the God Who has demonstrated His love for him, David acts in a profoundly illogical way. Interiorly, he contradicts the voice of God in his conscience regarding the sixth commandment. This means, in effect, that he chooses to live without God in the here and now of his decision. If the objection should be made that he did not intend to reject God but only to enjoy a forbidden pleasure, we can consider the teaching of St. James, that when it comes to our relation to God and His commandments, an all-or-nothing principle is at work.

> [10] For whoever keeps the whole law but fails in one point has become guilty of all of it. [11] For he who said, "Do not commit adultery," said also, "Do not kill." If you do not commit adultery but do kill, you have become a transgressor of the law. (James 2:10–11)

David's relation to God is not nine-tenths intact because he disobeys only one of the Ten Commandments. Because God gives each commandment from the totality of His love for man, to disobey any one of them is to reject the totality of His love. This is why to despise God's word is to despise God Himself.

By contradicting the truth of God's word, David fails to fulfill the primary duty of the fundamental vocation of every man, which is to render a sacrifice of one's entire life. St. Paul calls this "logical worship" (*logikēn*

---

132 In the same vein, St. Paul interprets the Galatians turning to a different gospel as turning away from God. See Gal 1:6.

latreian) (Rom 12:1),[133] which is "the rationally directed worship conformed to the *logos*,"[134] that is, "worship in harmony with the eternal Word and with our reason."[135] A striking witness to this fundamental human vocation comes in the Greek Stoic philosopher, Epictetus (50–135 A.D.).

> If I were a nightingale, I would do the work of a nightingale; if I were a swan, the work of a swan. But I am a rational being. I must sing hymns of praise to God. That is my work. I am doing it, and I shall not abandon my post as long as I am permitted to remain.[136]

Epictetus's rational hymns of praise give voice to all of creation's indebtedness to the Creator, Who provides for all of His creatures. Other creatures sing God's praise in their own way, by following the laws of their nature, but it is unique to man to do so knowingly and deliberately, that is, rationally. This is the law of his nature.

As pointed out earlier, the prophet Jeremiah similarly marvels at how effortlessly various animals give praise to God by complying with the laws of their natures, but he does so in order to contrast their compliance with the disobedience of God's chosen people: "Even the stork in the heavens knows her times; and the turtledove, swallow, and crane keep the time of their coming; but my people know not the ordinance of the Lord" (Jer 8:7). Similarly, Isaiah: "The ox knows its owner, and the donkey its master's crib; but Israel does not know, my people does not understand" (Is 1:3). For both prophets, man is like clay that dares to think that it knows better than the one who molds it: "He has no understanding" (Is 29:16).[137] For Isaiah, this metaphor corresponds to the thinking of those who "hide deep from the Lord their counsel" and keep their "deeds ... in the dark." Their attitude is, "Who sees us? Who knows us?" (Is 29:15). This describes the state of David's soul when he sins, and following, until his conversion, when his mind becomes a dark place because he hides his thoughts from the light of God's truth. Jesus,

---

[133] Most English versions translate this as "spiritual worship." But a problem with that translation is that it does not distinguish Paul's use of "*logikon*" here from his use of "*pneumatikos*" in other texts (such as Rom 1:11; 7:14; 15:27). Adhering closely to the Vulgate (*rationabile obsequium*), the Douay-Rheims Bible renders the phrase more literally as "reasonable service," which is fine so long as "reasonable" is taken in the anthropological sense of "rational" or "according to reason." The New Jerusalem Bible translates it as worship befitting "sensible people," that is, people whose actions are directed by the rule of reason. Joseph Fitzmyer translates it as "a cult suited to your rational nature" (Joseph Fitzmyer, *The Anchor Bible, Romans. A New Translation with Introduction and Commentary* [New York: Doubleday, 1993], 637). Stanislas Lyonnet confirms this interpretation when he writes that the phrase means "worship that is worthy of reasonable beings endowed with intelligence and freedom" (*Le message de l'épître aux Romains*, 140).

[134] Ratzinger, *Truth and Tolerance*, 130.

[135] Benedict XVI, Address to the Faculty of the University of Regensburg, September 12, 2006.

[136] *Discourses* I, xvi. Quoted in Jean Galot, *Abba Father* (New York: Alba House, 1992), 159.

[137] See also Is 45:9; 64:8; Jer 4:16; Rom 9:19–21.

Who perfectly knows what is in every man,[138] knows the reason for preferring darkness to light; it is "because their deeds were evil" (Jn 3:19). All sin entails a locking away of the conscience into a dark place in order to prevent the light of God's word—"The unfolding of your word gives light" (Ps 119:130)—from shining on immoral thoughts. In every sin, man tries to hide himself from God, as if he could prevent Him from seeing and knowing his secret intentions. This is the precise moment at which the sinner abandons his post of praising God for all that God has done for him. For, from what God has done for man the light of truth about God's love shines forth, and only when man sees the link between His love and His commandments is he able to obey them.

Jesus is "The Word ... the real light that gives light to everyone" (Jn 1:9 NJB). To shield one's conscience from Him is to shield it from His paschal mystery. It is to disdain, to have insufficient concern for, His self-sacrifice. For, it is in reference to His Cross that the Holy Spirit, the "light of consciences,"[139] convinces the world about sin and about God's merciful love.

There is a great difference between Epictetus's rational hymns of praise and those of David and God's people. The former are based only on a philosopher's understanding of the created order, while the latter, while not at all opposed to the former but in fact including this purely natural form of religion,[140] goes yet further. The logical worship of Jews and Christians is informed by faith in the marvelous works of God in behalf of His people. For Jews, this worship is a matter of the heart and is linked to the sacrifices offered to God in the Temple. For Christians, it is participation in *the* logical worship, the sacrifice of the Logos, Who became man in Jesus Christ. He is the temple of God.[141] He is the one who worships God in spirit and in truth.[142] By Baptism, Christians participate in His sacrifice and become temples of the Holy Spirit,[143] making their entire lives a spiritual sacrifice.[144]

The Lord's indictment against His people's failure to obey His commandments bears precisely upon the illogic of seeing His mighty works, which demonstrate His love, and then rejecting His love by despising His word, that is, His commandments. Again and again, God confronts the illogical behavior of His people, for example when He asks: "How long will this people despise me? And how long will they not believe in me, *in spite of all the signs* which I have wrought among them?" (Num 14:11). To listen to God's voice means more than simply to take it in by hearing, as if it were no different than any other noise that the ear

---

138 See Jn 2:25.
139 John Paul II, *Dominum et Vivificantem*, 45; see also *Dominum et Vivificantem*, 36 and 42.
140 "It belongs to religion to show reverence to one God under one aspect, namely, as the first principle of the creation and government of things" (Aquinas, *ST* II-II, Q. 81, a. 3).
141 See Jn 2:21.
142 See Jn 4:23–24.
143 See 1 Cor 6:19.
144 See 1 Pt 2:5.

registers. It means to live in obedience to all of His commandments *because* He has demonstrated His love through mighty works.

> ⁷ Today listen to the voice of the Lord:
> ⁸ Do not grow stubborn as your fathers did,
>   in the wilderness,
> when at Meribah and Massah
> ⁹ they challenged and provoked me,
> although they had seen all of my works. (Psalm 95:7–9 Liturgy of the Hours)

With his conversion, the hardened state of David's heart comes to an end. It begins with his heart being shattered by the realization that by despising and disobeying God's word he has set himself in opposition to His plan and thus to the future God has laid before him. And this, despite all of the works that God has done for Him! Thus, his conversion culminates in returning to the rationality of faith in the work of God's love, for Israel as a whole and for David individually, and to submitting himself anew to all that this implies. This is the essence of what it means to offer to God the sacrifice of a broken and contrite heart. It means to act logically again by returning anew to God's word, to God Himself, Whose interventions of wisdom and power, motivated by love, provide the foundation for the reasonableness of fully entrusting oneself to Him.[145] Jesus is in perfect continuity with this understanding God's works, His demonstrations of His love, as the foundation and motive of faith, when He says: "The works that I do in my Father's name, they bear witness to me" (Jn 10:25); "… believe the works, that you may know and understand that the Father is in me and I am in the Father" (Jn 10:38); "Do you not believe that I am in the Father and the Father in me? The words that I say to you I do not speak on my own authority; but the Father who dwells in me does his works. Believe me that I am in the Father and the Father in me; or else believe me for the sake of the works themselves" (Jn 14:10–11).

To entrust oneself to God for the purpose and meaning of one's existence is like following the regime of medication, diet, and exercise prescribed by a surgeon who has saved one's life through a heart and lung transplant. This great work of love bestows the gift of a new life, and now that the gift has been received, the recipient is responsible for it.[146] How long he will live with this gift depends entirely on his stewardship of it, that is, his rational custodianship, which is measured by fidelity to the surgeon's directives. In relation to the household of his own life, he is a "faithful and wise servant" (Mt 24:45). With a renewed understanding of what it means for life to be a gift, he can more intentionally embrace and live the purpose and meaning of life. This is the meaning of Jeremiah's

---

145 On faith as self-entrustment to God, see Vatican II, *Dei Verbum*, 5.
146 Think of the parable of the talents (see Mt 25:14–30).

prophecy[147] of a new covenant that will be written on the hearts of God's people, and of Ezekiel's prophecy[148] of God breathing into His people a new spirit.[149]

What is that purpose and meaning of life that God is so concerned that man receive from Him? Essentially, it is that man's vocation and fulfillment consist in being "set free from the hands of our enemies, free to worship Him without fear, holy and righteous in His sight, all the days of our life" (Lk 1:73–75 Liturgy of the Hours). John the Baptist's mission is to announce this freedom *from* enemies and freedom *for* worship, "to give knowledge of salvation to his people in the forgiveness of their sins" (Lk 1:77), that is, the experience of salvation that consists in the forgiveness of sins.[150] By the definitive revelation of God's mercy through His paschal mystery, Jesus Christ makes it possible to worship God without fear. That is, He has vanquished the enemy of sin and defeated the logic of sin by which the sinner is a prisoner to the doubt whether he is lovable, whether God is able to love him. This prevents the sinner from seeing God's commands for what they truly are, namely, His wisdom for the preservation of the gift of new life in His love. God's commandments are His wisdom regarding what His people must do and must not do in order to be good stewards of these gifts. To act logically in faith, then, is to obey God's commandments so as to live in the fullness of His gifts and to give Him honor by acknowledging Him as the Giver of both gifts: the first gift of life and freedom, and the second gift of His commandments, His law.

What, then, is the situation of the sinner, who despises God and His word, who acts illogically? Among the things that God has revealed through His word is that He is rich in mercy and always ready to forgive the repentant sinner. God seals the history that constantly confirms this when He sends His Son as the final word (*logos*) about His mercy. To refrain from confessing one's sins would be to despise this word, and thus God Himself. Jesus reveals that to harden one's heart against this word of God's mercy is the only sin that God cannot forgive. This is the blasphemy against the Holy Spirit: "every sin and blasphemy will be forgiven men, but the blasphemy against the Spirit will not be forgiven" (Mt 12:31). This

---

147 See Jer 31:31–34, and the elaboration on its fulfillment in Christ in Heb 8–10.
148 See Ezek 11:19; 18:31; 36:26–27.
149 See Stanislas Lyonnet's discussion of St. Paul's treatment of these two prophecies in "The Law of the Spirit and the New Covenant," Chapter Thirteen in *Le message de l'épître aux Romains* (Paris: Les Éditions du Cerf, 1971).
150 See I. Howard Marshall, *Commentary on Luke. New International Greek Testament Commentary* (Grand Rapids, MI: Eerdmans, 1978), 93. Fitzmyer remarks that "In the first part of the canticle [salvation] has more overtones of political deliverance from Israel's enemies; but now it is given a more spiritual meaning by the following prepositional phrase," which he translates "knowledge of salvation through the forgiveness of their sins" (Joseph Fitzmyer, *The Gospel According to Luke*, I-IX [Garden City, NY: Doubleday & Company, 1981], 386, 375). The two meanings, political and spiritual, are related. Political deliverance comes when the people's conversion is complete, as in Isaiah 40:2. It is therefore a sign of the interior renewal of faith.

sin "consists precisely *in the radical refusal to accept this forgiveness*"[151] that God always offers in the name of His mercy. This is the furthest limit of a hardened heart, "the radical refusal to be converted" despite having seen all of the evidence of God's mercy. The sinner "closes himself up in sin," refusing "to escape from one's self-imposed imprisonment and open oneself to the divine sources of the purification of consciences and of the remission of sins."[152]

With the help of God's word from Nathan, David escapes the irrationality of this auto-internment. His sin is rightly termed irrational because it violates two laws that are written in every human heart. The first law concerns man's relation to God. Because God is love and all He does is for man's good, to disdain His word is to deprive oneself of a good that God desires for man. When it is a question of mortal sin, this good is God Himself. The second law concerns man's relation to other men; it is known as the Golden Rule. How a person treats his neighbor reveals how he loves himself. Certainly, David would not want to be treated the way he treated Uriah, and this shows the inconsistency, the irrationality of his sin. David's conversion is a return to the total rationality of love, which is necessarily a triad of love of God, love of self, and love of neighbor.

For David to cease despising God's word by submitting to it anew in faith is for him to return to the most intelligent, the most rational, way of loving himself. And the only foundation for his hope in doing so is the conviction that God will not despise his broken and contrite heart. God's mercy is the only answer to the logic of sin, which leads to the conclusion that because by sinning man has despised the word of God, God would be in the right to despise man's words of contrition and repentance. Having rejected God's love, so this logic concludes, the sinner is unworthy of being loved anew. This is the logic of the symmetry between sin and punishment, that "one is punished by the very things by which he sins" (Wis 11:16).

Only if there is a logic that is higher than the logic of sin and the logic of justice is there any hope for the sinner, because these two logics dictate that sin be punished, even if it is eventually forgiven.[153] This is why God

---

[151] John Paul II, *Dominum et Vivificantem*, 46.
[152] Ibid.
[153] Several biblical texts straightforwardly, we might say, serenely and confidently, combine both God's punishment and His forgiveness. "Behold, happy is the man whom God reproves; therefore despise not the chastening of the Almighty. For he wounds, but he binds up; he smites, but his hands heal" (Job 5:17–18). "Yahweh our God, you answered them, you were a God of forgiveness to them, but punished them for their sins" (Ps 99:8 NJB). "... in my wrath I smote you, but in my favor I have had mercy on you" (Is 60:10). "'In overflowing anger for a moment I hid my face from you, but with everlasting love I will have compassion on you,' says the Lord, your Redeemer" (Is 54:8). "For I am with you to save you, declares the Lord; I will make a full end of all the nations among whom I scattered you, but of you I will not make a full end. I will chasten you in just measure, and I will by no means leave you unpunished" (Jer 30:11). "For the Lord will not cast off for ever, but, though he cause grief, he will have compassion according to the abundance of his steadfast love; for he does not willingly afflict or grieve the sons of men" (Lam 3:31–33). Wisdom literature develops this into exhortations to cooperate with the punishments from God by which He corrects those

has revealed a higher logic, which is the logic of His merciful love. This is "that greater reason which accepts into itself even darkness and irrationality and heals them."[154] The logic of sin is the logic of a failed vocation. Yet, since a vocation is received from the One Who calls, this implies that God's call has failed, which is untenable. And this leads us to the very heart of the promise that God makes through His prophets, namely, the promise of the grace by which God transforms the hearts of men from hearts of stone to hearts of flesh.[155] "Only this grace can resolve the contradiction between divine exigencies and human weakness.... In order for man to uphold His demands, God Himself has to take the initiative to transform him interiorly."[156]

Metaphorically, this interior transformation is the change from having a hardened heart to having a heart of flesh.[157] The reality to which this points is a change from a condition of "impenetrability of conscience"[158] to the rehabilitation of conscience so that it is open anew to the truth of God's word. The first effect of God's word[159] on a hardened heart is to strike a blow that pulverizes it.[160] The power of the Lord's voice to break cedars, to make the desert tremble, and to crush Israel's enemies[161] points to its power to shatter and to pry open a hardened heart. "Is not my word," God asks through Jeremiah, "like a hammer which breaks the rock in pieces?" (Jer 23:29).

Metaphors abound to convey the working of grace in conversion, for example, by comparing the effect of God's word to the work of a physician: God's word "must uncover sin so as to convert our hearts.... Like a physician who probes the wound before treating it, God, by his

---

whom He loves. "And thus, gradually you correct those who offend; you admonish and remind them of how they have sinned, so that they may abstain from evil and trust in you, Lord" (Wis 12:2). Clearly, the Lord's correction is an aspect of His mercy, by which He brings good out of the evil of sin. "But the Lord's compassion extends to everyone; rebuking, correcting and teaching, bringing them back as a shepherd brings his flock. He has compassion on those who accept correction, and who fervently search for his judgments" (Sir 18:13–14). God's punishment corrects, purifies, the desires, the preferences, the love of sinners: "You correct human beings by punishing sin, like a moth you eat away all their desires—a human being is a mere puff of wind" (Ps 39:11 NJB).

154 Ratzinger, *Truth and Tolerance*, 155–56.
155 See Pierre Grelot, *Sens chrétien de l'Ancien Testament* (Paris: Desclée, 1962), 357–58.
156 Ibid., 358.
157 See Ezek 11:19 and 36:26.
158 John Paul II, *Dominum et Vivificantem*, 47.
159 Several times the *CCC* identifies conversion as "the first work of the Holy Spirit's grace" (1989); "the first effect of the gift of love is the forgiveness of our sins" (734); "Transformation of the praying heart is the first response to our petition" (2739). "The first movement of the prayer of petition is asking forgiveness ..." (2631).
160 The *Catechism of the Council of Trent* elaborates on the metaphor of God's word effectively breaking a hardened heart: "literally means being broken into small pieces by a rock or some other hard substance. Used metaphorically as it is here, it means that our hearts, hardened by pride, are broken and crushed by penance" (*Roman Catechism*, Part II, 4 (Penance), trans. Robert Bradley and Eugene Kevane [Boston: St. Paul Editions, 1985], 268).
161 See Ps 29:5, 8; Is 30:31.

Word and by his Spirit, casts a living light on sin."[162] But it is St. Paul who most incisively describes, without images, the effect of the light of God's word in the consciousness of a penitent who looks back at his sin:

> [15] I do not understand my own actions. For I do not do what I want, but I do the very thing I hate. [16] Now if I do what I do not want, I agree that the law is good. [17] So then it is no longer I that do it, but sin which dwells within me. (Romans 7:15–17)

These verses describe what it means to act against, to violate, one's own conscience,[163] and they lay the foundation for the all-important distinction between the sinner and his sin.

The crucial element of this description is that St. Paul denounces sin as incomprehensible. Sin is irrational and thus contrary to man's rational nature in his relation to God, Who is Rationality, Logos. He identifies two desires in himself, corresponding to two laws: God's law and the law of sin.[164] When passing judgment on himself, he does so with a clear conviction that the desire to observe God's law defines who he really is, so that by obeying the law of sin he is in effect being unfaithful to himself and thus unfaithful to God.

The translation of the Jerusalem Bible brings out the interior dichotomy by contrasting a "true self" who acknowledges that God's Law is good and another "unspiritual self" that does not:

> [16] When I act against my own will, that means I have *a self* that acknowledges that the Law is good, [17] and so the thing behaving in that way is *not my self* but sin living in me. [18] The fact is, I know of nothing good living in me—living, that is, in *my unspiritual self*—for though the will to do what is good is in me, the performance is not, [19] with the result that instead of doing the good things I want to do, I carry out the sinful things I do not want. [20] When I act against my will, then, it is not *my true self* doing it, but sin which lives in me. (Romans 7:16–20, emphasis added)

The foundation for Paul's self-judgment is his memory of the judgment of conscience that he overruled when he (his untrue self) sinned.

---

162 *CCC*, 1848.
163 See Aquinas, *Commentary on St. Paul's Letter to the Romans*, Ch. 7, Lect. 3 (Marietti 563): "This can be taken in two ways: in one way of a person subject to sin, who understands in general that sin should not be committed, but overcome by the suggestion of the devil or by passion or by the inclination of a perverse habit, he commits it. Therefore, he said to do what he understands is not to be done, acting against conscience, just as 'the servant who knew his master's will but did not act according to his will'" (Lk 12:47).
164 See Rom 7:21–23.

That judgment of conscience remains a permanent plaintiff against him (his untrue self) and witness to the truth of God's word that he (his untrue self) has violated. Even if that truth is vulnerable to being overruled, it never surrenders its right to be acknowledged and obeyed. When that right has been violated, the ensuing remorse is a cry, like the blood of an innocent man who has been murdered, to God to set matters aright.[165] Ultimately, it is the blood of Christ that constitutes the perfect, definitive cry of innocent blood,[166] a cry of merciful love: "Father, forgive them." For, like Paul, who cannot understand his own behavior when he acts so as to despise God's law, "they know not what they do" (Lk 23:34). So, the fact that a person (his untrue self) violates the right of God's truth at one time does not attenuate that right at a later time. The cry of the blood of the innocent Christ amplifies that right, that is, His right to be heard not only by the Father but also by all who are made in God's image. Conversion entails acknowledging this right of the truth to determine one's freedom by agreeing with the voice and law of God heard anew in the conscience by one's true self. Conversion means that the true self takes sides with the truth against the untrue self. By conversion, the true self vindicates the right of the truth to prevail over the untrue self's claim to a "'right' to persist in evil."[167]

In conversion, then, two acts of conscience must be considered. First, there is the original judgment of conscience (I should do this, or not do that.) that the untrue self deliberately overrules. This act of conscience remains within the sinner as a profoundly personal "witness to the universal truth of the good, at the same time as the evil of his particular choice."[168] The second judgment of conscience takes place in the new moral context resulting from the violation of the first one. It bears upon righting the act of overruling the overruling of the first. It entails listening to the witness of the first one and vindicating the right of the truth that was violated by the untrue self. By "attesting to the fault committed," this second act of conscience, received by the true self, is a "verdict of the judgment of conscience [that] remains a pledge of hope and mercy."[169]

Applying St. Paul's text to David, it should be clear that at the moment of disobeying God's law, David does precisely what he (his untrue self) wants to do, despite the fact that it goes against God's law. In this act, he does not agree that the law is good. In other words, he does not agree with his own conscience, which is the very voice of God making His law known.[170] His sin consists in overruling the higher logic of God (the logic

---

165 "And the Lord said, 'What have you done? The voice of your brother's blood is crying to me from the ground'" (Gen 4:10).
166 See Lk 23:47 and Heb 12:24.
167 John Paul II, *Dominum et Vivificantem*, 46.
168 *CCC*, 1781.
169 Ibid.
170 "For man has in his heart a law written by God; to obey it is the very dignity of man; according to it he will be judged. Conscience is the most secret core and sanctuary of a

of man's true good) in the name of a lower logic of lust. Later, from the perspective of restored faith, he (his true self) makes a judgment about his sin based on the deeper and more lasting conviction that the law is good and should always be observed. From this perspective of faith, disobedience, that is, despising God and His word, is what he (his true self) hates, and the fact that he (his untrue self) has done precisely this leads him to acknowledge that he cannot understand his sinful actions.

Sin is the antithesis to the rational worship to which man is called. By condemning his sin as irrational, David returns to that rational worship by participating in "that greater reason which accepts into itself even darkness and irrationality and heals them."

The Sacrifice of Abraham: "God will provide ..." (Gen 22:8)

The testing of Abraham's faith when God instructed him to sacrifice Isaac sheds additional light on David's conversion into understanding the place of suffering in God's plan of love, and living it. For, suffering appears as irrational, incompatible with, a contradiction of the conviction of faith that God is love and that He is omnipotent.[171] The two sacrifices—Abraham's sacrifice of faith and David's sacrifice of a humble and contrite heart—are key moments in the divine pedagogy by which God leads those He loves to understand the depths of the evil of sin and the corresponding depths of His mercy. They are major moments of preparation for the definitive revelation of the place of suffering in the divine logic of love, in the paschal mystery of Christ.[172]

To turn to the sacrifice of Abraham in order to shed further light on David's sacrifice of a broken and contrite heart immediately confronts a difficulty. It is that while David's sacrifice is a conversion from sin—disdaining God and His word—to a renewed self-entrustment to God and His word, there is no mention of sin in the account of Abraham's sacrifice. Nevertheless, the test of Abraham's faith, which culminates in his readiness to sacrifice Isaac, certainly has sin as its general context. For, as a consequence of Adam and Eve's sin, the Creator's original mandate to be fruitful and to multiply is lived under a sign of contradiction. That is, man's vocation is constantly threatened. And while the threat may seem to come from exterior forces of hostility, whether enemies or the disorder of creation, the truth is that these threats from without are the result of the interior disorder of sin. Living under the sign of contradiction is the just punishment for sin of Adam and Eve. For, they accepted the serpent's contradiction of the truth that God is love. To live under the sign of

---

man. There he is alone with God, Whose voice echoes in his depths" (Vatican II, *Gaudium et spes*, 16).

171 The *CCC* addresses this head on: "If God the Father *almighty*, the Creator of the ordered and good world, *cares* for all his creatures, why does evil exist?" (*CCC*, 309, emphasis added).

172 Man is "absolutely ignorant" of the depths of the evil of sin and of the depths of God's mercy apart from the paschal mystery. See John Paul II, *Dominum et Vivificantem*, 32.

contradiction is to live with what one has chosen, as the prodigal son lived apart for his father, even though this contradicts the reality of his being the father's son. Like Adam and Eve, he chose to define what it means to love himself in a way that contradicted the truth of his vocation to be his father's son. The ensuing suffering that he experienced was his own doing, yet in God's plan of mercy it is meant to and in fact did lead him to reconsider things and to return to his father.

Abraham is the first in a long succession of men and women who confront the prospect of not being able to fulfill their vocation. In this case, it is the fundamental vocation to be fruitful and to multiply. This appears already in the account of the flood. Following the rescue of Noah and his family, the first thing God does is to renew the mandate to be fruitful and to multiply.[173] It comes to its Old Testament apogee with the Exile, when God's people confront the contradiction between their vocation and the fact that they "have become fewer than any nation ... because of [their] sins" (Dan 3:37). So, they beseech the Lord, reminding Him of His promise to Abraham: "For your name's sake do not give us up utterly, and do not break your covenant, and do not withdraw your mercy from us, for the sake of Abraham your beloved and for the sake of your servant Isaac and Israel your holy one, to whom you promised to multiply their descendants like the stars of heaven and like the sand on the shore of the sea" (Dan 3:35–36).

When confronted with the prospect of a failed vocation, the only hope is to appeal to the God of mercy. Because a failed vocation is the result of sin, this hope is essentially the hope to be restored to communion with God, to live once again with faith in His love, and to endure the threats to vocation as fitting into God's plan, as the just punishment for sin. Throughout its history, whenever the promised fulfillment of the blessing-mandate to be fruitful and to multiply is endangered, the prophets call the people to mimic Abraham by hoping against hope in the realization of the Lord's promise. When the sign of contradiction overtakes them because they have sinned by doubting God's love and disobeying His precepts, they must imitate Abraham and hope against hope in God's fidelity to His covenant. Indeed, the history of salvation is a chronicle of how God repeatedly renews this vocation-mandate to be fruitful and intervenes so that His people can fulfill it, as if He bore the primary responsibility for its fulfillment.

It is not at all an accident, therefore, that Abraham's faith is tested in the context of a confrontation between his desire to have a son and the impossibility of its fulfillment. We must not neglect to consider that God's intervention in Abraham's life presupposes the first intervention, that of creation and the gift of life itself, and that with this gift comes the desire to transmit life to children. Abraham's desire to have a son parallels Adam's desire to have "a helper fit for him" (Gen 2:20). Both are rooted in the

---

[173] "Bring forth with you every living thing that is with you of all flesh—birds and animals and every creeping thing that creeps on the earth—that they may breed abundantly on the earth, and be fruitful and multiply upon the earth" (Gen 8:17).

God-given dynamisms of their nature. And, just as Adam could not fulfill his desire by himself, but depended totally on God for its fulfillment, so too Abraham had no hope apart from a mighty deed by God. Because God approves of their desires and intends to fulfill them, He says to them, in effect, what Jesus would say to a man who had been an invalid for thirty-eight years, "Do you want to be healed?" (Jn 5:6); or, to two blind men: "What do you want me to do for you?" (Mt 20:32).

The hope of Abraham and Sarah for a son died, in effect, when they advanced beyond childbearing age. At the time of God's call and promise, the words of the disciples from Emmaus are aptly theirs: "We had hoped …" (Lk 24:21). God resurrects hopes that have died and been buried. He Himself is the "hope against hope" for those who, though living under a sign of contradiction, that is, confronting the prospect of an unfulfilled vocation, nevertheless believe in Him. He Himself is "the consolation of Israel" (Lk 2:25), Who defines Himself as seeing the distress of His people and hearing their cries,[174] Who sees their secret anguish and hears their silent sighs. He remembers His covenant of creation and, being faithful to His original intention in creating, brings their buried hope to life. Reflecting on this, Pope Francis writes of Abraham: "In the voice which speaks to him, the patriarch recognizes a profound call which was always present at the core of his being. God ties his promise to that aspect of human life which has always appeared most 'full of promise', namely, parenthood, the begetting of new life."[175]

The splendor of Abraham's faith is seen in the fact that he believes God's promise *despite* all the *evidence* that having an heir (and thus, also, inhabiting the promised land by his descendants and their nationhood) is impossible, and he believes *before* there is any *evidence* that Sarah has conceived. This is the precise opposite of the hardened heart, that refuses to believe God and to obey Him *despite* all evidence of His wisdom and power serving man out of love: "…. Although they had seen all of my works" (Ps 95:9 Liturgy of the Hours). Abraham's faith rests strictly on God's word, and now that "profound call which was always present in the core of his being" is fulfilled, and he has a future. His faith is manifested in his hope that, *despite* all the evidence indicating it is impossible,[176] *the Lord provides* for the fulfillment of his vocation. It is regarding this fulfillment of vocation that God intervenes a third time, when He requires Abraham to sacrifice Isaac. Once again, the overall context of sin is evident, as yet again Abraham confronts what it means to live one's vocation under a sign of contradiction. Yet again, the profound call within him seems to be unrealizable. In this great test the splendor of Abraham's faith consists in adhering to God's promise *despite* his inability to see how

---

174 See Ex 3:7; 6:5; 1 Sam 9:16; Neh 9:9; Job 34:28; Ps 69:34; 106:44.
175 Francis, *Lumen fidei*, 11.
176 "Abraham had certainty on the part of God promising, but the contrary appeared on the part of natural or human causes. Hence, he says, against the hope of natural and human causes he believed in hope of the divine promise" (Aquinas, *Commentary on St. Paul's Letter to the Romans*, Ch. 4, Lect. 3 [Marietti 367]).

sacrificing Isaac does not cancel it. For, he believes that God "cannot contradict himself; he must remember his marvelous deeds, since his glory is at stake, and he cannot forsake this people that bears his name."[177]

To believe that God cannot contradict Himself is the first principle of rational worship. This conviction leads Abraham to reason that God can raise Isaac from the dead.[178] It is precisely here that we see the parallel with David's sacrifice of a humble and contrite and his hope that "the Lord will look upon my affliction, and that the Lord will repay me with good" (2 Sam 16:12), and the justification for the interpretation of Psalm 51:4, advanced above. This faith and hope are the logical worship that is definitively revealed in the paschal mystery of Jesus Christ, in which it is the privilege of these two heroes of faith to participate in anticipatory manner.

The mercy by which God is faithful to Himself[179] is the only way that God can provide in a way that reconciles His promise with its apparent negation as a result of man's sin. Faith in God's mercy, which brings good out of evil and suffering, is the only foundation for a rational hope that evil and suffering will not have the final word, that with God all things, including the fulfillment of a vocation that seems unattainable, are possible. This kind of rational worship is evident in the great test of Moses' faith, when God threatens to annihilate His people after the great sin of the golden calf. At this moment, his mission, his vocation, to lead the people to the Promised Land is lived under the sign of contradiction. Moses' "hoping against hope" takes the form of confronting[180] God with the contradiction between His acts of liberating Israel from slavery and the threatened destruction of the same people. Following their apostasy, Moses "stands in the breach"—the breach between the two logics, of sin and mercy—before God in order to save the people.[181] "The arguments of his prayer—for intercession is also a mysterious battle—will inspire the boldness of the great intercessors among the Jewish people and in the Church: God is love; he is therefore righteous and faithful; he cannot contradict himself; he must remember his marvelous deeds, since his glory is at stake, and he cannot forsake this people that bears his name."[182] Clearly, God's intention is to

---

177 *CCC*, 2577.
178 "He reasoned that God was able to raise even from the dead" (Heb 11:19 NAB). The NAB's "reasoned" conveys better than the "considered" of other translations the sense of the Greek verb, *logizomai* (λογίζομαι) in a manner that comports with the discussion of logical worship.
179 In his encyclical on mercy, John Paul defines God's mercy as God's fidelity to Himself (see *Dives in misericordia*, 6, 7. 15). This is equivalent to the biblical theme of appealing to God to act in behalf of His people, especially in forgiving theirs sins, for the sake of His name: "For your name's sake, O Lord, pardon my guilt for it is great" (Ps 25:11). See also: Ps 79:9; Jer 14:7; Ez 20:44; Dan 3:34.
180 The *CCC* considers prayer of meditation as a confrontation that leads to conversion. It is a confrontation between the way things should be in our lives according to God's will and whatever contradicts God's will (see *CCC*, 2706; 2723). Similarly, Moses confronts the way things should be according to God's fidelity and mercy, on one hand, and on the other the potential contradiction of His fidelity and mercy.
181 Ps 106:23; cf. Ex 32:1–34:9.
182 *CCC*, 2577.

elicit this bold protest of faith and hope from Moses. He does not want to be alone in knowing the full extent of the logic of His mercy. He wants His people to know of His mercy, but He also wants Moses to know it first.

Confronting the apparent contradiction between God's word and promise, on one hand, and the prospect of their non-fulfillment, on the other, is the very essence of logical worship. Put another way, logical worship is the sacrifice of faith, the way that we make on offering of ourselves to God, the way that we entrust ourselves to His logic of love. It is our participation in God's own logic of merciful love. This is the sacrifice that atones for the irrationality of Adam and Eve, which Israel is constantly tempted to repeat. They despised God and His word by overruling the judgment of conscience rooted in the evidence of His love. Idolatry is to entrust oneself to a god who has not demonstrated his love. It is to accept the false testimony of another (the serpent, or other gods) when they provide no evidence of their love.

This is why the sacrifice of faith is *the* sacrifice that is acceptable to God. This becomes fully revealed in Jesus Christ, when He says *"Fiat"* to the sacrifice presented to Him. Catechized to associate the word *"fiat"* with the faith of Mary, Catholics rightly understand that *"Fiat"* is the proper response of man to God when He makes His will known. It conveys that primordial primacy of God's will over man's will. What, then, are we to make of those several times when Jesus, that is, God Himself, says *"Fiat"* to men?[183] In Jesus, God says *"Fiat"* to the cries of the brokenhearted, to the poor who place their hope in God alone. "Do you want to be healed of your tormented conscience?" "What do you want me to do for you?" The poorest of the poor are those whose hearts are broken by the apparent contradiction between a God of love and their suffering, especially the suffering of an accusing conscience and its attendant logic of sin. While Moses expressed his "hope against hope" in the form of a confrontation, these poor express it the form of petition: "Lord, if you are willing, you can cleanse me" (Mt 8:2 NJB). When it comes to the desire for a clean heart, for a purified conscience, His response is assured: "I am willing; be clean" (Mt 8:3 NJB). It would be a contradiction for a God of love to neglect the cry of the poor who only desire the very fulness of life that is His original intention. It would be a contradiction for the Messiah not to fulfill the prophecies regarding the restoration of sight to the blind and liberty for all those enslaved by sin and its consequences.[184]

The Second Vatican Council describes the vocation of all men as a quest to live a fully human life, that is, the fulfillment man's fundamental aspirations. The most fundamental of these is his search for the definitive

---

[183] To the Centurion, who intercedes in behalf of his servant, Jesus says: "Be it done for you as you have believed"—"Sicut credidisti fiat tibi" (Mt 8:13). To two blind men, who cry out to Him for mercy, Jesus says: "According to your faith be it done to you"—"secundum fidem vestram fiat vobis" (Mt 9:29). Finally, when the Canaanite woman begs Jesus to heal her daughter, Jesus replies: "Be it done for you as you desire"—"Fiat tibi sicut vis" (Mt 15:28).

[184] See Is 29:18; 61:1; Mt 11:5.

meaning of life. The Church's mission is to promote this fully human life by leading men to Christ, Who fully reveals man to himself.[185] At a time in history when the very existence of meaning and the possibility of discovering it are questioned, the Church proclaims that man is not deceiving himself when he embarks on a search for that meaning. Since creation is an expression of God's wisdom and goodness, a meaningful life is one that takes the truth about God and His plan of love for man as its foundation. This truth corresponds to man's most fundamental aspiration for meaning because he is "by nature and vocation a religious being,"[186] i.e., he is ordered to God by nature. As a result, his highest good can only be satisfied by this God Who "created man to make him share in His own blessed life."[187] The Council teaches that this profound desire for a fully human life, which is always present in the core of man's being, is currently lived under a sign of contradiction because of sin. This means that all men confront the fact that the fulfillment of their desire is simply beyond what they are able to attain on their own.

To live under a sign of contradiction is to be aware of the distance between one's desires and the possibility of their fulfillment. For men and women of faith, it is to confront the radical impossibility of living up to God's call, that is, to confront one's own incapacity to fulfill the vocation received from God—the vocation to love Him with one's whole heart, mind, soul, and strength, and one's neighbor as oneself. This distance and incapacity need not always be due to personal sin. To confirm this, one need only consider the response of the Blessed Virgin Mary to the announcement that she was to be the mother of the long-awaited descendant of David: "How shall this be?" (Lk 1:34). This is, essentially, the question that Abraham carries during his three-day journey to Mount Moriah: How shall God's promise be fulfilled if my son is sacrificed? It is the question that David, and everyone who sins, has to confront: How shall God's promise be fulfilled, now that I have sinned? There is only one answer: it will be fulfilled because He is the one holy God, because He is faithful to His love for us, because He is "rich in mercy" (Eph 2:4).

Man cannot see how his vocation and God's promises will be fulfilled. They are "shrouded in darkness."[188] The Virgin's "How shall this be?" necessarily accompanies faith and hope. For, "hope that is seen is not hope" (Rom 8:24). When what we see, despite efforts to break free, a pattern of recurring sin, when we see ourselves as "sold as a slave to sin" (Rom 7:14), then we find ourselves in the humanly hopeless situation of the descendants of Jacob in Egypt. Because we have confronted the limits of our own efforts to break free from sin, we are (finally) open to God's deeper grace—a deeper grace, because it is already a grace to do what we

---

185 See Wojtyła, *Sources of Renewal*, 279. The most elaborate explication and defense of this mission comes in the encyclicals of St. John Paul II, *Redemptoris missio* and *Fides et ratio*, and in the CDF document, *Dominus Iesus*, August 6, 2000.
186 See *CCC*, 44.
187 *CCC*, 1.
188 John Paul II, *Redemptoris Mater*, 26.

can to conquer sin. Precisely because we have made our best effort, we (finally) remember that God dwells "in thick darkness" (2 Chron 6:1). His ways are not our ways,[189] and there is a constant need that our understanding of what God has revealed be purified. We see this when Peter's faith in Jesus as Messiah has to be purified,[190] and when the apostles' understanding of the kingdom that He promises has to be purified.[191] We had thought that God's victory over sin will arrive with a suddenness comparable to the healing of blind men and lepers. We did not grasp the depths of the divine logic of love, according to which we are to enter ever more deeply into the paschal mystery. For, we are constantly tempted to hope that faith in God will exempt us from further suffering. We are constantly scandalized by evil and suffering, and learn only very slowly the place of suffering in God's plan.

This is why only faith in what God has accomplished in Christ and hope in His promises can remove this contradiction. Only He can fulfill man's desire to live a meaningful life, that is, a life that is worthy of a reasonable, rational, logical being. And because His mercy comes to us from His sacrifice on the Cross, man's living of a rational life only escapes being lived under a sign of contradiction by being lived as participation in the sacrifice of Christ, which constitutes logical worship. The logical worship of Christians is a participation in the divine logic of love. Everything God accomplishes in history, culminating in the Cross of Christ, is ordered by the goal of divine mercy, namely, the reconciliation of sinners with God. This logic is absolutely impenetrable apart from faith that is grounded in the experience of that very mercy. St. Paul conveys this by calling it "folly for those who are perishing," while "to us who are being saved it is the power of God" (1 Cor 1:18). The folly of the Cross of Christ is, in reality, the supreme wisdom of God—the final deduction from the divine logic of love. But, it is not a deduction that man is able to draw from what God has previously revealed, as if there were premises that, once known, could lead to the conclusion of the paschal mystery. The logic of divine love can only be known by revelation, and its coherence with what precedes it appears only in its own light. Faith is able to look backwards to perceive the culmination of the divine logic of love in the mystery of Christ, but even for the perfect faith of the Mother of God, the Cross appears as "the complete *negation*"[192] of what faith and hope previously held. Faith and hope are lived under a sign of contradiction to the very end and culmination of divine revelation. Only from the vantage point of the culmination and its effect in those who believe is one able to look back and to reconstruct as it were the order of the divine logic of love.

The perfection of the faith of Abraham and of Mary consists in their believing in the order of the divine logic of love even before it is fully

---

189 See Is 55:8–9.
190 See Mt 16:21–28.
191 See Acts 1:6–8.
192 John Paul II, *Redemptoris Mater*, 18.

revealed, in the face of its apparent contradiction by what they are experiencing. While for them this concerns the fulfillment of God's promises in history and does not directly concern the internal negation of sin, it is David's place in the history of salvation, that is, in the unfolding of the divine logic of love, to bear witness to the fact that the irrationality of sin does not negate God's fidelity to His own logic of love but rather serves to reveal it. God is the Master of history,[193] and this should be taken above all in relation to the interior history of consciences. His mastery is evident above all other things in the His redirection of human freedom from within that very freedom, and thus without any coercion. His greatest glory is the conversion of sinners for the fulfillment of the vocation to live a meaningful life, which is a life of constant conversion, which is the logical worship of God, which is participation in God's own logic of love, which is fully revealed in the Cross of Christ.

Now, however, "we walk by faith, not by sight" (2 Cor 5:7); we perceive God as "in a mirror, dimly" and only "in part" (1 Cor 13:12). "Even though enlightened by him in whom it believes, faith is often lived in darkness and can be put to the test. The world we live in often seems very far from the one promised us by faith. Our experiences of evil and suffering, injustice and death, seem to contradict the Good News; they can shake our faith and become a temptation against it."[194] This is why faith shows its maturity when a person continues "in hope to believe against hope" (Rom 4:18), when, like the Virgin Mary beneath the Cross, he "witnesses, humanly speaking, the complete negation of God's words"[195] and yet continues to believe and to trust in God.

Both Abraham and David, when confronted with what appears to be the complete negation of God's promise, continue "in hope to believe against hope," but with hearts that are broken. The brokenhearted are those who are distraught at the thought that God's promise may not be fulfilled, that they may not live to see His promise fulfilled. These are the brokenhearted whom God heals,[196] for whom the only consolation is to see the victory of the Lord, that is, the fulfillment of His promises.[197]

This is the state of the elderly Simeon, whom Joseph and Mary meet when they bring the infant Jesus to the Temple. Simeon lived "looking for the consolation of Israel" (Lk 2:25). This implies that he lived with a broken heart, which remains broken until the light of the Lord breaks through the darkness of sin and its consequences. Like the Hebrew slaves in Egypt, who saw only one generation after another born into slavery and die in slavery, he lived in the hope that believes against hope. There is nothing that can be done to hasten the fulfillment of this hope. There is only patience, waiting for the perfect moment, "the hour," that is known

---

193 See *CCC*, 269.
194 *CCC*, 164.
195 John Paul II, *Redemptoris Mater*, 18.
196 See Ps 147:3.
197 See Ps 34:18; Is 57:15; 61:1.

only to God as a conclusion of His logic of love. Once he sees Jesus and sees in Him the fulfillment of God's promises, he can exclaim: "Lord, now let your servant depart in peace, according to your word; for my eyes have seen your salvation" (Lk 2:29–30). Peace and consolation come with witnessing the fulfillment of promises. Until then, anguish, even desolation, accompanies those who "in hope believe against hope." It is the interior state of the shepherd until he finds his lost sheep, or the woman until she finds her lost coin, or the father until his lost son returns. For, his sheep is integral to the shepherd's vocation, her coin to the woman's vocation, and his son to the father's vocation. Until each is found, the prospect of a failed vocation remains. The only possible consolation is to be reunited with what has been lost.

David's heart is broken in the forgoing sense, for because of his sins he faces the prospect of the end of his reign, and with it the thwarting of God's promise that He would establish the throne of his descendant forever. Further, his conscience bears the weight of personal responsibility. In contrast to Abraham, David's dread is to know perfectly well that his sins are the cause of the prospect of a failed vocation as king. The refrain of enemies and of nations who observe his affliction, "Where is your God?" (Ps 42:3)[198] no longer comes from without but from within. Indeed, where was David's God when the king ordered that Bathsheba be brought to the palace and when he arranged for Uriah's death? Why was God not given the place that He deserves to have in David's conscience? Why did David prefer his own vision for his future to God's vision by despising His word and thus God Himself?

It is not true that David has no future. Rather, the truth is that he has a future that he has chosen for himself. And once he regains the perspective of faith he realizes that this is not the future that he truly desires. In his penitence, he desires the future that God has put before him, and with it the fulfillment His promises and the fulfillment of his vocation. The question that he must face is, is this the future that God too desires, or, have his sins altered that future? The answer depends entirely on whether God is merciful and forgiving. Thus, there is only one thing David can do, and that is to offer God the sacrifice of his broken and contrite heart, the sacrifice of logical worship, of faith in His mercy.

Despite the absence of an explicit awareness of sin in the case of Abraham, the similarities between the two sacrifices of faith invite further comparisons. Having considered Abraham's broken heart over the thought of losing his son and his consequent confrontation with the prospect of his life being reduced to being a contradiction, a failed vocation, our attention now turns to his simple yet profound profession of faith and continuing hope that God's promise will be fulfilled.

At the time of his test, Abraham expresses his faith and hope when he answers Isaac's question, "Where is the lamb for a burnt offering?" by saying, "God will provide" (Gen 22:7–8). This profession of faith and hope

---

198 See Ps 79:10; 115:2; Joel 2:17; Mic 7:10.

lived on in the memory of God's people. We read in Genesis, "So Abraham called the name of that place The Lord will provide; as it is said to this day, 'On the mount of the Lord it shall be provided'" (Gen 22:14). As in English, the root of the Hebrew word for "provide" is "to see." Literally, then, it means that the Lord sees ahead, into the future; He sees how the knot of contradiction will be untied, and He will see to it that it happens. He will provide for Abraham what Abraham cannot provide for himself. He will find a way for Abraham's vocation to be fulfilled, despite what he can only understand as its complete negation. What is it, precisely, that God sees? Might it be the broken heart of Abraham, anguished by the thought of losing the very son that God had given him, and miraculously so? Might it be that God sees in Abraham's broken heart a reflection of His own conflicted heart, depicted by Hosea, a heart overwhelmed by the thought of a failed vocation? Abraham, "the friend of God" (2 Chron 20:7; Is 41:8; Jas 2:23) is the first to participate in the conflicted love of God Himself and to offer the sacrifice of a broken heart.

Nearly a thousand years later, the Temple was built on the place called "the Lord will provide." This indicates that when Abraham's descendants think of worshipping of God and offering Him sacrifices, they aspire to reproduce the interior dispositions that elicit from God the same response He made to Abraham's sacrifice: "now I know that you fear God" (Gen 22:12). Thus, "Abraham's sacrifice stands at the root of the whole Israelite cult that is centered in the Temple."[199] It is "the paradigm and the justification for all the sacrifices of Israel."[200] The geographical significance of the Temple of Jerusalem derives from the faith that "enables Israel to perceive in Abraham's unconditional faith and obedience the ever-present model and inspiration for her many sacrifices."[201]

David is able to believe and to hope that God will not despise the sacrifice of his own broken and contrite heart because God did not despise Abraham's sacrifice of unconditional faith and obedience, offered from his broken heart. In contrast to Abraham, David's dread is to live with the knowledge that his vocation is threatened to fail because of his sin. Once he repents of despising God's word, he is constrained not to despise God's word regarding exterior kingdom by disregarding the kingdom within. Through his conversion, God initiates David into His logic of love and the logical worship of faith in His mercy. Now he can obediently live out what God's word requires, that is, the logical worship of hoping against hope that God will forgive Him. This faith in and obedience to God's word about His mercy, coming from a heart that is broken as it realizes that, from a merely human perspective there is no hope, is the sacrifice that is acceptable to God. God's mercy is the revealed doctrine that alone corresponds to Abraham's profession of faith and hope: "God will

---

199 Roch Keresztzty, *Wedding Feast of the Lamb. Eucharistic Theology from a Historical, Biblical and Systematic Perspective* (Chicago: Hillenbrand Books, 2004), 8.
200 Ibid.
201 Ibid., 9.

provide." Seeing a broken and contrite heart that professes faith in His mercy and hopes for forgiveness unfailingly elicits from God a response that is unimaginable for men, until it is revealed in Jesus Christ: *"Fiat!"* "Be it done for you as you have believed" (Mt 8:13).

The preceding invites us to discover the profound meaning of David's desire to build a Temple for God, a meaning that perhaps escaped the king at the time that he informed Nathan of his intention.[202] The Temple's association with the sacrifice of Abraham means that its essential purpose is to perpetuate Abraham's sacrifice of faith and obedience to the God Who in His mercy provides for man whenever his vocation is threatened. David's dream of building the Temple expresses his desire to "do what Abraham did" (Jn 8:39). In keeping with God's logic of love for David, it is not his place to construct the Temple. But it is his place to do what Abraham did. While in God's plan, Solomon will build the Temple, nevertheless He fulfills David's desire in a totally unexpected way. God grants the deeper desire of David's heart,[203] to do what Abraham did. God is more interested in the temple within, where the sacrifice of logical worship, that of a broken and contrite heart the believes in God's mercy, is offered. Before man constructs a Temple for God, God constructs a Temple for man. God fashions David's heart into a Temple, a place, an altar consecrated for the sacrifice of faith in God's mercy. David perpetuates the meaning of Abraham's sacrifice, not by constructing an edifice where sacrifices that are themselves only symbolic can be offered, but by becoming himself the sacrifice that is pleasing to God. David's broken and contrite heart is the Temple where God is worshipped "in spirit and in truth" (Jn 4:23–24).

God's mysterious fulfillment of David's desire to build a Temple confirms St. Paul's declaration that God "is able to do far more abundantly than all that we ask or think" (Eph 3:20). He sees to the depths of our desires, which we ourselves cannot fathom.[204] St. Augustine incisively formulates the principle: "The Lord is good, for He often does not grant what we desire, so that He may give us what we desire even more."[205] The place of Israel's second king is to immortalize the true meaning of sacrifice, as he does especially in Psalm 51, and to be a prophet of hope for

---

[202] See 2 Sam 7.
[203] What St. Augustine says of the prayer of his mother, St. Monica, applies here. For years Monica had prayed for her son's conversion. On the day that he was to leave for Italy, where in God's Providence the graces of conversion awaited him, she pleaded with God not to let him go. She could not see how his departure away from her could actually fit into God's plan of mercy for Augustine. Looking back, Augustine writes: "She remained praying and weeping. And what was she praying for, O my God, with all those tears but that You should not allow me to sail! But You saw deeper and granted the essential of her prayer: *You did not do what she was at that moment asking, that You might do the thing she was always asking*" (*Confessions*, 5, 8).
[204] "The heart is our hidden center, beyond the grasp of our reason and of others; only the Spirit of God can fathom the human heart and know it fully" (*CCC*, 2563).
[205] Augustine, "Letter to Paulinus and Therasia," quoted by Aquinas in *Summa contra gentiles*, III, 96.

all sinners that by His mercy God will always provide in order to fulfill the desires that He inspires in us.

Sinners are not deceived when in hope they believe against all hope in God's mercy and His desire to reconcile them to Himself. St. Thérèse of Lisieux assures us that "God cannot inspire unrealizable desires,"[206] and that He makes us desire what He wants to give us.[207] "Petition," St. Thomas tells us, "is like the interpreter of desire."[208] God works through our prayers; He "fulfills the holy desires" of the one who prays.[209] Whether or not a person is aware of it, the desire for something that God desires to give is the work of the Holy Spirit.[210] Enlisting St. Augustine, Benedict XVI incisively describes the situation of a heart that is simultaneously aware of its desire for God and of its incapacity.

> He defines prayer as an exercise of desire. Man was created for greatness—for God himself; he was created to be filled by God. But his heart is too small for the greatness to which it is destined. It must be stretched. "By delaying [his gift], God strengthens our desire; through desire he enlarges our soul and by expanding it he increases its capacity [for receiving him]."[211]

Sin profoundly magnifies man's awareness of being too small for the greatness to which God calls him. Many succumb to a false humility, which in reality is the sin of despair against hope, a form of despising God's word about His mercy. Only faith in God's mercy is able to defeat the logic of sin, which, as a logic of strict justice, is the premise of despair. This logic casts a dark shadow of doubt over the legitimacy of still desiring to receive God's love after having rejected it. It is precisely this awareness of possessing a desire that is unrealizable—and seemingly illogical—and yet continuing to hope in God for its fulfillment that constitutes hoping against hope and that gives rise to the prayer-sacrifice of a broken and contrite heart that appeals to God's mercy. This constitutes man's logical worship of God, a worship entirely grounded in faith in what God has revealed about His mercy. God's mercy and forgiveness—the conviction that God is more committed to the fulfillment of man's vocation than man himself is—are the sinner's only hope that his sins have not annulled God's promise, that therefore there is a future, that one's vocation has not

---

[206] Thérèse of Lisieux, *Story of a Soul. The Autobiography of St. Thérèse of Lisieux*, trans. John Clarke (Washington, D.C.: Institute of Carmelite Studies, 1975 [2nd edition, 1976]), 207.
[207] Ibid., 250.
[208] Aquinas, *ST* II-II, Q. 83, a. 1, ad 1.
[209] Aquinas, *Summa contra gentiles*, III, 95.
[210] Commenting on Rom 8:26, Aquinas says: "For the Holy Spirit makes us ask, inasmuch as he causes right desires in us, because to ask is to make desires known. Now right desires arise from the ardor of love, which he produces in us" (Aquinas, *Commentary of St. Paul's Letter to the Romans*, Ch. 8, Lect. 5; Marietti, 693).
[211] Benedict XVI, *Spe salvi*, 33, quoting from a homily of Augustine on 1 John.

been definitively canceled. An appeal to God's mercy is the sacrifice of faith in the God Who has revealed that He will always provide.

The Joy of Conversion

In the spiritual life, joy and sorrow are strictly coordinated because the spiritual life is participation in the paschal mystery, the essential dynamic of which is that death is transformed into life, the alienation of sin into reconciliation and communion, sorrow into joy. "Truly, truly, I say to you, you will weep and lament ...; you will be sorrowful, but your sorrow will turn into joy" (Jn 16:20); "So you have sorrow now, but I will see you again and your hearts will rejoice, and no one will take your joy from you" (Jn 16:22). This is the essential dynamic of love, from which sorrow and joy spring.[212] The joy of conversion is participation in Christ's own joy,[213] which is preceded by the suffering of His passion and crucifixion. But, we cannot remain at the level of Christ's physical suffering. For, that suffering is the outward manifestation—we can say, the sacrament—of His interior sorrow: "My soul is very sorrowful, even to death" (Mt 26:38).

So, to come to understand the joy that David anticipates as he confesses his sins, it is necessary further to sound the depths of his interior suffering, the torment of his conscience afflicted by unreconciled guilt. This torment of conscience is the Pit into which David has fallen by his own fault, which by God's mercy becomes the occasion for David to experience the truth about God's fidelity to His people, validated again and again throughout salvation history. Israel's life according to its covenant with God—occupying the land given by Him, there worshipping Him, and living in justice, with a mandated love of preference for the widow, the orphan and the poor—this life is constantly threatened by Israel's enemies. The people's first consciousness concerns its external enemies, those nations consumed with envy for their land. The lesson of Israel's history is God's fidelity, which frustrates the nations' designs, but does so in a manner that reveals the logic according to which "one is punished by the very things by which he sins" (Wis 11:16). Thus, the nations' ploys against God's people become their own undoing: "The nations have sunk down in the pit which they have made; In the net which they hid their own foot has been caught" (Ps 9:15). "They set a net for my steps; my soul was bowed down. They dug a pit in my way, but they have fallen into it themselves" (Ps 57:6).

Is this not what David experiences? Having "struck down Uriah the Hittite with the sword ... therefore the sword shall never depart from your house, for you have despise me" (2 Sam 12:9–10). What David did in secret, in order to safeguard his reputation among the people, God made

---

212 See *CCC*, 1765.
213 "These things I have spoken to you, that my joy may be in you, and that your joy may be full" (Jn 15:11). "But now I am coming to you [Father]; and these things I speak in the world, that they may have my joy fulfilled in themselves" (Jn 17:13).

public: "For you did it secretly; but I will do this thing before all Israel, and before the sun" (2 Sam 12:12). Like the wife of Hosea, David must be exposed before the people so that he can let go of all pretensions to being a righteous king and stand naked before God in his sinfulness. For, God, too, wields a sword:

> [12] Indeed, the word of God is living and active, sharper than any two-edged sword, piercing until it divides soul from spirit, joints from marrow; it is able to judge the thoughts and intentions of the heart. [13] And before him no creature is hidden, but all are naked and laid bare to the eyes of the one to whom we must render an account. (Hebrews 4:12–13)

All of this foreshadows the mission of Jesus Christ. The "righteous and devout" man, Simeon found the right words to express it when Joseph and Mary brought Jesus to the temple to present Him to the Lord. Precisely because he "looking forward to the consolation of Israel, the Holy Spirit rested on him" (Lk 2:25). Simeon understood that Israel's consolation requires its prior desolation of having its sins exposed, not only to the nations, but to the people themselves, so that they can repent of their sins and thereby be disposed to recent the new covenant in the blood of Christ.

The consolation of Israel is personified in David's confrontation with his own sin, repentance, conversion, and reconciliation with God. This is why he "is the first prophet of Jewish and Christian prayer."[214] What Christ will fully reveal is hidden but anticipated in the psalms, which in God's plan have a unique place in bearing witness to the kingdom within. Christ's mission is to establish the inner kingdom, and this entails "that the inner thoughts of many will be revealed." It entails, as well, that a sword will pierce" the soul of His mother (Lk 2:35). This, again, is the sword of God's truth, which must pierce everyone who is graced to perceive the causal relation between his sins and the suffering and death of Christ.[215] This is the realization of "*the entire dimension of evil* proper to sin" regarding which "man ... is absolutely ignorant apart from the Cross of Christ."[216]

David's place in salvation history is to bear witness to the other enemy, the interior enemy of sin, which even more fundamentally threatens the ability of God's people to live the covenant. In him we see that God's fidelity and victory are directed against David's *sin* and ordered

---

214 *CCC*, 2579.
215 See Zech 12:10: "And I will pour out on the house of David and the inhabitants of Jerusalem a spirit of grace and pleas for mercy, so that, when they look on me, on him whom they have pierced, they shall mourn for him, as one mourns for an only child, and weep bitterly over him, as one weeps over a firstborn" (Zech 12:10). St. John sees this fulfilled in the crucifixion and Jesus's body being pierced by a soldier's lance (Jn 19:34, 37). "It is in discovering the greatness of God's love that our heart is shaken by the horror and weight of sin and begins to fear offending God by sin and being separated from him. The human heart is converted by looking upon him whom our sins have pierced" (*CCC*, 1432).
216 John Paul II, *Dominum et Vivificantem*, 32.

to bringing *him* to fulfill his vocation. David is both the one chosen by God who enjoys His protection and the enemy of God who, by his sin, plots against others and thereby frustrates his own vocation. In his extraordinary transparency to himself, David's insights regarding the dynamics of sin and the work of God's mercy are so penetrating and lucid that in his psalms men and women of every temperament and culture discovered the truth about themselves in relation to God. "In the Psalms David, inspired by the Holy Spirit, is the first prophet of Jewish and Christian prayer."[217] Christians "make the Psalms their own ... in view of their fulfillment in Christ,"[218] that is, in view of His sacrifice and blood that purifies consciences. To pray the psalms is to confess one's sins and to profess one's faith in the fidelity and mercy of God.

As a fruit of his conversion and experience of God's mercy, David keenly grasps the irony of sin, so that in the presence of God he sings of "the wicked man [who] conceives evil, and is pregnant with mischief, and brings forth lies." Such a one "makes a pit, digging it out, and falls into the hole which he has made. His wickedness returns upon his own head, and on his own skull his violence descends" (Ps 7:14–16). When he sins, he, the king of Israel, is this wicked man, who conceived the evil of usurping another man's wife and arranged for that man's death. His marriage to Bathsheba was indeed based on a lie, the concealed truth about his treachery. Nathan's mission was to make him see that he fell into a pit of his own making, the pit of a conscience tormented by unreconciled guilt as a result of the violence that David himself inflicted on it. God alone can rescue him from this pit: God, "who forgives all your iniquity, who heals all your diseases, who redeems your life from the Pit, who crowns you with steadfast love and mercy" (Ps 103:3–4). Only God can put an end to a conscience writhing in the anguish of unreconciled guilt by drawing out from the pit of self-accusation: "At once, my bitterness turns to well-being. For you have preserved my soul from the pit of nothingness, you have thrust all my sins behind you" (Is 38:17 NJB).

To describe the living death of this Pit, the pervasiveness, depth, and intensity of his spiritual suffering, David (the Psalmist) frequently employs the metaphor of bones: they shudder (Ps 6:2); they are disjointed (Ps 22:14); they waste away (Ps 31:10); there is no health in them (Ps 38:3); they burn (Ps 102:3). Sin causes his whole being to be warped, broken, and insupportable. The distress of an accusing conscience causes a festering that reaches all the way to his bones, which can no longer function as they should. There is no support for his life; he is on the verge of total collapse. These images symbolize his moral life, which is in a state of total ruin because its support-structure, his conscience, is deformed.

In this desperate situation, David turns to God in the only way possible, by drawing from the collective memory of his people. "I remember the days of old, I meditate on all that you have done; I muse on

---

217 *CCC*, 2579.
218 *CCC*, 2625.

what your hands have wrought" (Ps 143:5). Another psalm vividly depicts the situation of desperation:

> ¹ I cry aloud to God, aloud to God, that he may hear me.
> ² In the day of my trouble I seek the Lord;
> in the night my hand is stretched out without wearying;
> my soul refuses to be comforted.
> ³ I think of God, and I moan; I meditate, and my spirit faints.
> ⁴ You keep my eyelids from closing;
> I am so troubled that I cannot speak. (Psalm 77:1–4)

In such a situation, when hope in chariots, horses, or princes is of no avail,[219] the only source of solace is to remember what God has done in the past as a sure foundation of hope that in His faithful love He will intervene anew.

> ⁵ I consider the days of old, I remember the years long ago.
> ⁶ I commune with my heart in the night; I meditate and search my spirit: […]
> ¹¹ I will call to mind the deeds of the Lord; yes, I will remember thy wonders of old.
> ¹² I will meditate on all your work, and muse on your mighty deeds.
> ¹³ Your way, O God, is holy. What god is great like our God?
> ¹⁴ You are the God who works wonders, who have manifested your might among the peoples.
> ¹⁵ With your arm you redeemed your people, the sons of Jacob and Joseph
> ¹⁶ When the waters saw you, O God, when the waters saw you, they were afraid; yes the deep trembled.
> ¹⁷ The clouds poured out water; the skies gave forth thunder; your arrows flashed on every side.
> ¹⁸ The crash of your thunder was in the whirlwind; your lightnings lighted up the world; the earth trembled and shook.
> ¹⁹ Your way was through the sea, your path through the great waters; yet your footprints were unseen.
> ²⁰ You led your people like a flock by the hand of Moses and Aaron. (Psalm 77:5–6, 11–20)

The omitted verses (vv. 7–10) place this remembering of faith in the context of a hope in distress, hope on the brink of despair. Anyone who takes God and the culmination of His logic of love in the paschal mystery seriously is thereby obligated to take sin seriously. To do so is to live a precipice spirituality by walking along the narrow path of conscience, where man's freedom and God's truth constantly meet. It is to live in constant

---

219 See Ps 20:8; 118:9; 146:3.

threat of losing one's balance and falling to the pit of sin, falling victim to the moral vertigo caused by a mere glance at the dark chasm of sin. Precipice spirituality requires the keenest focus, lest with a single misstep "I become like those who go down to the Pit" (Ps 28:1). Precipice spirituality is for those who understand the seriousness of the exhortation: "Watch, and be on your guard" (Lk 12:15 NJB); "Watch yourselves, or your hearts will be coarsened by debauchery and drunkenness and the cares of life" (Lk 21:34 NJB); "Be vigilant, stay firm in the faith" (1 Cor 16:13 NJB). Precipice spirituality is lived by custody of the heart, in order to be attentive and responsive to the voice of God, Whose voice echoes there: "More than all else, keep watch over your heart, since here are the wellsprings of life" (Prov 4:23 NJB); "And heed the counsel of your own heart [conscience], for no one is more faithful to you than it is" (Sir 37:13 NRS).

To sin is to "stray from the way of truth" (Wis 5:6), succumb to the vertigo of contemplated sin, and to fall into the pit. To avoid this disaster, one must be vigilant and focused on the narrow path of God's truth by remembering what He has accomplished in the past. And if one should fall into the pit, the remembering of God's past fidelity becomes the pledge for hope that He will intervene again in behalf of His faithful. Desperate to see His victory in the present moment, the practitioner of precipice spirituality cries out:

> [7] "Will the Lord spurn for ever,
> and never again be favorable?
> [8] Has his steadfast love for ever ceased?
> Are his promises at an end for all time?
> [9] Has God forgotten to be gracious?
> Has he in anger shut up his compassion?" (Psalm 77:7–9)

The thought that God's pattern of fidelity in the past may not be a guarantee of similar fidelity in his time of need gnaws at his hope: "And I say, 'It is my grief that the right hand of the Most High has changed'" (Ps 77:10).[220]

The only hope for a conscience imprisoned by the logic of sin—rejection of God's love means I am undeserving of being loved—is the logic of God's mercy. The wisdom passed on by Sirach indicates what is, precisely, that the exercise of considering the history of God's dealings with His people should lead a person to perceive:

> [10] Consider the ancient generations and see:
> who ever trusted in the Lord and was put to shame?
> Or who ever persevered in his commandments

---

[220] Though the ESV notably departs from this translation, which with slight variations is adopted by RSV, NAB, NAS, and NJB, it nevertheless conveys the sense of the transition from the (rhetorical?) questions of near despair to the act of remembering God's past acts of deliverance: "Then I said, 'I will appeal to this, to the years of the right hand of the Most High'" (Ps 77:10).

and was forsaken?
Or who ever called upon him and was overlooked?"
¹¹ For the Lord is compassionate and merciful;
he forgives sins and saves in time of affliction,
and he is the shield of all who seek him in truth. (Sirach 2:10–11)

To review the history of God's dealings with His people throughout salvation history, when in a state of hope on the brink, is to call to mind that the God of Abraham, of Isaac, and of Jacob has revealed Himself as "merciful and gracious, slow to anger, and abounding in steadfast love and faithfulness" (Ex 34:6). Salvation history is the recurring confirmation of this formulation of God in His relation to men. To petition the Lord, then, based on this doctrine, is, essentially, to "appeal to the oaths and covenants given to our fathers" (Wis 18:22). It is not a plea that God should accede to man's wishes, but that He should be *faithful to Himself*—though now the desire of man and the desire of God are one. For the man of the Old Testament, all of this is compacted into a prayer that is, in effect, doctrine in the form of petition: "Though our iniquities testify against us, act, O Lord, *for your name's sake*; for our backslidings are many, we have sinned against you" (Jer 14:7); "Do not spurn us, *for your name's sake*; do not dishonor your glorious throne; remember and do not break your covenant with us" (Jer 14:21).

This is the faith that drives David's prayer, and his conviction that the confession of sins with a broken and contrite heart is an acceptable sacrifice to God. This act of faith leads him to hope that joy will accompany his conversion, and so he prays: "Let me hear joy and gladness; let the bones that you have crushed rejoice" (Ps 51:8 NRS). "Restore to me the joy of your salvation" (Ps 51:12). For the man of faith, the joy of salvation is more than the end of the just punishment that purifies faith and hope. That kind of joy, which is real and has its proper place in the spiritual life, corresponds to the imperfect contrition for sin. A deeper joy of salvation accompanies perfect contrition for sin, which is sorrow for sin "when it arises from a love by which God is loved above all else."[221] When God is loved in this way, the greatest concern is for the glory of His name. That glory resides in every act of His fidelity to Himself and His promises, every act that reconfirms the truth that He is "merciful and gracious, slow to anger, and abounding in steadfast love and faithfulness" (Ex 34:6). This is realized when He forgives sins and restores His people to faith. Thus, the sinner plays his own role in the glorification of God's name, simply by turning to Him in the humility of hope on the brink, in the desperation of precipice spirituality, remembering in His presence the history of His mercy, and beseeching Him to work a new marvel of mercy, for the glory of His name: "Help us, O God of our

---

221 *CCC*, 1452.

salvation, *for the glory of your name*; deliver us, and forgive our sins, *for your name's sake!*" (Ps 79:9).

This joy in what God accomplishes *for* the sinner and *for* the glory of His name is rooted in a profound awareness of faith that nothing escapes God's sovereignty and that therefore even sin is made to serve how He reveals Himself. This faith-awareness is evident when David attributes the crushing of his bones to God: "the bones that *you* have crushed" (Ps 51:12). Here, David expresses himself in the mode of his religious culture, which is profoundly aware that every event in one way or another falls within God's plan.[222] The prime example of expressing this awareness is God revealing to Moses that He will harden Pharaoh's heart.[223] Yet, elsewhere we read that Pharaoh himself hardened his heart.[224] Similarly, God's people can pray: "O Lord, why do you make us err from your ways and harden our heart, so that we fear you not?" (Is 63:17). Yet, God Himself exhorts the same people, "Harden not your hearts" (Ps 95:8). To attribute to God the hardening of a heart or the crushing of bones is a way of expressing the conviction that God foresees everything and the everything depends on Him, not only for its existence but also for its actions. For, "in him we live and move and have our being" (Acts 17:28).

David knows that his unbearable state is the result of his sins: "Against you, you only, have I sinned, and done that which is evil in your sight" (Ps 51:4). Because the effect of his sin reaches to the very foundation of his being, his very bones, and thus to the very foundation of his relationship with God, David turns to the God who created that foundation and can restore it. Man cannot reach to the depths of the wound caused by his sin. Only God can restore life. He alone can revive a conscience crushed to death by the weight unreconciled guilt.

Especially during Lent, the Church takes to herself David's plea to be set free from the distress of conscience by the truth of God's mercy.

> [17] Relieve the troubles of my heart,
> and bring me out of my distresses.
> [18] Consider my affliction and my trouble,
> and forgive all my sins. (Psalm 25:17–18)

> Set me free from my distress, O Lord.
> See my lowliness and suffering,

---

[222] "Thus there is no reason why God should not have knowledge of individual effects, or why He should not directly regulate them by Himself, even though He may carry them out through intermediate causes. However, in the very execution He is, in some fashion, in immediate touch with all effects, to the extent that all intermediate causes operate in virtue of the first cause, so that in a certain way He Himself appears to act in them all" (Aquinas, *Compendium of Theology*, ch. 135). See also *Summa contra gentiles*, Bk. II, ch. 67 ("That God is the Cause of the Operation of All Things that Operate").
[223] See Ex 4:23; 7:3.
[224] See Ex 8:15, 32; 9:34.

and take away all my sins.225

> Be merciful, O Lord, to those who approach you in supplication, and, accepting the oblations and prayers of your people, turn the hearts of us all towards you.226

Lent only amplifies the prayer that the Church renews with every celebration of the Eucharist, when, following the recitation of the Lord's Prayer, the celebrate prays:

> Deliver us, Lord, we pray, from every evil,
> graciously grant peace in our days,
> that, by the help of your mercy,
> we may be always free from sin
> and safe from all distress, as we await the blessed hope
> and the coming of our Savior, Jesus Christ.

The psalm-prayer following Psalm 51 in the Liturgy of the Hours (Friday Morning Prayer, all four weeks) recapitulates, in terms of conscience, several of the themes—conscience, joy, glory—that have been discussed:

> Look upon our contrite heart and afflicted spirit and heal our troubled conscience, so that in the joy and strength of the Holy Spirit we may proclaim your praise and glory before all the nations.

Conscience is the spiritual organ by which man is able to hear God's voice of moral truth. For the seeker of truth, for the person whose conscience is right and receptive, God's truth "makes its entrance into the mind at once quietly and with power."227 God's truth comes to him like the "still small voice" (1 Kings 19:12) that Elijah experienced as his hope was being purified. In contrast, for a hardened heart, God's voice is an overpowering force, like the "great and strong wind [that] tore the mountains, and broke in pieces the rocks" (1 Kings 19:11), and the earthquake and fire that preceded the Lord's coming to Elijah as a still small voice. Indeed, "The voice of the Lord breaks the cedars ... shakes the wilderness ... makes the oaks to swirl" (Ps 29:5, 8, 9). The voice of the Lord both shatters and crushes, and comforts and heals. Its crushes in order to humble, by shattering the stronghold of pride. It humbles as a prelude to comforting, so that God's voice may find a home in the contrite heart.

The crushing, shaking, shattering effect of God's word lasts only for so long as the conscience is unable to recognize it and to receive it as a still small voice, and it can only do this once the stone-hard resistance of

---

225 Entrance Antiphon, Friday, First Week of Lent.
226 Prayer over the Offerings, Thursday, First Week of Lent.
227 Vatican II, *Dignitatis humanae*, 1.

impenitence is pulverized. The joy for which David prays is the joy of conversion, which brings an end to the judgment that crushes, shakes, and shatters the soul and ushers in a new season of being at home with God's word. The irrationality of despising God's word relinquishes to rationality, affliction cedes to gladness, sorrow transforms into joy, and the petition is granted: "Make us glad as many days as you have afflicted us, and as many years as we have seen evil" (Ps 90:15). When God forgives and reconciles, mourning turns into dancing, desolation into consolation, sorrow into joy. But, He forgives and reconciles only when the sinner's "period of service is ended" and his "guilt has been atoned for" (Is 40:2 NJB),[228] precisely by "bearing sufferings and trials of all kinds and ... accept[ing] this temporal punishment of sin as a grace."[229] By accepting the affliction of an accusing conscience as the just punishment of sin, that very punishment is transformed into the sacrifice of a humble and broken heart that is acceptable to God.[230]

At this precise point, when his conversion becomes a participation in God's work of turning the anguish of conscience into the joy of a new experience of His liberating mercy, David's conversion anticipates and participates in the paschal mystery of Christ, which is the one and only sacrifice that is acceptable to God. This is the "good" with which David intuits the Lord will bless him for enduring the affliction of the just punishment for his sins.[231] By confessing his sin and witnessing to God's mercy, David cooperates with the God "who encourages all those who are distressed" (2 Cor 7:6 NJB) and gives Him glory.

David's reference to joy and gladness thus aligns his interior state with that of St. Paul's mysterious rejoicing over his suffering: "Now I rejoice in my sufferings for your sake, and in my flesh I complete what is lacking in Christ's afflictions for the sake of his body, that is, the church" (Col 1:24). What Psalm 51 discloses about David's conversion glorifies the God of mercy and gives hope to all who confront the logic of sin. In this way, he prefigures the mission of St. Paul, who wrote about himself in order to exalt the God of mercy and to encourage sinners: "I received mercy for this reason, that in me, as the foremost, Jesus Christ might display his perfect patience for an example to those who were to believe in him for eternal life" (1 Tim 1:16). In this way, God is "justified in His words and blameless in His judgment."[232]

---

228 Because of their fundamental convergence, the variations in common English translations of Isaiah 40:2 are worth noting: "... her warfare is ended, that her iniquity is pardoned" (RSV, ESV); "... she has served her term, that her penalty is paid" (NRS); "... her service has ended, that her guilt is expiated" (NAB); " ... her warfare has ended, That her iniquity has been removed" (NAS); "... her evil is come to an end, her iniquity is forgiven" (DRA).
229 *CCC*, 1473.
230 In theological terms, punishment is transformed into satisfaction. See Jean-Hervé Nicolas, "Miséricorde et sévérité de Dieu," *Revue Thomiste* 94 (1988): 204–205.
231 See the discussion of 2 Sam 16:12, above.
232 See Ps 95:4 and the discussion of it above.

Everyone who by Baptism has entered into the paschal mystery is called to this kind of rejoicing in suffering: "Rejoice in so far as you share Christ's sufferings, that you may also rejoice and be glad when his glory is revealed" (1 Pet 4:13). In fact, Christians are only God's children and "fellow heirs with Christ, provided we suffer with him in order that we may also be glorified with him" (Rom 8:17). The Church, especially in the perfecting of Baptism in the celebration of the Eucharist, is the sacrament, that is, the sign and instrument, of the conversion that is a participation in Christ's paschal mystery and in the joy of the resurrection. The Church's mission is to live and to radiate the joy of conversion, the victory of God's mercy over sin, and thereby to give glory to God and comfort and hope to all whose bones have been crushed, to all who are afflicted by an accusing conscience.

This mission of joy is for all who cooperate with the grace that Christ merited in order to vanquish the evil of sin. Only the Holy Spirit, who searches the depths of God and of man, can disclose the full truth about sin and about God's mercy. Only He can convince the world about sin in a way that is simultaneously a convincing about God's mercy and redemption in Christ. And He does this in reference to the paschal mystery, which reveals both *"the entire dimension of evil* proper to sin"—the "mystery of iniquity" (2 Thess 2:7)—and *"the full dimension of the* ... 'mystery of religion' (1 Tim 3:16)."[233] The Holy Spirit is God's gift to those who accompany Christ into His paschal mystery. "From the greatest moral evil ever committed—the rejection and murder of God's only Son, caused by the sins of all men—God, by his grace that 'abounded all the more' (Rom 5:17), brought the greatest of goods: the glorification of Christ and our redemption"[234] by the gift of the Holy Spirit.

In light of the preceding, David's prayer for the joy that accompanies conversion is in effect a petition for the Holy Spirit. For, joy is a name for the Holy Spirit.[235] He is the gift that comes to us only after and because of the passion and death of Christ.[236] The Spirit's dwelling within those who believe in Christ and who participate in His paschal mystery is that Joy that

---

[233] John Paul II, *Dominum et Vivificantem*, 32.
[234] *CCC*, 312.
[235] "The Holy Spirit, in the Gospel according to Luke, is joy, in John's Gospel he is the same reality: joy is the Holy Spirit and the Holy Spirit is joy or, in other words from God we do not ask something small or great, from God we invoke the divine gift, God himself; this is the great gift that God gives us: God himself. In this regard we must learn to pray, to pray for the great reality, for the divine reality, so that God may give us himself, may give us his Spirit" (Benedict XVI, Lectio Divina, February 12, 2010).
[236] "Here it should be noted that, while all the other promises made in the Upper Room foretold the coming of the Holy Spirit *after* Christ's departure, the one contained in the text of John 16:7f. also includes and clearly emphasizes the relationship of interdependence which could be called *causal* between the manifestation of each: "If I go, I will send him to you." The Holy Spirit will come insofar as Christ will depart through the Cross: he will come not only *afterwards*, but *because of* the Redemption accomplished by Christ, through the will and action of the Father" (John Paul II, *Dominum et Vivificantem*, 8).

lay ahead of Christ and for the sake of which He endured the Cross.[237] Our conversion is rightly described as "a death event" because it is a participation in the death and resurrection of Christ. And for this reason, we too endure the pain of conversion for the sake of that same Joy.

St. Paul exhorts all Christians: "And you became imitators of us and of the Lord, for you received the word in much affliction, with the joy of the Holy Spirit" (1 Thess 1:6). In context, the affliction to which St. Paul refers here is the tribulation resulting from persecution. Its source, then, is exterior. Nevertheless, the strength to remain faithful in the midst of such trials derives from the interior conversion that entails the confrontation with the logic of sin and the acceptance of the affliction of an accusing conscience as sin's just punishment. This is participation in Christ's own being "very sorrowful, even to death" (Mt 26:38) because of the sins of the world. Since all forgiveness of sins comes through the paschal mystery and conforms the one forgiven to the one Who suffers in order to forgive, the word of God can only be received with interior, spiritual affliction or tribulation, which leads to Joy.[238]

> What God says to us is his truth, not ours; it becomes ours only when he utters and gives it to us, and we conform to it. For that reason it becomes a judgment on us in so far as we do not submit to God but rebel against him. We can only penetrate the truth of the Word as persons judged, recognizing the condemnation of their state as "outside the word." This act of judgment follows ineluctably and its necessity cannot be evaded or denied, once God pronounces his verdict upon sin, and on the old sinful world, which happened preeminently on the Cross.[239]

All of this is recapitulated, definitively promulgated as it were, the moment Christ pronounces the words "for you," "for many," and "for the forgiveness of sins" in the institution of the Eucharist: "This is my body which is given *for you*" (Lk 22:19); "this is my blood of the covenant, which is poured out *for many for the forgiveness of sins*" (Mt 26:28). The faith of David on display in his appeal to God's mercy and the faith of Catholics who approach Mercy Incarnate in the Eucharist is certainly creedal in the sense that it entails adherence to what God has revealed about Himself. For David, this is the history of God's marvelous works, and for Catholics it entails all of the doctrine that is summarized in the

---

237 See Heb 12:2.
238 The pattern of the Joy of the Holy Spirit following the suffering of purification from sin is foreshadowed in the dove, a symbol of the Holy Spirit, that returned to Noah with an olive leaf (Gen 8:11), indicating that the flood waters that purified the earth of sin were receding. This points to the significance of the Holy Spirit descending upon Jesus at His Baptism (see Lk 3:22). The Holy Spirit, the Spirit of Holiness, can only lite on that which is pure and sinless.
239 Hans Urs von Balthasar, *Prayer*, 175.

Creed. But, the adherence of faith cannot be reduced to assent to objective truths about God and what He has revealed. The Creed itself points to this in the two phrases, "for us men and for our salvation" and "for our sake." To profess one's faith is to profess that one has been enriched and transformed by God's love. It is to profess that God's love is efficacious, that it changes the human condition—that it has changed *my* condition, that I have been transformed and enriched. And, this awareness is the source of joy in the Holy Spirit.

David believes this in this "for me" dimension of God's love: "This I know, that God is *for me*" (Ps 56:9). "Come and hear, all you who fear God, and I will tell what he has done *for me*" (Ps 66:16). The great lesson of salvation history is that all that God does is for our sake and for our salvation. Faith is "knowing that one is loved by God,"[240] not only because He has told us this, but because His word of love is efficacious. It is every bit as efficacious in forgiving sins—"Your sins are forgiven" (Mt 9:2; Lk 7:48)—as it is in healing physical infirmities—"Rise and walk" (Mt 9:5)—and even in restoring those who have died to life: "Lazarus, come out!" (Jn 11:43); "Child, arise" (Lk 8:54); "Young man, I say to you, arise" (Lk 7:14). When Jesus says, "I forgive you; your sins are forgiven," those who are spiritually dead for having cut themselves off from God's love are restored to life.

This is why, "Faith is more than the mere acceptance of certain abstract truths: it is an intimate relationship with Christ, who enables us to open our hearts to this mystery of love and to live as men and women conscious of being loved by God."[241] "This is faith: being loved by God and letting oneself be loved by God in Jesus Christ."[242] St. Paul professes his faith in the profoundly personal terms of the "for me" correlation to Christ's love: "I live by faith in the Son of God who loved me and gave himself for me" (Gal 2:20). Pope Benedict XVI calls this St. Paul's "personal profession of faith," and comments:

> His faith is the experience of being loved by Jesus Christ in a very personal way. It is awareness of the fact that Christ did not face death for something anonymous but rather for love of him—of Paul—and that, as the Risen One, he still loves him; in other words, Christ gave himself for him. Paul's faith is being struck by the love of Jesus Christ, a love that overwhelms him to his depths and transforms him. His faith is not a theory, an opinion about God and the world. His faith is the impact of God's love in his heart.[243]

---

[240] Benedict XVI, Message for Lent, 2013 (dated October 15, 2012).
[241] Benedict XVI, Homily, August 20, 2011.
[242] Benedict XVI, General Audience, February 16, 2011.
[243] Benedict XVI, Homily, June 28, 2008.

This is the kind of faith that makes it possible for anyone afflicted by an accusing conscience to approach God. With the fulness of Christian revelation, this affliction is not reducible to an act of merely transgressing a divine commandment. The paschal mystery reveals that to sin is indeed to despise the word of God, as Nathan reproaches David, but now that word is not something that God has revealed but the Revealer Himself. Christ's passion and death reveal the effect that sin has on the Word of God Himself. Jesus' "for you," "for many," "for the forgiveness of sins" assure the conscience afflicted by the logic of sin that sin cannot cancel God's love *for me*. For, He speaks His words of love—"for you," "for many," "for the forgiveness of sins"—from within the very suffering that our sins have inflicted upon Him! That suffering unleashes God's love for sinners!

In this way, the affliction of conscience entails the dread of realizing that I am implicated in the crucifixion of Christ, that I am the cause of His suffering and death on the Cross, that I have entered into the paschal mystery as an active participant in Christ's suffering and death—as a member of the Sanhedrin that falsely condemns Him, as a Pilate who tries to remain uninvolved, as a soldier who tortures Him, as a Peter who denies Him. That is the perspective of faith, an unavoidable corollary derived from the fact that the meaning Jesus attributes to His suffering and death is that of a sacrifice *for* sinners.

There is a perfect correspondence, a symmetry as it were, between the physical appearance of the crucified Christ and the condition of the sinner's conscience. His lacerated and disfigured body was foreseen by Isaiah: "As many were astonished at him—his appearance was so marred, beyond human semblance, and his form beyond that of the sons of men" (Is 52:14). "The whole of this body, hands, feet and every bone, ... is in a state of utmost tension: bones, muscles, nerves, every organ, every cell is stretched and strained to breaking point.... the terrible tension driving its way into hands, feet and every bone: driving its way into his entire body which, nailed like a mere thing to the beams of the Cross, is about to be utterly 'voided' in the convulsive agony of death."[244] By looking upon His mutilated body, the sinner sees the condition of his own disfigured conscience, contorted to the point of being beyond recognition.

There is no joy in realizing that the crucified Christ is the one whom my sins have pierced.[245] There is no joy in seeing the wretched state of my own conscience as the reflection of what His body was reduced to. This definitive, christological dimension of the logic of sin, cut off from the truth about God's mercy, can only lead to the experience of life being an unbearable burden. Judas' hanging of himself is the definitive conclusion drawn from the logic of sin, the inevitable outcome of precipice spirituality when the fatal vertigo of a conscience tormented by unreconciled guilt triggers a freefall into the dark despair of the Pit. For, isolated from the

---

244 Cardinal Wojtyła, Meditation on the 11th Station of the Cross (*Sign of Contradiction*, 192).
245 "The human heart is converted by looking upon him whom our sins have pierced (cf. Jn 19:37; Zech 12:10)" (*CCC*, 1432).

revelation of God's mercy, one cannot see the full truth about the affliction of conscience. One cannot see that it is a gift of grace, a participation in the Son of God's own suffering caused by sin.[246]

Conversion is the resurrection of a conscience that has died to the truth. In His mercy, the risen Lord says what He once said to the entombed Lazarus: "Arise! Come out!" Because He says this to sinners precisely as the Risen One, that is, as the one who Himself died because of sins, conversion is always a participation in His dying and rising. The Word of God that was put to death by being despised, rejected, and disobeyed, rises to speak anew the living truth in the conscience. Conversion is the reliving of the paschal mystery, in which the desolation of death leads to the joy of new life.

St. Augustine and St. Thomas concur that the very anguish of conscience over sin, viewed now in relation to faith and hope in God's mercy, can be a source of joy.

> A man may be displeased at having sinned, and be pleased at his displeasure together with his hope for pardon, so that his very sorrow is a matter of joy. Hence Augustine says (*De poenitentia*, Ch. XIII): "The penitent should ever grieve and rejoice at his grief."[247]

David's joy in conversion is a participation in God's joy over the restoration of Jerusalem. It is, as already discussed, joy in the victory of God's fidelity and mercy over man's infidelity and sin. It is joy in the glory of God. And, just as the Holy Spirit is Joy, He is also Glory.[248] This is to say that man redeemed from his sins by Christ, man living in the joy of knowing that He is loved by God by the witness of the Holy Spirit, man, fully alive in Christ by the Holy Spirit and empowered to make a gift of himself by fulfilling the commandments to love God and neighbor, man who praises God above all for His mercy, fully revealed in the paschal mystery, man for whom, therefore, the Eucharist is the center of his life— this man is the glory of God.[249] Again, the joy that David associates with conversion anticipates the christological fulfillment of the theme of sorrow being turned into joy. For those who accept, as the just punishment, that their sins are the cause of Christ's suffering, their conversion and restoration to the love for which they are made is the cause of His joy, the very Joy for the sake of which He endured the Cross.[250]

Imagine the lost sheep, whose absence so distresses its shepherd that he simply cannot go on with his day. So great is his affection for his sheep that all other activities cease until he finds his precious lost sheep. Now imagine

---

246 See John Paul II, *Dominum et Vivificantem*, 45.
247 Aquinas, *ST* III, Q. 84, a. 9, ad 2.
248 See *CCC*, 690, 693, 697, 705.
249 See John Paul II, *Dominum et Vivificantem*, 59.
250 "... let us run with perseverance the race that is set before us, looking to Jesus the pioneer and perfecter of our faith, who for the joy that was set before him endured the Cross, despising the shame, and is seated at the right hand of the throne of God" (Heb 12:1–2).

this sheep being graced to transcend his own fear over being lost, and that instead of thinking of himself he begins to think of his shepherd and the state of his anguished heart. And so, this sheep begins to do what he can to find his way home, knowing that the anguish of his shepherd's heart will only cease when the two are reunited. The same sheep who by wandering away distresses his shepherd's heart has the power to bring him joy.

Or, imagine a different version of the Parable of the Prodigal Son. Imagine that the older son goes looking for his brother in order to inform him that his absence is causing their father such grief that he is dying of a broken heart, and begs him to return home *for the sake of his father*. Imagine that this news allows him to see the full truth about his sin in relation to his father, that it has struck a mortal blow to his love, and that this realization shatters his self-centeredness.

To love is to unite oneself with another. Love unites two destinies, so that the sorrows and joys of the one who is loved become the sorrows and joys of the one who loves. Thus, to love is to cede to the one whom you love the power to inflict grief and the power to cause joy. Thus, God's love for His people is revealed when He sorrows and delights over Jerusalem, depending on the city's prosperity, which depends on the fidelity of its inhabitants. The paschal mystery of Jesus Christ reveals that God Himself is afflicted when those whom He loves reject His love and turn away from Him, and He rejoices over the conversion of sinners, when they open themselves anew to His love, which takes the form of mercy because mercy is love that keeps loving when it has been rejected.

Sinners have the power to inflict paschal suffering on the Sacred Heart of Jesus, but they also have the power to elicit that joy for the sake of which He embraces that suffering. As He endured the Cross for the sake of that joy, sinners endure their own cross of an accusing conscience for the sake of that same joy. The greatest of sorrows is transformed into the greatest of joys. In the last of the beatitudes, Jesus declares blessed those who participate in His suffering over sin: "Blessed are you when men revile you and persecute you and utter all kinds of evil against you falsely on my account. Rejoice and be glad, for your reward is great in heaven, for so men persecuted the prophets who were before you" (Mt 5:11–12).

The joy of conversion, then, is twofold. It is the joy to which sinners can look forward as the fruit of conversion and reconciliation with God. It is participation in Christ's own joy over repentant sinners. It is also the joy for the sake of which those who are reconciled with Christ participate in His suffering for the conversion of sinners. This joy even accompanies participation in Christ's suffering because one has come to see its place in the redemptive plan of God's mercy.

This is the foundation for St. Thérèse of Lisieux believing that God had granted her power over His own heart.

> "I confide in Jesus," she says, "I relate to Him in detail my infidelities, thinking in my daring abandonment to acquire in

this way more power over His Heart and to win more fully the love of Him who is not come to call the just but sinners to repentance."[251]

Such is the boldness, the *parrhesía* of her faith and hope in the mercy of God, Who never fails to attend to the cry of the poor. For, "He delivers the needy when he calls, the poor and him who has no helper" (Ps 72:12). The sinner has no other helper because only God can forgive sins. He is the only hope of those afflicted by the poverty of an accusing conscience, the poverty of unreconciled guilt, the realization that one is deprived of love for having rejected it. This is the greatest of all forms of poverty. And when a person acknowledges this poverty as contrary to his true happiness and desires anew to be loved by God, St. Thérèse further assures us that "God cannot inspire unrealizable desires."[252] If ever there were a desire inspired by God it is the desire to be forgiven by Him and to be reconciled with Him, the desire to be loved by Him. For, God is love, and in the suffering of Christ He has revealed the full extent of the evil of rejecting His love, and, from the heart of Christ's sacrifice He sends the Holy Spirit to convince the world concerning sin and concerning God's merciful love. By this action of the Holy Spirit, He makes us desire what He desires:

> Have I any pleasure in the death of the wicked, says the Lord God, and not rather that he should turn from his way and live? (Ezekiel 18:23)

> As I live, says the Lord God, I have no pleasure in the death of the wicked, but that the wicked turn from his way and live; turn back, turn back from your evil ways. (Ezekiel 33:11)

Again, St. Thérèse assures us that God makes us desire what He wants to give us.[253] "The more God wishes to bestow on us the more He makes us desire."[254]

Christ has instituted this dynamic of mirroring desires in the sacraments of Baptism and Penance, wherein "the encounter of God's thirst with ours" takes place. These sacraments are the realization of the truth that "God thirsts that we may thirst for him."[255] So long as a penitent approaches the mercy of Christ in these sacraments with true contrition, he is assured by Christ's own pledge and knows in advance that he will be forgiven.

---

[251] Vernon Johnson, *Spiritual Childhood* (New York: Sheed and Ward, 1954), 93.
[252] Thérèse of Lisieux, *Story of a Soul. The Autobiography of St. Thérèse of Lisieux*. John Clarke, trans. (Washington, D.C.: Institute of Carmelite Studies, 1975 [2nd edition, 1976]), 207.
[253] "He has always given me what I desire or rather He has made me desire what He wants to give me" (ibid., 25).
[254] Thérèse of Lisieux, "Act of Oblation as a Victim of Divine Love," June 9, 1895.
[255] *CCC*, 2560.

In christological terms, to rejoice in this suffering means to perceive that mysterious necessity that the Messiah "should suffer these things and enter into His glory" (Lk 24:16). For the repentant sinner, this corresponds to the necessity of the just punishment for sin called moral suffering or remorse, which if accepted and borne with awareness of its place in God's plan, becomes a salvific moment in the individual's participation in Christ's redemptive suffering. Believing this, the anguish of conscience is a reason for joy.

The logic of contrition and conversion, then, is that the sinner's love for God is not sufficiently mature and strong so as to enable him to avoid sinning in the first place. Yet, like David and St. Peter, his love is sufficiently mature and strong so as to enable him to be grieved by his sin. It is this love, manifesting itself now in penitential sorrow, that is the source of joy. For, the sinner realizes that it is right and just that he should so grieve. Imagine a sequel to the parable of the prodigal son, in which years after his conversion and reinstatement as his father's son he sins again, leaving his father's house in search of some illusory promise of happiness. Imagine his humiliation and self-accusation, but imagine above all else his memory of his father's joyous welcome when he returned home. Now he sees his new form of destitution and of humiliation in light of his father's mercy, which recognizes in precisely this experience of destitution and humiliation, this experience of an accusing conscience, the son's return to truth about his sin, which can only mean that he has returned to the truth about his true happiness as son of his father. This return to the truth about himself in relation to his father is the essence of his return to his father. All that remains is for this interior return to express itself in the exterior, physical return. During his return home, he can see the rightness and justness of the suffering that caused his interior return, and rejoice in it in anticipation of his father's joy upon his return.

Such is the sacrifice of a broken, humble, and contrite heart, which is pleasing to God. A sacrifice is an offering to God for the purpose of obtaining a benefit from Him. God is love and desires to give, and what He desires to give most is Himself. To offer such a heart to God is simply, and only, to offer nothing but a desire—a desire pleasing to God, to be sure, but a desire ineffective in itself to remedy the misery of sin. God's desire is the cause of forgiveness and reconciliation, but He desires the sinner's cooperation, and that cooperation is simply his desire to be loved.

The liturgical offering of bread and wine in Mass symbolizes this humble recognition of total dependence upon God. At the Offertory, every believer can make his own the words of St. Andrew, who with a little boy offered to Jesus just a little bit of bread and a few fish, realizing how disproportionate they were to the need: "but what are they among so many?" (Jn 6:9). The bread and wine that priests take into their hands symbolize the desire of each of the faithful to be nourished so as to live up to the word of God that was proclaimed in the Liturgy of the Word. Just as the bread and wine are acknowledged to be God's gifts, so too this desire is already a gift of grace. But of itself it is not enough. Making an offering of it, we recognize that unless Jesus bless it and multiply it, our desire to be loved by Him and to love Him in return is not enough. Only Christ multiplies it by uniting it with His paschal charity does it become strong enough for us to love God "to the end" (Jn 13:1).

Just as by faith we know in advance that God is pleased with this offering and will bless it and multiply it, David knows that God will not spurn the desire of his humble and contrite heart. Christians know that the reason is that in it He sees the pierced Sacred Heart of His own Son. David can make the offering, but God must do the cleansing. This is clear in David's petitions: "Wash me thoroughly from my iniquity, and cleanse me from my sin!"—for I cannot; "Purge me with hyssop, and I shall be clean; wash me, and I shall be whiter than snow" (Ps 51:2, 7)—for I can neither purge nor wash myself. For, only God's mercy is able to wash away the sin that has rejected His love. Because it is the nature of love to be a gift, the repentant sinner is totally dependent upon God. His hope is in what God has revealed about his humble and contrite heart being the sacrifice that He will never spurn.

On man's part, then, conversion is the desire to receive God's love anew. In this the parallel between the spiritual death of sin and physical death is exact. For, for man who is made in the image of Love, "to live is to love, and to love is to live."[256] Only the One Who is Life and Love and Who has created man for life and love can restore them when they are lost by sin. Scripture calls this a "new creation."[257]

It is possible that David's reference to hyssop is based on the ritual for cleansing lepers.[258] In his time, the scourge of leprosy was a kind of death, certainly a prelude to the death of the body, but also death to living in society, and thus death to love. For people with faith, leprosy was an inescapable occasion to be aware of total dependence upon God. Once the gift of health was lost, only a miraculous intervention by God could restore it. David sees his sins as a spiritual leprosy. They have defiled him and cut him off from Life and Love. If God does not exercise His sovereign power to heal him with the hyssop of mercy, David will remain a man whose fundamental way of relating to others—and to himself—is to cry out: "Unclean, unclean" (Lev 13:45). For his spiritual leprosy, David seems to intuit that his tears of contrition, signs of the broken and contrite heart that is a sacrifice acceptable to God, are the hyssop through which the Lord cleanses sins.[259]

The definitive answer to David's plea to be cleansed of sin will come when the Son of God heals the lepers of His day[260] as a sign of His

---

256 John Paul II, Homily, February 20, 1981, 3.
257 See 2 Cor 5:27; Gal 6:15.
258 See Lev 14:1–7, 33–53. See Jacques Guillet, "Le Psaume Miserere," in *La Maison Dieu*, No 23 (1953): 65–66.
259 David's tears of repentance, then, anticipate the conversion of Christian Baptism and the tradition of associating tears with Baptism, even using the expression "baptism of tears."
260 See Mt 8:2–4; 26:6; Lk 7:22; 17:12–19.

authority to heal the leprosy of sin.[261] It is noteworthy that in the account of the healing of ten lepers, the one who returns to praise God for the gift of his healing receives an additional gift from Jesus. He is the only one who hears Jesus say, "Your faith has saved you" (Lk 17:19 NAB). Jesus has more to give than just to heal leprosy. His cures of physical illness are intended to be a first act of love for men in their need, a contact at the level at which so many live and measure their happiness, namely, physical well being and prosperity. The remarkable thing is that the very process of exercising His saving power over physical ailments becomes the occasion for the one being healed to discover that there is more to Jesus than just this power over the forces of nature. The leper, the man born blind, the woman with a hemorrhage[262]—all these approach Jesus in the hope of being healed of their ailment, and they all leave having received a far superior gift, the gift of faith.

This inseparability between physical and spiritual healing in Jesus' mission, as well as the order between the two, especially in the case of leprosy, casts an important light on Jesus' proclamation that He did not come to abolish the Law but to fulfill it.[263] His power to heal lepers effectively renders obsolete all of the Law regarding leprosy.[264] The Law, as St. Paul so clearly sees, could only put a curb on sin and its consequences. Concerning leprosy, the regulations of the Law intended to curtail its extension. That is the most that any spiritual discipline or set of spiritual exercises can accomplish. Even under the New Law, so long as these are understood as man's efforts to develop virtues in order to obtain victory over sin. This is not, however, an adequate understanding of the New Law of Christ. Christian action is always a response to the love of God, Who first loves us, and a cooperation with this same love, which must always have the primacy. Christian action is the fruit of the gift received. The apostles can acquire and distribute the food that Jesus multiplies, but only He can multiply it. The woman with a hemorrhage can make the effort to seek Jesus, but only He can heal her. Blind men can cry out to Him, expressing their desire to be healed, but of itself their desire is not sufficient for their healing. Only when Jesus receives the desire and unites it to His own desire are man's desires and efforts fulfilled.

The metaphor that takes sin as the enemy and the life of faith as a battle against this enemy can lead to the misunderstanding that sin is something real, with its own existence. But it is not. Sin is a void, the absence of love, and only the One Who is Love can fill this void. Just as God brings beings into existence from nothing, so only He can make love present where sin has vacated it. This is what redemptive substitution means.

---

[261] See Mk 2:1–12.
[262] See Mt 9:22; Lk 18:42.
[263] See Mt 5:17.
[264] See Lev 13:45–14:57.

What confers on substitution its redemptive value is not the material fact that an innocent person has suffered the chastisement deserved by the guilty and that justice has thus been in some way satisfied.... The redemptive value comes instead from the fact that the innocent Jesus, out of pure love, entered into solidarity with the guilty and thus transformed their situation from within. In fact, when a catastrophic situation such as that caused by sin is taken upon oneself on behalf of sinners out of pure love, then this situation is no longer under the sign of opposition to God, but, on the contrary, it is under the sign of docility to the love which comes from God (Gal 3:13–14).... Thus this "substitution" signifies the "superabundance" of love which overcomes every deficiency of human love, every negation and contrariety linked with human sin in every dimension.[265]

St. Francis of Assisi conveys the essentials of this kind of substitution in the prayer that is attributed to him: "Lord, make me a channel of Your peace, that where there is hatred, wrong, discord, error, doubt, despair, shadows, sadness ... I may bring love, the spirit of forgiveness, harmony, truth, faith, hope, light, joy." The answer to the evil of sin is a substitution that Cardinal Ratzinger calls "a replacement of the subject." Drawing on the Church's faith in the Sacrament of Baptism as participation in the paschal mystery of Christ, an event of dying and being raised to new life, he describes conversion as

> something more radical than a mere revision of a few opinions or attitudes. It is a death event.[266] In other words it is the replacement of the subject. The 'I' ceases to be independent and to be a subject existing in itself. It is torn from itself and inserted into a new subject. The 'I' does not perish, but in effect it must let itself fall completely in order to be received within a larger 'I' and together with it be conceived anew.

---

265 John Paul II, General Audience, October 26, 1988, 4.
266 Ratzinger may be thinking of a text of Basil the Great here: "The plan of God and our Redeemer for human beings consists in calling them back from exile and bringing them back from the alienation which came about because of disobedience.... For the perfection of life it is necessary to imitate Christ, not only in terms of the meekness, humility, and patience exhibited in his *life*, but also in terms of his *death*.... How do we achieve a similarity to his death? ... What is to be won by this emulation? First of all, it is necessary to break through the form of our past life. According to the word of the Lord this is not possible if one is not reborn (cf. Jn 3:3). For rebirth is ... the beginning of a second life. To begin a second life, however, one must put an end to the first.... [W]hen lives change direction, there is obviously a death necessary between the lives which ends what has gone before and begins what is to follow" (quoted in *A New Song for the Lord. Faith in Christ and Liturgy Today* [New York: Crossroad Publishing Company, 1997], 19–20).

> The replacement of the subject, about which we are speaking, cannot be brought about by the subject himself. That would be illogical and even senseless. In such a case the subject would still be at work but in the futile effort of trying to break out of his own subjectivity. The replacement of the subject involves a passive element that Paul calls death, and for good reason, since it has to do with a participation in the event of the Lord's Cross. It can take place only from the outside, starting from the other. Christian conversion breaks down the barrier between the 'I' and the "other" and so must begin with this other and can never be accomplished in the isolation of the self.[267]

Faith is the awareness that as a result of encountering God's mercy in Christ this substitution of life in Christ for the void of sin has taken place. To believe in Christ means to acknowledge that He has received my desire to be liberated from slavery to sin, accompanied by the remorse of a humble and contrite heart, as an acceptable sacrifice, and united my intention to His intention. As a result, my very being bears witness to the liberation that He has brought about, even as the restored wholeness of a leper or a blind man bears witness to His healing power. And since this liberation occurs by way of substitution, faith entails professing, with St. Paul, "I have been crucified with Christ; it is no longer I who live, but Christ who lives in me; and the life I now live in the flesh I live by faith in the Son of God, who loved me and gave himself for me" (Gal 2:20).

Once again, we see how David's experience of his sin and of God's mercy places him at the heart of the mystery of Christ. Even though the definitive revelation of divine mercy must wait for a full millennium, the mystery of Christ is already at work in the heart of the king whose name is in one of the titles most frequently used for Jesus: son of David.[268] The forgiveness of sins is God's work, yet He desires a genuine cooperation on our part. The wonder of God's grace is seen in those who, like David, offer to God the sacrifice of a humble and contrite heart. By itself this offering cannot bring about the forgiveness and reconciliation with God that is sought, just as the humble offering of a small boy's five loaves and two fish was too little to feed a large crowd. It is always possible to repeat the words of Andrew, and to attend to the great discrepancy between what is offered and the intended goal: "What are they among so many?" Yet, faith inspires us to make the offering, confident that what for men is impossible is not impossible for God, "for all things are possible with God" (Mk 10:27). God will always be faithful to Himself and, just as Jesus received the bread and fish offered to Him and the intention that accompanied that

---

[267] Joseph Ratzinger, Address at St. Michael's College in Toronto, April 15, 1986. See also his *Principles of Catholic Theology*, 55–67.
[268] See Mt 1:1; 9:27; 12:23; 15:22; 20:30–31; 21:9, 15; 22:42.

offering, so He loves to bless and to multiply the intentions of humble and contrite hearts. He accomplishes this by uniting them to the sacrifice of His own pierced heart, which He offers to the Father as His own intention for the forgiveness of sins, knowing that it is the only sacrifice acceptable to the Father. Because by faith we know as it were in advance that the Son's sacrifice is accepted by the Father, we can be certain and know in advance that God will not spurn a humble and contrite heart that approaches Him in the Sacrament of Confession and unites itself with His sacrifice in the Eucharist. A natural result of our knowledge, implicit in the above remarks, is that we become more aware that God wishes to extend this same mercy to others.

Solidarity with Sinners

In the first sketched portrait of David, before his conversion, a sense of his own innocence accompanies the bold confidence he has in God's protection. David could count on God to fulfill His promises because he considered himself blameless. After all, isn't it an article of faith that if God's people listen to Him and adhere to His precepts, He will be their God and they will be His people?[269] At this early stage in his spiritual journey, David seems to have no awareness of his own limitations, weakness, and capacity to be unfaithful and to turn away from God. Psalm 17 has already been quoted as indicative of David's state of mind at this stage in his life. Another psalm is no less apropos.

> [1] Vindicate me, O Lord,
> for I have walked in my integrity,
> and I have trusted in the Lord without wavering.
> [2] Prove me, O Lord, and try me;
> test my heart and my mind.
> [3] For your mercy is before my eyes,
> and I walk in faithfulness to you.
> [4] I do not sit with false men,
> nor do I consort with dissemblers;
> [5] I hate the company of evildoers,
> and I will not sit with the wicked.
> [6] I wash my hands in innocence,
> and go about your altar, O Lord,
> [7] singing aloud a song of thanksgiving,
> and telling all your wondrous deeds.
> [8] O Lord, I love the habitation of your house,
> and the place where your glory dwells.
> [9] Sweep me not away with sinners,
> nor my life with bloodthirsty men,
> [10] men in whose hands are evil devices,

---

269 See Jer 7:23; 11:24.

and whose right hands are full of bribes.
¹¹ But as for me, I walk in my integrity;
redeem me, and have mercy on me.
¹² My foot stands on level ground,
in the great congregation I will bless the Lord. (Psalm 26:1–12)

Similar to the Pharisee whom Jesus contrasts to the humble tax collector as both pray in the Temple,[270] it is not humility and contrition that fill David's soul when he thinks of God's house. Rather, he considers how his integrity separates him from sinners.

The difference in the way David expresses himself in several other psalms points to a transformation that results from his conversion. In the *Miserere*, the psalm so named by the first word of the Latin translation, which means, "Have mercy," he straightforwardly acknowledges his sin and petitions the Lord that He not cast him away from His presence.[271] If "presence" is a reference to the glory of God in the Tent of Meeting (or the Temple), then it is clear that David is expressing a sense of unworthiness. This is confirmed by his insight that the sacrifice that is acceptable to God is a broken and contrite heart. Penitence is the disposition that gives man access to God's presence. It is the state of "truth in the inward being" (Ps 51:6) when a person is aware of having sinned and with faith in God's mercy "takes sides with the truth against himself." David's newly acquired awareness of sin leads him to declare: "Behold, I was brought forth in iniquity, and in sin did my mother conceive me" (Ps 51:5). From seeing sin only in others he comes to see it in himself. God has answered his prayer that He clear him of his "hidden faults" (Ps 19:12).

This reference to hidden faults indicates that David has come to understand the condition of his own heart prior to the intervention of God's word through Nathan. His faults remain hidden from him until God's word uncovers them and brings them to light. What does it mean to avoid the encounter with God's word in the conscience, to harden one's heart against God's word so as to make it impenetrable to His truth? In the light of his encounter with God's mercy, David knows. One of the fruits of conversion is the clarity with which he is able to see and the lucidity with which he is then able to describe this state of impenetrability of conscience:

¹ Transgression speaks to the wicked deep in his heart;
there is no fear of God before his eyes.
² For he flatters himself in his own eyes
that his iniquity cannot be found out and hated. (Psalm 36:1–2).

In a telling verse of the *Miserere*, David interjects that he will teach God's ways to sinners so that they may return to Him: "I will teach transgressors your ways, and sinners will return to you" (Ps 51:13).

---

270 See Lk 18:10–14.
271 See Ps 51:11.

David's graces of repentance are not just for him. God wants to reach others through him and with his cooperation. David's heightened sense of sin and of God's mercy constitute a mission: "Every one to whom much is given," Jesus teaches, "of him will much be required; and of him to whom men commit much they will demand the more" (Lk 12:48). The king's new mission concerns that kingdom of another order, the kingdom within, of which the son of David, Jesus of Nazareth, is king.

David's awareness of the link between his experience of being saved by God's mercy and the mission to bear witness to it so that sinners will return to God reproduces the movement of Psalm 22, the first words of which Jesus makes His own as He hangs on the cross: "My God, my God, why have you forsaken me?" (Ps 22:1). Certainly, also, He made His own the desperate cry of the one who seems to be abandoned:

> [19] O Lord, do not be far away!
> O my help, come quickly to my aid!
> [20] Deliver my soul from the sword,
> my life from the power of the dog!
> [21] Save me from the mouth of the lion!
> From the horns of the wild oxen you have rescued me. (Psalm 22:19–21)

Then, anticipating that the Father will answer this prayer for deliverance, by His resurrection that bears witness to the Father's power and mercy, Jesus perfectly fulfills the mission to proclaim the marvelous work of God:

> [22] I will tell of your name to my brothers and sisters;
> in the midst of the congregation I will praise you:
> [23] You who fear the Lord, praise him!
> All you offspring of Jacob, glorify him;
> stand in awe of him, all you offspring of Israel!
> [24] For he did not despise or abhor
> the affliction of the afflicted;
> he did not hide his face from me,
> but heard when I cried to him.
> [25] From you comes my praise in the great congregation.
> (Psalm 22:22–25)

Like Jesus, David fulfills his mission as king through teaching and through sacrifice. Regarding teaching, St. Thomas comments that those who have not experienced God's mercy should not exercise the office of teaching about God, since they do not know Him according to His greatest attribute. It is only "after God has restored to him the perfect spirit that it is right that such persons should both have doctrine and teach others: 'I will give you pastors according to my own heart and they shall feed you with knowledge and doctrine' (Jer 3:15)."[272] St. Thomas remarks that this teaching is ordered both to the contemplation of God and to the conversion of sinners. The two are inseparable, since the conversion of sinners is God's greatest work and the effect of His greatest attribute, mercy. He also states that it is the fruit of his love for God. Having been loved by God, David now has a mission to love others as God has loved him. David accomplishes this mission also through the sacrifice of praise. The experience of God's mercy opens his lips to praise God for His chief attribute of mercy. The entire Psalter may be considered the fruit of David's conversion and as a sacrifice of praise and thanksgiving[273] that, being observed by sinners, elevates their minds to the truth about God's mercy, gives them hope, and instructs them about the perfect spiritual sacrifice that Jesus Christ will definitively offer to God. This anticipates the witness and pedagogical value of Christian liturgy. "For the liturgy, 'through which the work of our redemption is accomplished,' most of all in the divine sacrifice of the Eucharist, is the outstanding means whereby the faithful may express in their lives, and manifest to others, the mystery of Christ and the real nature of the true Church."[274]

David's mission of mercy is directed to those who, like him, have confronted the reality of sin within themselves. David understands them, he knows them, because he knows himself. He is like a recovering alcoholic who has a special empathy for other alcoholics who have not yet taken sides with the truth against themselves, or like a woman in whom there has been an unleashing of a special love for women shackled by post-abortion syndrome because she has emerged from that dark night of crippling regret. David no longer considers himself set apart from sinners, but one among them. Having experienced the cleansing power of God's mercy, he is like a leper who, having encountered Jesus and having been healed by him, rushes off to inform the entire colony of lepers that there is hope for them. His mission is to resurrect necrotic hope. His own being, renewed by the love of Christ, is all the evidence they need. David has

---

272 Aquinas, *Commentary on the Psalms*, Psalm 50 [51] (Marietti, 507).
273 "The flow of the psalms in some ways follows the fortunes of David's kingdom, and key royal psalms occur at strategic locations in the literary structure of the Psalter. In this way, the Psalter presents a spirituality of prayer and praise that is grounded on the promises of the Davidic covenant and radically open to the fulfillment of those promises in the New Covenant (see especially Ps 89). The theme of the Psalter can be summarized by the well-known refrain, "Give thanks to the Lord, for he is good; his *mercy* [Hebrew *hesed*] endures forever." Once it is understood that *hesed* refers specifically to *covenant fidelity*, it becomes apparent that the Psalms as a book constitute one act of praise to God for his faithfulness to his covenant promises" (John Bergsma and Brant Pitre, *A Catholic Introduction to the Bible, Vol. I: The Old Testament* [San Francisco: Ignatius Press, 2018], 534). "In sum, the movement from lament to thanksgiving for deliverance is typical of a great many psalms. In fact, generally speaking, the Psalter itself moves from a concentration of lament psalms in book 1 to a concentration of thanksgivings and hymns in book 5. Thus we can say that many individual psalms, and the Psalter as a whole, display a "*todah* shape" (Bergsma and Pitre, *A Catholic Introduction*, 585).
274 Vatican II, *Sacrosanctum Concilium*, 2.

been brought out of the darkness of sin, and now his mission is to lead others out of darkness into the light of God's mercy.[275] David knows that the desire of every sinner for liberation from unreconciled guilt is, in reality, a desire to encounter Jesus: "We wish to see Jesus" (Jn 12:21).

The same sense of solidarity with sinners appears in Psalm 32. Here, too, David's worship springs from the depths of his experience of God's mercy, yet he also speaks for all who have confronted their sin and encountered God's healing mercy. He begins with a beatitude:

> ¹ Blessed is he whose transgression is forgiven,
> whose sin is covered.
> ² Blessed is the man to whom the Lord imputes no iniquity,
> and in whose spirit there is no deceit. (Psalm 32:1–2)

The repentant king's liturgy of praise issues from the liturgy of his sacrifice of a broken and contrite heart. His experience of God's mercy becomes liturgy. Just as the whole being of a healed leper proclaims the efficacious love of God, so David's whole life is a liturgy, a "spiritual worship" (Rom 12:1). He has been "transformed by the renewal of [his] mind" (Rom 12:2), bringing a radical change in the way that he relates to God and to men. Thanks and praise interpenetrate as he sings of what God has done *for him*. Having been healed of the leprosy of sin, the truth about man's sin and God's mercy constitutes the very meaning of life.

To drive home the tremendous blessing of having been forgiven, David describes what life is like so long as man does not confess his sins to God.

> ³ When I declared not my sin, my body wasted away
> through my groaning all day long.
> ⁴ For day and night your hand was heavy upon me;
> my strength was dried up as by the heat of summer. (Psalm 32:3–4)

With these words, David describes life in the Pit, the absence of the blessing. The joy of conversion and reconciliation with God becomes a lens through which he can see his former state. This is the condition of a person burdened by an accusing conscience. Cut off from His mercy, the thought of God only adds to the burden of life for a person who is aware of his sin.

St. John Paul II does not hesitate to interpret these verses as describing the experience of unreconciled guilt in one's conscience.

> Above all, the person praying describes his very distressful state of conscience by keeping it "secret" (cf. v. 3): having committed grave offenses, he did not have the courage to confess his sins to God. It was a terrible interior torment,

---

275 See Jn 8:12; 12:46; 1 Jn 2:8.

described with very strong images. His bones waste away, as if consumed by a parching fever; thirst saps his energy and he finds himself fading, his groan constant. The sinner felt God's hand weighing upon him, aware as he was that God is not indifferent to the evil committed by his creature, since he is the guardian of justice and truth.

Unable to hold out any longer, the sinner made the decision to confess his sin with a courageous declaration that seems a prelude to that of the prodigal son in Jesus' parable (cf. Lk 15:18). Indeed, he said with a sincere heart: "I will confess my offense to the Lord." The words are few but born from conscience: God replies immediately to them with generous forgiveness (cf. v. 5).[276]

Unable to hold out any longer! With missionary zeal, David sets before us two contrasting ways to live. In the spirit of Moses, it is an appeal to reflect and to be reasonable: "I have set before you life and death, blessing and curse; therefore choose life, that you and your descendants may live" (Dt 30:19). For, "He who conceals his transgressions will not prosper, but he who confesses and forsakes them will obtain mercy" (Prov 28:13).

The Burden of Sin and the Sabbath Rest

David's experience of God as a burden seems to contrast with Job's anguished question to God, "Why I have I become a burden to you" (Job 7:20). For both God and for His image, sin is a burden. For David, the thought of sin, cut off from God's mercy, becomes a crushing weight: "Day and night your hand was heavy upon me" (Ps 32:4[277]); "For my iniquities have gone over my head; they weigh like a burden too heavy for me" (Ps 38:4). The contrast of Judas and St. Peter proves the gravity of this burden. Both betrayed Jesus. For Peter, who considers the truth about sin along with the truth about God's mercy, there is repentance and new life, while for Judas, who holds out in not confessing his sin, in refusing to believe in mercy, the truth about his sin is an unbearable burden, there is despair and death.

In the Book of Job, Israel wrestles with the possibility of a sin that remains hidden from them.[278] For, according to the prevailing theology of the time, misfortune such as that experienced by Job must be a divine punishment for sin. Job projects his experience of conscience onto God.

---

[276] John Paul II, General Audience, May 19, 2004, 2–3.
[277] Similarly, Job: "Today also my complaint is bitter, his hand is heavy in spite of my groaning" (Job 23:2).
[278] See Barthélemy, *God and His Image*, Chapter 1: The Wrong View of God: Job.

Unreconciled guilt is a burden because sinful man is a burden to God.[279] He could live in peace and enjoy his life but for the awareness that God keeps oppressing him with a sense of guilt. Job, that is, Israel, would find solace and resolution in the Christian faith that conscience is the faculty that detects the voice of God and that the same God Who fashions man to experience guilt provides an answer to it by becoming man and offering Himself as a sacrifice for the expiation of this guilt. In Christ it is true that sin is a burden for both God and for man. In His three falls while carrying the Cross and in His death, Christ reveals that man cannot shoulder this burden, that its weight crushes him. And in His resurrection He reveals that only God can remove it.

A "theology of burden" is not complete without consideration of the prophet Jeremiah. There were many among the people of his time who hardened their hearts against him because they found his oracles to be hard sayings, inconvenient truths that conflicted with what they expected God would say. When they saw Jeremiah approaching the city, they derided him with the sarcasm of referring to his message—which is the word of God—as "the burden of the Lord." In His displeasure, God instructs Jeremiah what to say in response:

> [33] "When one of this people, or a prophet, or a priest asks you, 'What is the burden of the Lord?'; you shall say to them, 'You are the burden, and I will cast you off, says the Lord.' [34] And as for the prophet, priest, or one of the people who says, 'The burden of the Lord,' I will punish that man and his household. [35] Thus shall you say, every one to his neighbor and every one to his brother, 'What has the Lord answered?' or 'What has the Lord spoken?' [36] But 'the burden of the Lord' you shall mention no more, for the burden is every man's own word, and you pervert the words of the living God, the Lord of hosts, our God. [37] Thus you shall say to the prophet, 'What has the Lord answered you?' or 'What has the Lord spoken?' [38] But if you say, 'The burden of the Lord,' thus says the Lord, 'Because you have said these words, "The burden of the Lord," when I sent to you, saying, "You shall not say, 'The burden of the Lord,'" [39] therefore, behold, I will surely lift you up and cast you away from my presence, you and the city which I gave to you and your fathers.'" (Jeremiah 23:33–39)

Verse 36 is yet another illustration of the principle "that one is punished by the very things by which he sins" (Wis 11:16). The lesson here is that the alternative to accepting the truth of God's word about sin and the corresponding burden of taking sides with the truth against oneself

---

279 Later there is a recognition that because of His transcendence, neither do man's sins in any way negatively detract from God's perfection, nor does his righteousness positively add anything to His glory. See Job 35:6–8.

is to reject His word and to justify this rejection by claiming that it is burdensome. Here, "burdensome" means "unreasonable, not in keeping with man's way of thinking"—as absurd as clay correcting the potter: "You turn things upside down! Shall the potter be regarded as the clay; that the thing made should say of its maker, 'He did not make me'; or the thing formed say of him who formed it, 'He has no understanding'?" (Is 29:16). And with this, the real issue is unmasked: the creature stands in judgment of his Creator rather than to stand before the judgment of his Creator.

Because of sin, all men experience life as burdensome, particularly the interior life, the moral life. Fleeting moments when life is not onerous teach us that it does not have to be this way, that the suffering and arduousness of life's struggles are not inherent in life. Man yearns for a life free from suffering and from the toil that seem unavoidable. The biblical account of creation and the revelation of heaven and eternal life vindicate man's intuition that life should not be burdensome and toilsome. We have to learn to see the time in which live in light of the perfect harmony of the Garden of Eden and the fulness of life in heaven. It was not that way— burdensome and toilsome—in the beginning, and it will not be that way in the end. This is the foundation of our hope. The burdensome character of life is another dimension of the contradiction that sin introduces into our experience of life. And because sin has been vanquished, so too has the burdensome aspect of life.

For all who labor and are heavy burdened, the theology of the Sabbath rest validates their longing for a burden-free life. Jesus is the Sabbath rest[280] because He alone can take away the burden of sin and its effects.

The penitent man's desire to be forgiven, to have the burden of sin lifted off of him, is already a participation of faith in God's own desire to liberate men from sin. This divine desire is revealed in and points to the theological meaning of the Sabbath rest. Rest can be understood merely as being freed from labor and from the toil that accompanies it, or as enjoyment of the fruits of labor. Rest is not the cessation of activity. Rather, it is the highest and most fulfilling of all activities. This is why the Sabbath can symbolize the enjoyment of communion with God in heaven. The whole point of the Sabbath day is that man should refrain from those activities by which he participates in God's work of creation so that he might participate, consciously and intentionally, in the rest of God, that is, in His joy over the creation of man in His image and likeness. The weekly injunction to live a burden-free life[281] is for the sake of remembering not only God's work of creation, but especially His great work of liberating Israel from the burden of slavery in Egypt.[282] The Promised Land is a new Eden, the place where God's people can fulfill their vocation to be fruitful and to multiply and to worship God, and thereby bear witness to His efficacious love.

---

280 See Mt 11:28.
281 See Jer 17:21–27.
282 See Neh 13:19; Ps 81:6; Is 9:4

Just as the gift of life in the Garden of Eden is pure gift for Adam and Even, so too life in the Promised Land is pure gift for Israel. This sheer gratuitousness means that there is nothing that man has to do or can do to gain it. It can only be received. Yet, once it is received man becomes responsible for it. The gift becomes a vocation,[283] and this means that the gift can be lost. Just as Adam and Eve sinned against their vocation and forfeited life in the Garden, so too Israel fails to be a good steward of the gift of the Promised Land by sinning against its vocation to worship the God, "without fear, holy and righteous in His sight" (Lk 1:74–75 Liturgy of the Hours). The institution of the Sabbath is entirely at the service of fostering Israel's fidelity to its vocation to worship God by enjoying the blessings of His benevolence and by the rituals that manifest the full meaning of this fullness of life as gift from God for the sake of communion with God.

Yet, time and again the rest of the Promised Land would be disrupted as a result of Israel's sins. Even before entering into the rest of the Promised Land, Israel learns that though it is pure gift, man must freely open himself to this gift by the obedience of faith. Failure to obey God's voice is forfeiture of this rest in the fulfillment of vocation. For, to sin is become a slave again,[284] in effect, to return to the oppression of Egypt, and those who do not listen to God's voice will not enter into the rest He has prepared for them, the Promised Land.[285] Over time, God's people would long for a day of perfect rest. But since it is necessary to be perfectly obedient to His word in order to enjoy this rest, this means that Israel's eschatological hope is for the grace of a perfect obedience of faith. A perfect keeping of the Sabbath is a sign of that this perfect rest and perfect obedience of faith have arrived: "According to the testimony of the prophets, [the Sabbath's] observation was a condition for realizing the eschatological promises (Jer 17:19–27; Is 58:13f)."[286]

Observance of the Sabbath, however, can be misunderstood to mean that by keeping the Law regarding the Sabbath God will respond with the reward of fulfilling His promises. It is better to understand the relation between the Sabbath and the fulfillment of God's promises in terms of the graces by which the faith of God's people is definitively purified so that they can now observe the Sabbath as God has always intended. This is in keeping with St. Paul's teaching on the newness of Christ and the limits of the law, as well as his teaching on Abraham's works of circumcision and offering Isaac as the fruits of his justifying faith and not the means by which his faith acquired its justifying power.

In Jesus Christ, God fulfills His eschatological promises first by being Himself their realization—through His complete self-entrustment and

---

[283] John Paul II insightfully links the gift of the capacity to love with the vocation to love. See John Paul II, *Familiaris consortio*, 11.
[284] "Every one who commits sin is a slave to sin" (Jn 8:34).
[285] See Ps 95:11.
[286] Ceslas Spicq and Pierre Grelot, "Sabbath," *Dictionary of Biblical Theology*, Updated Second Edition, ed. Xavier Léon Dufour (Frederick, MD: The Word Among Us Press, 1988), 511s.

obedience to the Father—and second, by drawing people into a participation in His fullness.287 He accomplishes this by forgiving their sins and writing His law on their hearts. Jesus reveals the fulfillment of the Sabbath when He lifts the burdens of human infirmity by healing on the Sabbath.288 As signs that confirm His authority to forgive sins,289 His miracles of healing, especially on the Sabbath, point to His Paschal Mystery and to His authority to lift the burden of an accusing conscience. He thereby brings to fulfillment the vocation of every man and woman, which consists in complete self-entrustment and obedience to the Father. To believe in His merciful love, which is His power to forgive sins, is to enter into His own rest in communion with the Father.290 This rest is the heaven He desires for us. Since the only obstacle to this rest is sin, He leads us into it by forgiving our sins. God's mercy, then, fully revealed in Jesus Christ, is the fulfillment of the Sabbath, the definitive act of doing that good for which the Sabbath was instituted, namely, to worship God. Only in Him can man find rest from carrying the burden of sin. To approach Him for mercy and forgiveness is to enter into God's rest.291

The Groaning of Creation

The intensity of the hope of enjoying a peaceful conscience by coming to rest in renewed communion with God is correlative to the intensity of the experience of the restlessness caused by a conscience burdened by unreconciled guilt. The more intense the pain that accompanies an illness the more motivated one is to find a cure. It is axiomatic that the more one progresses in the spiritual life by loving God more and more perfectly, the more one will suffer as a result of sin.

David conveys this suffering of his soul through vivid descriptions of his body. His soul is listless, in the survival mode of the desert for being unable to escape the sapping heat of the sun. There is no oasis, no shade, no prospect for a respite from his torment. He is alive, but there is no joy in living because of the constant threat of non-existence. The conditions for a flourishing life are not present. The senses that ought to register sweetness, beauty, and melody only take in their opposites: bitterness, disfigurement, and discord. All that he experiences produces anguish. He can only groan. "Woe is me! for the Lord has added sorrow to my pain; I am weary with my groaning, and I find no rest" (Jer 45:3).

David knows that the cause of his groaning is the failure to confess his sins. "When I declared not my sin, my body wasted away through my groaning all day long" (Ps 32:3). On the Cross, Jesus utters similar words

---

287 See Jn 1:16.
288 See Mt 12:9–12; Lk 13:10–16; 14:1–6; Jn 5:1–18; 7:23; 9:1–16.
289 See Mt 9:2–7.
290 "Here below, the 'rest of the soul' is to live in harmony with the will of God (Jer 6:16); even more, it is to be united with God, to live with Him" (Ceslas Spicq, *L'Épître aux Hébreux, II: Commentaire* [Paris: J. Gabalda et Cie, 1953], 103).
291 See Heb 3–4, esp. 4:9–16.

on behalf of all humanity: "My God, my God, why hast thou forsaken me? Why art thou so far from helping me, from the words of my groaning?" (Ps 22:1). There is only one remedy to humanity's groaning, and that is the sacrifice of a humble and contrite heart, the total entrustment of oneself to God's mercy as the only hope for the forgiveness of sins.

What David so graphically depicts is what St. Paul calls the groaning of creation as it labors under the futility of its state of contradiction. On one hand, all creation strains toward its fulfillment, which consists in the harmony of its order. On the other hand, it ceaselessly confronts its own incapacity to attain that fulfillment. Creation lives under the sign of contradiction, the constant threat to the fulfillment of vocation. In such a state, existence is in conflict with itself; all creation is consigned to moaning.

> [22] For the creation was subjected to futility, not of its own will but by the will of him who subjected it in hope; because the creation itself will be set free from its bondage to decay and obtain the glorious liberty of the children of God. We know that the whole creation has been groaning with labor pains together until now; [23] and not only the creation, but we ourselves, who have the first fruits of the Spirit, groan inwardly as we wait for adoption as sons, the redemption of our bodies. (Romans 8:22–23)

The epicenter of this futility and groaning is the human conscience. Like the Law of the Old Covenant, conscience makes the truth known, but by itself it is inefficacious with regard to performance. The person who desires to follow God's law as known in his conscience cannot fail to discover his inability to do so, and so he groans. He does not let go of his desire, which would remove the conflict, but neither does his hope relieve his anguish because he realizes that some kind of death must occur—death to his old self, who resists God's truth—for his desire to be fulfilled, and this thought of death he finds repulsive.[292] Keeping his sins to himself,

---

[292] Commenting on another text in which St. Paul considers the groaning that is the condition of Christians waiting for the consummation of their hope for eternal life, Aquinas defines groaning as the result of the confrontation between man's desire and the delay in its fulfillment. His analysis leads him to define the confrontation as a conflict between two desires: "The condition of the desire is natural, delaying the desire of grace, because we would prefer to be found clothed and not naked, i.e., we would prefer that the soul attain to glory without the body's being dissolved by death. The reason for this is that there is a natural desire in the soul to be united to the body; otherwise, death would not be a punishment. And this is what he says: For while we are still in this tent, i.e., who live in this mortal body: 'Since I know that the putting off of my body (tent) will be soon' (2 Pet 1:14), we sigh, i.e., inwardly in the heart, and not outwardly with our voice: 'We moan and moan like doves' (Is 59:11), because it is hard to think of death, and yet burdened as with something against our desire, in that we cannot attain to glory without the putting off of the body" (Aquinas, *Commentary on St. Paul's Second Letter to the Corinthians*, Ch. 5, Lect. 1, [Marietti 159]). The key is Aquinas' mention of punishment. Man would like to have his desire for eternal life fulfilled, and though drawn to this fulfillment in hope he has an aversion to the "price"

David is in a similar position. He knows that he should confess his sins to God, but consideration of the price that comes with it prevents him from doing so promptly. And so he groans. He cannot know that answer to this groaning is Christ's death on the Cross to prove God's love for us. For He alone is able to pay the price.[293] But he does believe in God whose past acts of fidelity and mercy are a pledge of His future fidelity and mercy, which will be definitively revealed in the paschal mystery. What Jesus says of Abraham is operative here: "Your father Abraham rejoiced that he was to see my day; he saw it and was glad" (Jn 8:56). David, too, by his faith, sees the day of Jesus and rejoices in it. For, groaning cannot be final because "God is greater than our hearts" (1 Jn 3:20).

Groaning has its place in God's plan. Like all suffering it is meant to inform us and to motivate us. It informs us that something is profoundly not right, that we have been wounded by the misuse of our own freedom. And it prompts us to seek a remedy. It is here that faith in God's revelation is so profoundly liberating. How many go in search of remedies that do not correspond to the actual issue because they do not rightly understand that it is an issue of the misuse of freedom, of the rejection of love, of sin—an offense against God? And, in God's plan, the groaning caused by an accusing conscience is meant to last only for so long as taking responsibility for one's state, the beginning of repentance, is not yet acquired. The "period of service is ended" (Is 40:2 NJB) the moment that perfect contrition is acquired—which means that even those who are baptized shall have to live with it throughout their pilgrimage of faith. How much unnecessary groaning there is in the world for lack of faith in God's merciful love!

St. Paul vividly describes this state of knowing-yet-being-powerless in his Letter to the Romans:

> [21] So I find it to be a law that when I want to do right, evil lies close at hand. [22] For I delight in the law of God, in my inmost self, [23] but I see in my members another law at war with the law of my mind and making me captive to the law of sin which dwells in my members. [24] Wretched man that I am! Who will deliver me from this body of death? (Romans 7:21–24).

This puts into words the groaning of all men of all time, and it does so in christological terms. God's merciful love, fully revealed in Jesus Christ, is the only answer to the questions that spring forth from an accusing conscience. To live in denial, or to find some pseudo-explanation for the gnawing of the consciences, or simply to avoid the issue by escaping into

---

that comes with it, namely, the death-to-self suffering of conversion, which in God's plan is necessary (see Lk 24:26, 46 and Acts 3:18; 17:3; 26:23 on the necessity that the Christ should suffer in order to enter into His glory). If embraced, this becomes the sin of presumption by which a person hopes to obtain his forgiveness without conversion (see *CCC*, 2092).

293 "You were bought with a price" (1 Cor 7:23; 6:20).

work or pleasure or technology induced mindlessness (through drugs, mesmerizing electronics, extreme sports)—all of these will only prolong the purifying "period of service." So long as David avoids the truth about his sins and refuses to confess them, his life is nothing more than a pseudo-existence, an endless, agonizing sequence of incurable, festering, moral purulence.

Complementing David's description of how he wastes away so long as he does not confess his sins is the image of opposing the power of a river: "Do not be ashamed to confess your sins, do not struggle against the current of the river" (Sir 4:26 NJB). The strongest swimmer cannot swim upstream. He may hold his own for a while, but once his strength is exhausted, the force of the river wins and takes him along its course. Resisting the natural dynamism to acknowledge and to confess one sins depletes man's vitality. To attempt to do so consumes everything, to the last reserves of one's forces. The wise man passes on the wisdom that he no doubt learned as David did: go with the flow!

All of nature, like the river, is governed by an order the corresponding inexorable laws that only a fool would attempt to circumvent. The God of nature, the Creator, is the source of that order and its intrinsic laws. This is why all acts contravening the order of nature are offenses against God, Who has put the highest order in man, who is made in His image. A sinful act that breaks the law of his own nature destroys both the order God established in him and his relation to the God of that order. This is why sin is by nature self-destructive, even suicidal. Sin is disordered desire, which leads man to seek some momentary prize or satisfaction, like the wife of another man, but at the twofold price of losing his communion with God and living with an accusing conscience.

Wisdom consists in acknowledging that God's order precedes one's freedom and regulates it. It entails acceptance of the limits this order places on freedom, and this disposition of the will makes it possible to contemplate God's watercourses with veneration of their order and grandeur. For a person aware of sin, wisdom consists in going with the flow of his own nature, riding the waves of truth that flow from his conscience, and arriving at the peaceful delta where this river flows into the ocean of God's mercy.

The accusation and remorse of conscience are fundamental elements of this order of God's wisdom. They are essential elements of the just punishment for sin, and to acknowledge it as such is the first step in conversion: "to do its work grace must uncover sin so as to convert our hearts and bestow on us 'righteousness to eternal life through Jesus Christ our Lord' (Rom 5:21). Like a physician who probes the wound before treating it, God, by his Word and by his Spirit, casts a living light on sin."[294] Thus, the first step beyond a futile clinging to an illusory happiness and towards a real hope that truly satisfies one's deepest desires

---

[294] *CCC*, 1848.

entails a recognition of the desolation brought on by sin. This step is exhibited in the following psalm:

> [1] O Lord, rebuke me not in your anger,
> nor chasten me in your wrath!
> [2] For your arrows have sunk into me,
> and your hand has come down on me.
> [3] There is no soundness in my flesh
> because of your indignation;
>   there is no health in my bones
> because of my sin.
> [4] For my iniquities have gone over my head;
> they weigh like a burden too heavy for me.
> [5] My wounds grow foul and fester
> because of my foolishness,
> [6] I am utterly bowed down and prostrate;
> all the day I go about mourning.
> [7] For my loins are filled with burning,
> and there is no soundness in my flesh.
> [8] I am utterly spent and crushed;
> I groan because of the tumult of my heart.
> [9] Lord, all my longing is known to you,
> my sighing is not hidden from you.
> [10] My heart throbs, my strength fails me;
> and the light of my eyes—it also has gone from me.... (Psalm 38:1–10)

Arrows that strike, festering flesh, bones that are too weak to support the body, a burden too heavy to carry, sighing, burning, being crushed, eyes that cannot detect the light—all of these images convey the state of a person living—but really, barely living—with unreconciled guilt, expending all of his energy resisting the flow of the river of truth. Yet, it is just this recognition—the cause for despair apart from faith and hope in God's mercy—that becomes a saving grace for David. David experiences his anguish in the presence of God, Whom he knows is not indifferent to his groaning in desolation.

Professing Faith through Supplication

While Psalm 38 and other penitential psalms vividly describe the state of the sinner's soul, Psalm 51 conveys the faith-inspired turn to God in a straightforward supplication for mercy and restoration. It is rightly considered a profession of faith in God that takes the form of a confession of sins. It is a hymn that extols the triumph of God's faithfulness over man's unfaithfulness, the victory of divine mercy over man's sin. The two, God's mercy and man's sin, are correlative; each enters into the definition of the other. To grasp God's mercy in depth requires a correspondingly deep grasp of the evil of sin, and vice versa. By confessing his sins to God, David bears witness to the mercy of God, without which he would never approach Him. Faith in God's mercy makes it possible to live in "the certainty of being loved"[295] by Him, especially when the "logic of sin"[296] would dictate precisely the opposite.

The Psalm is a profession of faith because every petition in it—nineteen in all—is rooted in the truth about God. Prayer of petition is always and necessarily based on doctrine. We pray as we believe and we believe as we pray. Prayer of petition and doctrine are so intrinsically bound to one another that it is possible to say that petition *is* doctrine expressed in the form of a desire that God do what only He can do, that His will be done. David asks God to have mercy on him and to blot out his offenses *because* he believes that God is merciful. Thus, faith is an assent to the truth about God's mercy, but it is more than that. Faith also gives rise to prayer of contrition based on this truth. Prayer of contrition is always an appeal to God's mercy.

This relation between doctrine and petition is so much a part of Catholic life and liturgy that it merits the status of being a law: *lex orandi, lex credendi*. The law of prayer is the law of faith.[297] The Church's prayers *are* doctrine formulated to express the desires of her heart. For example, in the *Agnus Dei*, we address Christ according to one of His revealed titles and functions: "Lamb of God, Who takes away the sins of the world." This truth about Him gives us the courage to hope, and to express this hope in the supplication: "have mercy on us." Similarly, the petition of the Hail Mary, "pray for us sinners," is preceded by a doctrinal summary of what we believe about Mary. We ask her to pray for us *because* of what we believe about her unique role in God's plan of salvation. She is our Mediatrix because she is full of grace, blessed among women, and Mother of God. In the Lord's Prayer, what Jesus reveals about the Father is the foundation for the seven petitions. The seven petitions of the Our Father give expression to the desires of those who know the Father as Jesus does.[298]

The first truths about God that the sinner must know is that He is "merciful and gracious, slow to anger, and abounding in steadfast love and

---

295 *CCC*, 2778.
296 Recall that the "logic of sin" entails a world of "perfect" justice, "an eye for an eye" (*lex talionis*) wherein a sin against an all wise and good God deserves nothing less than death as its punishment. For man, spiritual death is life without love, which is hell. Since sin entails a rejection of God's love, the just punishment for it is to live without His love, as the prodigal son lived without his father and the benefits of being his son.
297 See *CCC*, 1124, which includes the original and longer form of this famous dictum: *ut legem credendi lex statuat supplicandi*: "That the law of supplication may be the foundation of the law of faith" (Prosper of Aquitaine).
298 "The Lord's Prayer is most perfect.... For since prayer interprets our desires, as it were, before God, then alone is it right to ask for something in our prayers when it is right that we should desire it. Now in the Lord's Prayer not only do we ask for all that we may rightly desire, but also in the order wherein we ought to desire them, so that this prayer not only teaches us to ask, but also directs all our affections" (Aquinas, *ST* II-II, Q. 83, a. 9).

faithfulness" (Ex 34:6), that He is a Father who is "rich in mercy" (Eph 2:4), that "God proves his love for us in that while we were still sinners Christ died for us" (Rom 5:8 NAB), and that He welcomes the return of sinners with joy, like the father of the prodigal son.

Man's Obedience and God's Mercy, Glory, and Holiness

The repentant sinner who believes in God's mercy is able to supplicate God for forgiveness, and by doing so He also proclaims His glory and exalts the holiness of His name. For, God's glory is the manifestation of His holiness, that is, His divine fulness of perfection, which supersedes the logic of sin with the higher logic of mercy:

> [8] How can I give you up, O Ephraim! How can I hand you over, O Israel! How can I make you like Admah! How can I treat you like Zeboiim! My heart recoils within me, my compassion grows warm and tender. [9] I will not execute my fierce anger, I will not again destroy Ephraim; for I am God and not man, the Holy One in your midst, and I will not come to destroy. (Hosea 11:8–9)

The restoration of man from the deprivation of love to being loved and being able to love is the glory of God,[299] His greatest work, the definitive evidence of the efficacy of His merciful love. The act of believing in the God of mercy is the great transformation of man that redounds to God's glory. Faith is the astounding effect of all of God's mighty works in behalf of man.[300] And, as we have seen, because mercy is God's greatest attribute in relation to us, St. Augustine exhorts us to praise God, that is, to give Him glory, above all for His mercy. With this we see that Vatican II's renewal of the call to holiness is a call to conversion, a call to rediscover the doctrine of divine mercy, and a call to renew the fundamental vocation of the Church, which is to give glory to God.

A compelling logical sequence binds these three terms—mercy, glory, holy—together. By His mercy, God forgives sins and thereby accomplishes what only He can accomplish, namely, the renewal of the human heart. For, because sin is an offense against God, only He can forgive and thereby transform hearts that have become inert to His truth and love—hearts of stone—into hearts of flesh that draw their life from His love. While this transformation takes place in the secret of each person's heart, it bears an observable fruit. The great sign of this transformation is to obey His commandments, which Jesus summarized: "A new commandment I give to you, that you love one another; even as I have loved you, that you also love one another" (Jn 13:34). The sinner who once disobeyed God's commandments now obeys them, and he does so not out

---

[299] See John Paul II, *Dominum et Vivificantem*, 59.
[300] See Rom 4:20 and 1 Pet 1:7.

of fear of punishment but out of the deep conviction—so deep as to be engraved on his heart[301]—that God is love and that because He gives His commandments out of love they are light and life for man.[302] This free adherence to God in the free obedience to His commandments constitutes God's glory because it is faith in action. It is the irrefutable evidence that His love is efficacious in re-orienting man's freedom without in any way violating that freedom. Israel's very existence as God's people who are obedient to Him in faith[303] constitutes the glory of God.[304] This obedience of faith is marvelously encapsulated in what the Virgin Mary says about herself: "Behold, I am the handmaid of the Lord" (Lk 1:38). And because the definitive source of His people's transformation is God Himself, His holiness, Mary links *what He has done for her* to His holiness: "he who is mighty has *done great things for me*, and holy is his name" (Lk 1:49). There is no explanation beyond God Himself for His election of His people and the marvelous deeds by which He liberates them to worship Him. God's holiness is, essentially, the perfection of His love,[305] and when His people see what He has done for them out of love, they acknowledge the holiness of His name[306] and obey His commandments. To be the glory of God is the Church's fundamental vocation, the vocation that Mary personifies. This is what the *Catechism* means when it teaches:

> Christians of the first centuries said, "The world was created for the sake of the Church." God created the world for the sake of communion with his divine life, a communion brought about by the "convocation" of men in Christ, and this

---

301 "I will put my law within them, and I will write it upon their hearts" (Jer 31:33).
302 "Your word is a lamp to my feet and a light to my path" (Ps 119:105). "For the commandment is a lamp and the teaching a light" (Prov 6:23). God's commandments are "commandments of life" (Bar 3:9). The Bible constantly links the commandments with life. See Deut 4:40; 6:2; 1 Kings 3:14; Neh 9:29; Sir 45:5; Mt 19:17; Jn 12:50. St. Paul makes it clear that this link between God's commandments and life is established from the beginning (see Rom 7:10), when God gave a commandment to Adam and Eve in order that they should not die (see Gen 2:17).
303 On the obedience of faith, see: Rom 1:5; 16:26; 2 Cor 10:5–6; Heb 11:8. Though Jesus did not have faith, obedience is nevertheless the hallmark of His relation to His Father. See: Jn 4:34; 5:30; 6:38; Phil 2:8.
304 "I will show myself holy among those who are near me, and before all the people I will be glorified" (Lev 10:3).
305 "God's holiness is not merely an incandescent power before which we are obliged to withdraw, terrified. It is a power of love and therefore a purifying and healing power" (Benedict XVI, Homily, April 13, 2006). Jesus "teaches us that the heart of holiness is love, which leads even to giving our lives for others (cf. Jn 15:13). Therefore, to imitate the holiness of God, as it was made manifest in Jesus Christ his Son, 'is nothing other than to extend in history his love, especially towards the poor, the sick and the needy (cf. Lk 10:25ff.)'" (John Paul II, *Ecclesia in America*, 30).
306 When the descendants of Jacob see what God has done to restore His people in Jerusalem, they will "will acknowledge my name as holy, he will acknowledge the Holy One of Jacob to be holy and will hold the God of Israel in awe" (Is 29:23 NJB). The first petition of the Our Father is precisely that people will come to recognize the holiness of God's name by reason of what He accomplishes through Jesus Christ in men, that is, in the Church. See *CCC*, 814.

"convocation" is the Church. The Church is the goal of all things, and God permitted such painful upheavals as the angels' fall and man's sin only as occasions and means for displaying all the power of his arm and the whole measure of the love he wanted to give the world.[307]

The power to obey God's commandments of love, especially for the poor and for enemies, flows from the conviction of faith that everything He does for His people, including the commandments He enjoins upon them, He does out of love. It comes from the experience or being loved by God in our own poverty, the poverty of our sin, which makes us God's enemies.[308] Because the root of disobedience is doubt about His love, conversion into renewed obedience must be based on a renewed conviction about His love. And this is no merely theoretical renewal of conviction. If that were the case, redemption would be nothing more than a teaching acquired through study. Rather, conversion into obedience based on a renewed conviction about God's love comes with a new encounter with that love. It is a new experience of God's mercy, which gives rise to a new song in praise of God's marvelous deeds. For Israel, to sing a new song to the Lord is to make a profession of faith regarding His mighty deeds, and to do so with joy. Israel's first song follows God's liberation of Israel from slavery in Egypt.[309] From that time forward, whenever God intervenes in a new historical or personal situation, the proper response is to sing a new song.[310]

The great prophecies of Ezekiel and Jeremiah confirm this. In both texts in which Ezekiel prophesies that God will change His peoples' hearts of stone to hearts of flesh,[311] the first effect is that they will obey His commandments. Obedience is also a defining quality of the new covenant of Jeremiah: The new covenant will differ from the old covenant, which God's people broke.[312] To understand this emphasis on obedience it is necessary to grasp that in the Bible disobedience is the great sign of a lack of faith in God's love. Sin begins with doubt about God's love.[313] The restoration to obedience that the prophets envision is the undoing of the disobedience of Adam and Eve. Since their sin, God has been at work to restore His people to obedience, not just any obedience but an obedience of faith rooted in the conviction that God is love. This conviction is the fruit of the experience of His mercy, by which He continues to love His people even after they have sinned by disobeying His commandments. God responds to man's rejection of His love and consequent disobedience by

---

307 *CCC*, 760.
308 See Rom 5:6–10. God proved His love for us through Christ dying for us while we were still weak, while we were still sinners, while we were still His enemies.
309 See Ex 14:31–15:21.
310 See Jud 16:13; Ps 33:3; 40:3; 96:1; 98:1; 144:9; 149:1; Is 42:10; Rev 5:9; 14:3.
311 See Ezek 11:19–20 and 36:26–27.
312 See Jer 31:32–33.
313 See *CCC*, 215, 397, 399. John Paul II calls it suspicion of God's love. See *Dominum et Vivificantem*, 37–39.

giving them greater and greater demonstrations of His love so that they no longer isolate His commandments from His love. This logic of ever-greater demonstrations of His love reaches its unsurpassable limit in the paschal mystery of Jesus Christ, which is the definitive proof of God's love.[314] God has nothing further to give because, quite literally, He has given everything, His very self.

"Teach me wisdom in my secret heart" (Ps 51:6).

David's petition that God instruct Him in wisdom in his secret heart is his version of the prophecies of Jeremiah and Ezekiel, that God write His law on His people's hearts, or that He give them new hearts. David beseeches God to work in him a transformation that he cannot bring about by himself. He seeks a wisdom that will put an end to his disobedience. For, in Israel's understanding, wisdom and the law of the covenant are inseparable. Wisdom is the gift to live according to, to obey, God's law.[315] But there are two ways to obey God's law, out of fear of punishment, and this is only the beginning of wisdom, and out of an internalization of God's law that is so complete that there is no longer any distinction between His vision for one's fulfillment and one's own. Wisdom is the gift by which the two, God and man, have become one regarding the judgments by which a person pursues his fulfillment. It is man's participation in God's providence and governance in relation to the hearts of men.

To elaborate on this, it is helpful to realize that there is a consistent structure in God's covenants. The essentials of this structure are the following. First, God takes an initiative of love in order to bestow a gift upon those whom He loves. Second, once God bestows this gift, He gives commandments, which are His wisdom regarding what His people must do and must not do in order to be good stewards of the original gift. This is in keeping with man's dignity and freedom. Once man receives God's gift, he becomes responsible for it. So, in the covenants there are two acts of divine love. In the first, God bestows an original gift. In the second, He bestows a second gift in the form of the knowledge man must have in order to preserve the original gift.

This structure is evident in creation. First, God imparts the gift of life, and then He gives the commandment, which is at the service of the preservation of the gift of life.[316] Thus, God's law is a "law of life"[317] and His commandments are "commandments of life."[318] The structure is also evident in the covenant of Sinai. First, God bestows the gift of freedom to

---

314   See Rom 5:8.
315   See Deut 4:6–8; Ps 19:7; Sir 1:26; 15:1; 19:20; 32:2; 39:1; Jer 8:8.
316   See Gen 2:17. For St. Paul, the commandment is "ordained to life" (Rom 7:10 DRA). It is not a means for attaining life, since life is a gift. Rather, it is the means for preserving life. "He who keeps the commandment keeps his life; he who despises the word will die" (Prov 19:16).
317   See Sir 17:11 and 45:5.
318   See Bar 3:9. See also Deut 30:16–20.

the Hebrew slaves in Egypt, then He gives the commandments, which are entirely at the service of safeguarding that freedom.[319] Wisdom is the gift by which God's people grasp this relation of law (second gift) to life and freedom (first gift). It is wisdom to realize that God's love for man corresponds to man's love for himself. As a result, to obey the Lord's commandments is the definitive fulfillment of man's love for himself. To disobey His commandments, that is, to sin, is a truly suicidal act.[320] Wisdom brings life while the folly of sin brings death.

This structure of the covenants is the scriptural foundation for a proper understanding of Christian moral teaching and what the *Catechism* means what it teaches, "The commandments ... come in the second place."[321] We do not justify ourselves by keeping the commandments. Rather, we keep the commandments because we are justified.[322] Israel does not earn its freedom from slavery by keeping the commandments, nor do Adam and Eve gain their existence by obedience. Obedience is always the result of God's people experiencing His love for them and thereby coming to trust that His commandments are meant to serve them. This is very clear in the brief "introduction" to the Ten Commandments: "And God spoke all these words, saying, 'I am the Lord your God, who brought you out of the land of Egypt, out of the house of bondage. You shall have no other gods before me" (Ex 20:1–3). This means: "I have demonstrated my love for you [For slaves, the definition of being loved is to be set free!] by making a first gift of freedom to you. Now, with these commandments, I give you another gift: the gift of wisdom regarding what you must do, and what you must not do, in order to continue to live with my first gift of freedom."

God rightly expects His people to obey Him precisely because they have witnessed His mighty works of love in their behalf. The same divine love that motivates His mighty works of liberation imparts to His people the wisdom they need in order to remain free. This is the thrust of the message of the prophets, who give voice to Israel's memory of the great test at Meribah.[323] To despise God's word, as David did,[324] is to prefer some other word to that of the God Who has demonstrated His love. It is to entrust oneself to another who has no right to be trusted because he has not demonstrated his love as God has. The great lesson of salvation history is, put negatively, not to harden one's heart against His words of knowledge

---

[319] "The ten commandments, like the whole Law which is their commentary, have no other aim in view than to preserve Israel from a twofold slavery into which both ancient and modern civilizations have fallen and continue to fall" (Barthélemy, *God and His Image*, 75).

[320] "As a rupture with God, sin is an act of disobedience by a creature who rejects, at least implicitly, the very one from whom he came and who sustains him in life. It is therefore a suicidal act" (John Paul II, *Reconciliatio et paenitentia*, 15).

[321] See *CCC*, 2062.

[322] This is essentially St. Paul's argument, in Romans 4, that Abraham was justified by faith prior to his obedient observance of any command from God.

[323] See Ex 17:7; Num 20:13, 24; 27:14; Deut 6:16; 9:22; 33:8; Ps 81:7; 95:8; 106:32.

[324] See 2 Sam 12:9. See also Num 15:31; Isa 5:24.

and wisdom,[325] which are words of life:[326] "O that today you would listen to his voice! Harden not your hearts" (Ps 95:7–8). Positively, the lesson is to listen to God's word and to keep it. Thus, Jesus says, "Blessed rather are those who hear the word of God and keep it!" (Lk 11:28). To listen to God and to obey His commandments, based on the memory of His demonstrations of love, is true wisdom.

> [6] Keep them and do them [God's commandments]; for that will be your wisdom and your understanding in the sight of the peoples, who, when they hear all these statutes, will say, "Surely this great nation is a wise and understanding people." [7] For what great nation is there that has a god so near to it as the Lord our God is to us, whenever we call upon him? [8] And what great nation is there, that has statutes and ordinances so righteous as all this law which I set before you this day? (Deuteronomy 4:6–8)

Leading His people into this wisdom is the goal of God's plan of love. When people sin by despising His word, they fall back into some form of slavery. In God's plan, this punishment is medicinal. It is meant to place them in a new situation of slavery and dependence on Him so that they can experience His merciful love anew and, based on this new experience, come to a renewed trust in Him and obey His commandments.

"Restore to me the joy of your salvation" (Ps 51:12). With these words, David reveals his keen understanding of God's mercy and the structure of the covenants He establishes with those to whom He shows mercy. For, salvation is inseparable from observing the commandments.[327] And this gives us the key for interpreting a text of Hebrews: "Christ became the source of eternal salvation to all who obey him" (Heb 5:9). Salvation is not a reward for obedience. Rather, obedience is the fruit of salvation and thus the sign of salvation. Obedience is rooted in the experience of the undeserved gift of liberation from evil and suffering.

This is the wisdom for which David prays. He knows that God's forgiveness cannot mean simply the suspension of punishment, for, that would void punishment of its very purpose and leave the sinner in his state of suspicion of God's love and the resulting disobedience of His commandments. David knows that forgiveness must be something positive, a true reconciliation, a restoration of communion with God. This is why, in the midst of his confession of sins, he requests: "teach me wisdom in my secret heart" (Ps 51:6). This is equivalent to the petition: "create in me a clean heart" (Ps 51:10). Wisdom is the unction that purifies hearts. For, it is the heart that discerns the difference between good and evil, and a clean

---

325 See Prov 19:27; Sir 39:6.
326 See Deut 32:47; Ps 119:37; Acts 7:38; Phil 2:16; 1 Jn 1:1.
327 See Ps 119:117, 146, 155; Heb 5:9.

heart is able to "call good and evil by their proper name."[328] This is the true wisdom[329] that proves itself by keeping God's commandments.[330] This wisdom and obedience are the magnificent good that God brings out of the evil of sin by forgiving. The wisdom that is unique to Israel is the wisdom that expels the folly of doubting God's love by remembering His marvelous works, and which bears the fruit of obedience to God by keeping His commandments. It is a wisdom rooted in faith in God's first gift, the gift of His mercy. It is a wisdom of mercy and conversion. Obedience is the fruit of belief in and experience of God's merciful love, and the event that engraves the conviction that He is love on the hearts of men is the encounter with His merciful love.

Just as for slaves the definition of being loved is to be set free from slavery, and a leper's definition of being loved is to be set free from leprosy, so for sinners, the definition of being loved is to be set free from the fear of not being loved. But this cannot be an imaginary lesson, as if it sufficed simply to envision, no matter how vividly and intently, what it is like to doubt God's love. To this, God could respond in kind, and devise of plan of salvation that is nothing more than a myth about His mercy—an envisioned mercy, but not an Incarnate Mercy. The wisdom for which David prays is accessible only to the brokenhearted, that is, to those humbled by the awareness of their own sins. Humility makes a person teachable, receptive to the gift of wisdom: "with the humble is wisdom" (Prov 11:2). Wisdom consists in seeing reality in light of the full truth about man's sin and about God's mercy. The greatest obstacle to this is pride, which blinds a person to his faults and thereby diminishes or altogether removes his sense of dependence on God's mercy. Humility rests on the truth about human weakness and sin, and it thereby disposes man to be open to God's mercy. Humility of mind leads to faith in God's mercy, and humility of will leads to hope in that same mercy. The story of Naaman, the leper, exemplifies this.[331] Naaman knows the truth about himself; he cannot deny the truth about his leprosy. In his humble state, he learns of the healing power of the God of the prophet Elisha, and he begins to hope that he might be healed. Yet, only when Naaman's servant dispels his pride, which flared up because what Elisha instructed him to do seemed too little to him, does he follow the prophet's instructions and is healed. It is wisdom to submit to the power and mercy of the living God. Imparting such wisdom through forgiving men's sins, so that sinners approach Him, is God's greatest work, the work that gives Him the greatest glory.

The perceptive probing of Psalm 51 into the thoughts of a repentant heart brings to light a fundamental dimension of Israel's faith. The great

---

328 John Paul II, *Dominum et Vivificantem*, 43. See Is 5:20: "Woe to those who call evil good and good evil."
329 See 1 Kings 3:9; 2 Sam 14:17, 20. See also Gen 3:5. Mature Christian faith is the power to distinguish good from evil (see Heb 5:14). In this way, all the faithful participate in the charism of kings to know the difference between good and evil.
330 See Ps 19:7; Prov 28:7; Sir 1:26; 6:37; 15:1; 19:20; 33:2.
331 See 2 Kings 5:1–7.

lesson of Israel's history is that the ability to love the Lord with one's whole heart is a gift that accompanies the experience of His mercy. It is the gift that comes with the humility of enduring the punishment for hardening one's heart against God and the purification that comes with turning to Him anew in humility and faith and hope in His mercy. It is highly significant that Jeremiah's new covenant, in which God writes His law on His people's hearts, and Ezekiel's new hearts of flesh, are gifts that accompany Israel's repentant return to the Lord. Similarly, in two texts of Deuteronomy, loving God with one's whole heart is the fruit of a repentant return to the Lord.[332] The school of true wisdom is humble conversion and the experience of God's mercy. This is why David's supplication for the gift of wisdom in his secret heart is a petition that is ultimately fulfilled when God sends His Son into the world in order definitively to reveal His mercy. Through David, God is fashioning hearts in the Old Testament to desire what He desires. These are the hearts of the poor and humble, "who rely solely on their God's mysterious plans" and who are "the great achievement of the Holy Spirit's hidden mission during the time of the promises that prepare for Christ's coming."[333] For, Jesus Christ is the wisdom of God,[334] Who definitively reveals God's mercy so that those who believe in Him can live in "the certainty of being loved,"[335] a certainty that expels all suspicion about God's love so that in loving obedience they can fulfill the whole of God's law by loving their neighbors as themselves.[336]

Mercy: God's Victory over the Anguish and Futility of a Failed Vocation

At the time that Nathan comes to him, David is the epitome of a heart that is "hardened against turning to the Lord" (2 Chron 36:13). His heart—which the Bible variously describes as uncircumcised, false, stubborn, rebellious, and therefore anguished, faint, smitten, stricken, grieved—is precisely the wilderness into which God leads sinners so that He can speak anew to them.[337] God will give to David a new heart[338] so that he will know Him[339] in the full biblical sense of what it means to know: David will experience God's mercy.

---

332 See Deut 4:29–31; 30:1–3, 6. 6:5; 10:12; 11:13; 13:3.
333 *CCC*, 716.
334 See 1 Cor 1:21–24.
335 *CCC*, 2778.
336 "Owe no one anything, except to love one another; for he who loves his neighbor has fulfilled the law. The commandments, 'You shall not commit adultery, You shall not kill, You shall not steal, You shall not covet,' and any other commandment, are summed up in this sentence, 'You shall love your neighbor as yourself.' Love does no wrong to a neighbor; therefore love is the fulfilling of the law" (Rom 13:8–10).
337 "I am going to seduce her and lead her into the desert and speak to her heart" (Hos 2:16 NJB).
338 See Jer 32:39 and Ezek 36:25.
339 See Jer 31:33 and 24:7.

The victory of God's mercy over David's sin makes his conversion, and Psalm 51, a light for all who are curious about the claims of the God of Israel, for all who are ready to make judgments about Israel's God based how He deals with Israel's king. Anyone who visits his own heart in its desert-state can search through the history of religions and discover in David (and in Israel) the light of truth regarding God's response to man's sin. The heart that, as a result of sin, becomes a wasteland of unreconciled guilt and doubt about the very meaning of life—because man is made for love and by sinning he has rejected love and made himself unlovable—can identify with King David and his joy of discovering that in His mercy God continues to love those who have rejected His love.

With man's need to encounter God's mercy in mind, and reflecting on St. Mark's observation that Jesus looked upon the rich young man with love,[340] John Paul II gives a penetrating description of the desperate need to know God's love of a heart crushed by the awareness of sin. For, "Man cannot live without love. He remains a being that is incomprehensible for himself, his life is senseless, if love is not revealed to him, if he does not encounter love, if he does not experience it and make it his own, if he does not participate intimately in it."[341] And this need for God's love is most intense when the logic of sin dictates that man deserves to live deprived of the very Love for which he is made.

> Man needs this loving look. He needs to know that he is loved, loved eternally and chosen from eternity. At the same time, this eternal love of divine election accompanies man during life as Christ's look of love. And perhaps most powerfully at the moment of trial, humiliation, persecution, defeat, when our humanity is as it were blotted out in the eyes of other people, insulted and trampled upon. At that moment the awareness that the Father has always loved us in his Son, that Christ always loves each of us, becomes a solid support for our whole human existence. When everything would make us doubt ourselves and the meaning of our life, then this look of Christ, the awareness of the love that in him has shown itself more powerful than any evil and destruction, this awareness enables us to survive.[342]

In his penitential psalms, David multiplies images to convey precisely what John Paul II so vividly depicts. Both his sin and the prospect of defeat at the hands of his enemies plunge his heart into a dark despondency, for both, he thinks, indicate that God's reign has been overthrown. Emissaries of despair, both bear the writ of indictment: "Where is your God?" For God to be vanquished, regarding either His interior or His exterior

---

340 See Mk 10:21.
341 John Paul II, *Redemptor hominis*, 10.
342 John Paul II, Letter to the Youth of the World, *Dilecti amici*, 1985, 7.

kingdom, is a contradiction around which all that is intelligible collapses. If God can fail in His vocation to be God, then no vocation of man can be fulfilled, and all is contradiction. Thus, David's heart is like a land that, for lack of water, cannot fulfill its vocation to bring forth a harvest. His bones cannot fulfill their vocation of supporting the weight of his being.[343] Groaning is not a momentary action, something that he does, it is virtually equated with his existence.[344] With so many images of creation being subjected to futility,[345] David conveys his awareness that by his sins he has placed himself in a state of contradiction and futility as his vocation to be loved and to love seems hopelessly unrealizable.

Though David remains close to God by reason of his office as king, this is no consolation to him at the moment that he becomes aware of his sin. For, that is not the primary closeness for which he is made, nor is it the closeness that is most important to God. So long as his heart is far from God,[346] David is in the same situation that the prophets decry when the people offer God their outward sacrifices but hold back their hearts. When it is not accompanied by inward closeness, outward closeness—the keeping of ritual, legal, and moral precepts—is not only without value;[347] it also entails a self-condemnation.[348] Only when God rebuilds the walls of Jerusalem, that is, when He makes David's heart an interior fortress of God-fearing virtues, "then will [God] delight in right sacrifices, in burnt offerings and whole burnt offerings" (Ps 51:19).

Blessed are Those who Confess Their Sins

Because He is love, because He is merciful love, God cannot remain indifferent to the suffering of sinners. Their groaning under the oppressive weight of unreconciled guilt is the cry to which He is especially attentive. These are the poor for whom He has a preferential love, for they truly are the poorest of the poor.[349] With faith in God's mercy, David confesses his sins.

> [15] But for you, O Lord, do I wait;
> it is you, O Lord my God, who will answer....

---

343 See Ps 32:3; 38:3.
344 See Ps 32:3–5; Ps 38:8.
345 See Rom 8:20.
346 See Is 29:13–14.
347 Circumcision, cut off from interior worship of God in the Spirit, has no value. See Gal 5:6; 6:15 and Phil 3:3. Paul rightfully sees the fruit of this closeness in "keeping the commandments" when he declares: "For neither circumcision counts for anything nor uncircumcision, but keeping the commandments of God" (1 Cor 7:19).
348 St. Paul applies this logic to his teaching on the Eucharist: "Let a man examine himself, and so eat of the bread and drink of the cup. For any one who eats and drinks without discerning the body eats and drinks judgment upon himself" (1 Cor 11:28–29).
349 "Indeed, just as he is not truly happy who abounds in riches, delights in pleasures, possesses honors in abundance, but he who delights in God; so, he is not miserable who is poor, wretched and feeble and weak, but he who is a sinner" (Aquinas, *Commentary on the Psalms*, Psalm 50 [51] [Marietti, 501]).

> ¹⁸ I confess my iniquity,
> I am sorry for my sin. (Psalm 38:15, 18)

Similarly, in Psalm 32, David repents of having kept his sins hidden so that he can repent of his sins:

> I acknowledged my sin to you,
> and I did not hide my iniquity;
> > I said, "I will confess my transgressions to the Lord;"
> > then you forgave the guilt of my sin. (Psalm 32:5)

The confession of sins and God's response of mercy are the cause of the blessing with which he begins the Psalm:

> ¹ Blessed is he whose transgression is forgiven,
> whose sin is covered.
> ² Blessed is the man to whom the Lord imputes no iniquity,
> and in whose spirit there is no deceit. (Psalm 32:1–2)

It is wisdom worthy of being passed from one generation to the next not to resist the natural flow of conscience to confess one's sins to God. And for those who obey this wisdom, there is the blessing of living in the certainty of being loved by God.[350] Blessed are those who humbly acknowledge their moral wretchedness! Doubly blessed are those who do not lose hope and look for someone to rescue them from this state! Superabundantly blessed are those who discover in the mercy of Jesus the answer to their question, "Who will deliver me?

---

350 On the certainty of being loved by God, see above all *CCC*, 2778. See also Benedict XVI, *Spe salvi*, 26; Address, June 5, 2006; Message for 50th World Day of Prayer for Vocations, April 21, 2013.

Conclusion:
Conversion as Descent into Humility in order to Ascend to the Inner Kingdom of Prosperity Measured by Divine Mercy

Near the outset of these reflections on David's conversion the question was asked whether the bold confidence he exhibited toward God was in some way inappropriate. If the essential difference between David before and after his sin and conversion consists in his humility and apparent withdrawal of confidence in God's protection and the assurance of success, does this mean that such confidence is something antithetical to a right relationship with God that needs to be purified?

What becomes clear in David's conversion is that the object of his confidence undergoes a radical transformation. In the first stage of his life, David understands God's promises and protection to be assurance of victory in battle and of prevailing over his enemies. He could request a trial with no doubt about the outcome. He was assured of being vindicated, and judgment would fall on his adversary. This changes as a result of his sin and conversion. The second king of Israel comes to realize that there is an enemy within, namely, sin. By his adulterous and murderous actions, and his impenitence, he despised the word of the Lord. As a fruit of his conversion and deeper humility, he is no longer eager for his day in court: "Enter not into judgment with your servant; for no man living is righteous before your" (Ps 143:2). An appeal to the divine tribunal under these circumstances could only mean that the judgment would go against him, for God cannot judge against Himself. This awareness leads David to pray in a wholly new manner, calling upon God to look upon his afflictions as an acceptable sacrifice.

In addition, Augustine's insight (discussed in Chapter One) into the perilous nature of prosperity as the occasion of David's fall into forgetfulness of what God had done for him invites us to ask whether there are parallels to his situation today. One possible parallel may be found in the situation of the Church in the United States over recent decades and the scandal of clergy sexual abuse. Has the prosperity that Catholicism has enjoyed in the United States contributed to the current crisis? There can be no question about the Church's social and economic prosperity. By the late 1990s, Catholics had arrived. A disproportionate number of Catholics held positions as U.S. representatives and senators. A similar disproportion pertained with regard to the number of CEOs of Fortune 500 companies, and Catholics contributed more to the economy than any other religious group. At the same time, by the end of the Second Millennium there were numerous indicators of decline: closing of inner-city parishes; closing of schools; decline in Mass attendance and in Confirmations of those who had been baptized; liquidation of ecclesiastical property; decline in the understanding of faith (despite "improved" methods of catechesis); decline in vocations to religious and clerical life; a moral secularization of an alarming number of the faithful.

Prosperity is not *ipso facto* threatening to robust faith. Jesus' words, "it will be hard for a rich man to enter the kingdom of heaven" (Mt 19:23), are relevant. Typically, people do not become prosperous by accident. Prosperity is the fruit of focused effort, and this is an indicator that it is a high value, a priority. There is nothing intrinsically evil, nothing sinful, about prosperity and the activities ordered to acquiring it. But perhaps this is plays into it being such a great threat to putting God first, and a potent stratagem of the evil one. For, there are only so many hours in a day, and if all those hours are consumed by efforts to achieve material prosperity, God is effectively crowded out. So, the issue is not about the moral *quality* of acts ordered to prosperity, which should be presupposed to be upright, but about the *quantity* of those actions. The issue, in other words, is whether those striving for prosperity keep it in perspective. Are they committed to the practices that keep faith alive and promote its continuing maturation, such as: prayer, sacraments, devotions, catechesis, ecclesial service? Faith is a fragile gift. As these spiritual actions diminish, as people spend less time in the presence of God and expose themselves more and more to the secular values of the surrounding culture, it is to be expected that they become self-satisfied with what *they* have accomplished—their prosperity—and that they develop a certain arrogance in relation to their own freedom—precisely the dispositions that precipitated David's tragic fall into sin.

The essence of Jesus' mission, which is prefigured in the mission of Nathan, and which the Church continues, is to make present the merciful love of God for the forgiveness of sins. The Church has accomplished this mission in every kind of social, cultural, political, and economic condition. Awareness of sin and living in total dependence on God's mercy are essentially independent of these circumstances. This explains the often-misunderstood instructions of St. Paul to slaves, which are in fact an application of the general principle: "Everyone should remain in the state in which he was called" (1 Cor 7:20). Many Catholics live a mature faith despite the lack of support from the surrounding, secular culture, even the hostility of that culture against faith. But, the essential autonomy of faith in relation to culture should not lead to a fatal presumption regarding the influence of culture on people of faith. There is no doubt that a secular culture of economic prosperity has contributed to the loss of faith of many. There is wisdom in the verse: "For the scepter of wickedness shall not rest upon the land allotted to the righteous, lest the righteous put forth their hands to do wrong" (Ps 125:3).

Conclusion

Just as Jesus is not at home on earth but speaks of heaven as His true home, so Christians should understand that "we have no lasting city" here on earth, "but we seek the city which is to come" (Heb 13:14). Our time on earth is a pilgrimage of faith, not a time of rest. This awareness keeps all things in perspective, especially the primacy of the interior kingdom in relation to any exterior kingdom. The entails the elevation of moral conscience to the summit of the hierarchy of values and thus the radical relativization of all things that do not bear an essential relation to moral conscience. The petition of the Lord's Prayer, "Thy will be done on earth as it is in heaven," which follows and explicates the preceding petition, "Thy kingdom come," is answered with every cooperation with grace at work in conscience. To seek the truth, to acknowledge the truth, and to conform to the truth are the actions proper to those who show that they are "of the truth" by listening to the voice of Christ the King (Jn 18:37). For, all of the works of the King of heaven are truth (Dan 4:37).

St. Thomas Aquinas very precisely translates the theology of the priorities of the inner kingdom into prayer:

> Grant to me, Lord my God:
> that I not fall into imperfection
> in prosperity or adversity;
> that I be neither exalted in the former,
> nor disconsolate in the latter;
> that I rejoice in nothing
> unless it leads me to You;
> that I sorrow in nothing
> unless it turns me from You.

Another problem with earthly prosperity is that it can too readily be taken as a blessing, as an indication of God's favor in response to doing His will. This idea is well represented in the Old Testament, yet even here there are already indications of a more spiritual understanding of the signs of divine favor. The kingdom that Jesus establishes is "not of this world" (Jn 18:36) because He is "not of this world" (Jn 8:23). This is why the Church, which is "the kingdom of Christ now present in mystery,"[1] is "present in this world and yet not at home in it."[2] She must never lose awareness of being "like a stranger in a foreign land."[3] To preserve this awareness, Christians must live the evangelical counsels of poverty, chastity, and obedience. For, Christ's disciples are "not of world" (Jn 15:19) because they are born anew, from above, even as Jesus is from above. This means that they must live in the world as He did, drawing from the same source of life from which He draws rather than from the world. Jesus' manner of living in the world reveals not only that He is from above

---

1   Vatican II, *Lumen gentium*, 3.
2   Vatican II, *Sacrosanctum Concilium*, 2.
3   Vatican II, *Lumen gentium*, 8, quoting St Augustine.

but also that He will return to the Father. We call that manner of living the evangelical counsels, which necessarily accompany the perfection of charity to which all are called.

The Second Vatican Council calls on the entire Church to follow Christ in His total dedication to the Father and to fulfilling the mission the Father entrusts to Him. This means that the Church and all of her members must follow Christ in His poverty and obedience, and in keeping with their vocation, in His chastity.[4] The ministry of priests, in a special way, calls for them to be conformed to Christ in His obedience, celibacy, and poverty.[5]

The counsels accompany the perfect charity of Christ. For Him, they are pure fruit of perfect charity. Theologians call this the affective living of the counsels. He had no need to live the counsels ascetically (the effective practice of the counsels) as means to promote a more perfect charity, because His charity was always perfect. The members of the Pilgrim Church must live the counsels in both ways. They experience them affectively, for example, when at times of prayer they are so completely absorbed in love of God that all other loves are rightly ordered. They practice the counsels effectively as means of denying themselves lawfully desired goods for the sake of arriving at that detachment that becomes more and more perfect as charity becomes more and more perfect.

Charity is the very essence of Christ's kingdom and, therefore, it is present in mystery in the Church. Charity "is the soul of the holiness to which all are called."[6] And because charity cannot be perfect without poverty, chastity, and obedience, the Church lives her holiness as Christ did, by living poverty, chastity, and obedience. It should not be a total surprise, then, that when the Second Vatican Council initiated a renewal in the Church that consists essentially in the call to holiness a new phase in the ages-old spiritual battle should ensue. The enemy of Christ and of His Church is irrevocably set against the participation of men and women in the holiness of God. He defines victory negatively, as thwarting the spread of the civilization of love from heaven to earth. He is totally opposed to God's will being done on earth as it is in heaven. This means that he is opposed to the Pilgrim Church's participation in Christ's way of life, through the effective affective realization of the counsels.

St. Augustine's reading of David's fall provides a warning against all things that can be the occasion for distracting us from the single-hearted love of God that the evangelical counsels both express and safeguard. It shows us that it is possible to be absorbed in doing the Lord's will in the sphere of external mission while neglecting the internal mission of conversion into the perfection of charity. The enemy wages battle on all three fronts of poverty, chastity, and obedience. The attack is seldom direct. It is, rather, incremental, beginning with insinuations that: a radical embrace of the counsels is simply not necessary; the Church must, after all,

---

4   See Vatican II, *Lumen gentium*, 8, 42.
5   See Vatican II, *Presbyterorum ordinis*, 15–17.
6   *CCC*, 826.

bear witness to the goodness of creation; detachment from earthly goods for the sake of witness to hope in the eschatological promises of Christ can be a deterrent to mission; at all costs, extremes must be avoided; the counsels may have had their place in prior epochs and the cultures of another time, but they must be reinterpreted and updated in keeping with the new realities of our times.

The heavier artillery enlisted by the enemy's assault on the counsels takes the form of attacking the foundational principles of moral theology. It is to be expected that the most powerful created intellect, corrupted by pride, would have a strategy for undermining the most fundamental and important principles of Christian life. He accomplishes this today by perverting the magnificent fruits of a new historical awareness and of historical theology by insinuating that in the end there is no foundation for faith in universal truths. Masked as intellectual humility, historical relativism undermines the bold confidence, the *parrhesía* of faith. Why should today's believers and their clergy make costly sacrifices to conform to the demands of the Gospel if those demands change with the times? Why should we assume that norms that were meaningful in another era are meaningful in ours? The devil knows that the absolutely indispensable condition for conversion is an absolutely unshakable certitude in the truth of what God has revealed in Christ. When theologians betray their mission and theology degenerates into cataloguing so many schools or methods or approaches to understanding the Christian mystery, and when students are constantly reminded that these are after all only approximations of the truth that we cannot fully comprehend, should it be a surprise that a proposal for a Catechism for the Universal Church is met with protestations that a consciousness of theological pluralism simply precludes the possibility of expressing the faith in a way in which all can discover their faith in it?

It is not necessary to continue beyond identifying confusion about conscience and God's mercy as ordinances manufactured by the enemy to assail the Church's faith regarding the evangelical counsels. The point is that it is a consummate victory of the Church's enemy when the faithful—clergy, religious, and laity—come to be convinced that they can follow Christ without embracing the counsels (in a way that is commensurate with their vocation, to be sure). The scandal of clergy sexual abuse is only the most notorious indication that the Church in the United States, today, is like David in his time of prosperity. While certainly the response to this scandal entails legal and economic dimensions, in the end the only response that is adequate is a deep conversion, rooted in humility and a new awareness of total dependence on God's grace and mercy, and a rediscovery of the necessity of a new commitment to live the evangelical counsels.

Regardless of contemporary applications, there is no doubt that David's experience of sin and of God's mercy leads him to discover a deeper form of God's fidelity, corresponding to a deeper form of evil and suffering that he encountered in his own heart and conscience. He passes from preoccupation with a temporal kingdom to being focused on a spiritual kingdom. He intuits that the persecution and humiliation he experiences are tied to his sin and deserved, and that if God should withdraw His protection in the sphere of the king's dealings with others He will never fail to respond to a broken and contrite heart, because the sole preoccupation of such heart is God Himself. A broken and contrite heart desires only that God forgive the sin that separates the sinner from God. It is a heart that loves God for His own sake and not for the sake of any gift that He might bestow—except the gift of Himself! For, to love God for His own sake includes loving Him for His plan of totally gratuitous of love, and for His fidelity to that love, which is His mercy. To know His mercy is to know that its efficacy does not depend on any measure of human status[7]—except the status of man's heart. Human status is measured by comparing men among themselves,[8] while the status of the heart is measured directly by each one's relation to God. God's self-giving is in no way affected by human status. His love is impartial regarding the interior kingdoms of hearts and consciences. It reaches every broken and contrite heart, whether of male or female, of slave or free, of Jew or Gentile, prelate or laity. This is why David's conversion transcends Israel as a political unity and is universal as a paradigm of conversion.

David's hope that God look upon the affliction, which he knows to be the effect of his sin, foreshadows and participates in the affliction of Jesus Christ, which was caused by the sins of men. The heavenly Father will look upon the affliction of His Son offering Himself in sacrifice on the Cross and show mercy to Him by raising Him from the dead. David's conversion is a participation in Christ's resurrection. Though he is never baptized, he receives the regenerating graces of Baptism, and becomes subject to the King Who reigns in consciences and thus he becomes a member of the Kingdom of Christ that is mysteriously present in the Church.

David: True Prophet Who Bears Witness to Christ

The extraordinary events of David's life, especially the path to which he was called by God to be king, should not obscure the profound points of contact between his life and the lives that most disciples of Christ live. Even a brief reflection leads us to see that our very existence, our vocation to life, is no less extraordinary than David's vocation to be king. Both originate in God's completely gratuitous initiative of love, and both can only come to fulfillment by Divine Providence, by God's grace.

David's experience of conversion sheds light on a vital dimension of every Christian journey of faith. Every vocation is in fact twofold. The first and most fundamental vocation is the call to holiness, the perfection of

---

7   This is what Scripture means when it attributes to God the quality of not showing partiality. See Deut 10:17; 2 Chron 19:7; Acts 10:34; Rom 2:11; Gal 2:6; Eph 6:9; Col 3:25; 1 Pet 1:17. Because Christians are sharers in the divine nature (see 2 Pet 1:4), they too must treat others without partiality. See 1 Tim 5:21; Jas 2:1, 9.

8   Think of Jesus' teaching on the Pharisee and the tax-collector in the Temple (Lk 18:10–14), and the quarrelling among the apostles over who was greatest (Mk 9:33–35).

charity, and communion with God in Christ[9]—the kingdom within. Along with this, God calls each one to participate in the mission of Christ by exercising the gifts given by the Holy Spirit for building up this kingdom, the Church. This second vocation is not really distinct from the first. Rather, it specifies the call to holiness and communion with God. The concrete manner in which a person strives towards the perfection of charity is determined by the duties and circumstances that come with this second vocation.

The (second) vocation to participate in Christ's mission is always more visible than the interior (first) vocation of the spiritual life. This is why the first threats to vocation of which one is aware are exterior: the seminary rector whose recommendation might mean the end to a priestly vocation; the lack of financial resources needed to complete an important work of the apostolate; health conditions that impede the way one envisions fulfilling his mission; anyone who seems to be placing obstacles to what the Lord is asking of me. Prayers of petition often reflect this, focusing more on the means to the fulfillment of vocation in the second sense, as a function in the Church, than on the graces needed for holiness. When these prayers concern the conversion of those who appear to be obstacles to the fulfillment of what I consider to be God's will, the conversion I have in mind is nothing more than a change of mind regarding the precise point of opposition to my plans, not the total conversion of another's soul for the sake of holiness and God's glory.

Two things become clear at this point. The first concerns attachment to how *I* understand *my* vocation and how best to fulfill it. It is time to regain perspective when the first reaction to what appear to be impediments to my mission is to think of them as interventions of forces opposed to God's plan. Any threat to my mission then confirms its divine origin as well as how I understand it. But it must be asked: Are the two identical? Might this perceived threat be a providential occasion for purification, not only of my zeal but also of how I understand my mission? Have I become more attached to the gift of my mission than to the Giver of the mission? Following on this—and this is the second thing that becomes clear—is that an unpurified zeal for mission reduces one's relationship with God to mere utility. God is seen primarily as the source of all the grace and means required for the fulfillment of the mission. This is mirrored in relationships with others. All relationships and encounters are sized up uniquely on the calculation of whether they have something to contribute to my mission, as if this mission were virtually identical with the mission of the Church as such. When zeal for mission makes its success the dominant criterion for relating to God and to others, there are two inevitabilities. First, the fruit that it bears will in some way be tainted because of the bias of one's personal understanding of his vocation. Second, there will need to be a providential purification of that misunderstanding.

---

9 The universal call to holiness is set forth as Chapter Five of the Dogmatic Constitution on the Church, *Lumen gentium* of Vatican II.

Zeal for mission is laudable, and no resource or energy should be spared when it comes to doing God's will. Nevertheless, but it should not overshadow zeal for holiness or even substitute for it. It is common to both missions that they are received from God and that His grace sustains them. This is why it is easy to confuse them, or even conflate them. But might it be that the temptation to overvalue one's mission is rooted in a kind of spiritual insecurity? Might the inversion of priorities by which a person exaggerates success in the apostolate as a criterion for his relationship with God be compared to the attitude of certain Pharisees at the time of Christ for whom prayer was a parade of things they had done for Him?[10] Might I find it less demanding to throw myself into my exterior mission than to confront the sin within that is an obstacle to the interior mission of holiness?

Even more fundamentally, the question of the criteria for measuring success in the apostolate must be posed. Jesus describes His own mission in terms of seeds, and not just any seeds but the smallest of seeds, the mustard seed.[11] An inexperienced person might simply pass over such a small seed as unpromising. Yet, it is precisely this small seed that "when it has grown it is the greatest of shrubs and becomes a tree" (Mt 13:32). And for this remarkable growth to take place, the mustard seed, like all seeds, only if it "falls into the earth and dies" is it able to "bear much fruit" (Jn 12:24).

Bearing fruit is primarily a function of remaining attached to the Vine.[12] As pleasing as it is to God that a person should take this mission seriously, it is even more pleasing to Him that the one He calls to be His associate in mission understands that all mission is rooted in communion with Him.[13] Communion, that is, holiness, comes first, and this is pure gift from God, pure mercy. Perhaps that is the reason why it takes so long for the heart to become attuned to the primacy of communion in holiness. A desire to do things for God, as good and holy as that is, can all too easily lead to forgetting that everything begins with God's initiative, and to measuring one's relation to God on the basis of exterior criteria rather than on the basis of the perfection of charity. Our activity in doing what is good is so close to us, and it is so profoundly related to the very dignity of being made in God's image, that the evil one prizes its corruption, which begins with the attenuation of the link of the exterior mission to the interior mission.

As image of God, man is made to act as God acts. God loves, and this means that He imparts the goodness of being and all of the enhancements of their being to creatures. Human dignity consists in cooperating with God in loving, that is, in communicating the good to others. This is what it means to be God's associate in mission. The trouble is that when we think of mission too often it is primarily in terms of efficiency and the effort we need to make. We think that the fruit we can expect is proportionate to our efforts. We do not think of the power of the good to attract. And so all of

---

10   See Lk 18:12.
11   See, for example, Mt 13:31–32; 17:20; Lk 13:19; 17:6.
12   See Jn 15:1–8, 16.
13   See John Paul II, *Christifideles laici*, 32.

our energies quickly become channeled in the direction of various activities that are calculated to result in the diffusion of the good. There certainly is a time and a place for this, but to the extent that this mindset crowds out the action of God, not deliberately but in fact, it becomes a perversion of what is most noble in us.

Jesus warns us about this in His teaching about those who prophesy, cast out demons, and accomplish great works in His name.[14] These activities, good in themselves, are not infallible indicators of communion with God. They are only expressions of communion with Him when they are performed solely because they are received as the mission that He entrusts to us. Taking them on because they appeal to us for any reason other than that they are God's will for us is to take them on for merely human motives. Even an originally pure motive is not insurance against corruption. We can presume that David assumed his office as king of Israel with the purest of motives. But the moment his pure motive is set aside, he becomes like the seeds in the parable of the sower that make a promising beginning but end up "choked by the cares and riches and pleasures of life, and their fruit does not mature" (Lk 8:14). Abuse of office is the inevitable result, as it is perverted to serve the office holder rather than those it is meant to serve. The mission of service flows from abundance, not need. Communion with God, which meets all needs, is the only insurance against abuse of office. The clergy sexual abuse scandal that has rocked the Church in recent decades confirms this. And this cannot be separated from a devaluation of the Eucharist as the source and summit of the Church's life and the privileged means by which Christ continues to build His Church as the communion of men with God.[15] The gift of communion with God always comes first. Our participation in Christ's mission presupposes this gift. In fact, our participation in His mission is this very communion in action.

In light of these considerations the lesson in David's encounter with Nathan on the occasion of the king's decision to build a temple for God is perhaps more applicable to our own time than might appear at first. The impression is given that God is aware of David's need for conversion, of his propensity to think in terms of doing things for God. There is a logic, then, in David's desire to express his gratitude for all that God has done for him. Such a logic is based on facts. It is true that God had chosen David and rid him of his enemies. But it is also true that God desires the transformation of David's heart. Once this transformation occurs, his perspective changes. Formerly, defeat at the hands of his enemies and suffering were taken as signs that God had abandoned him. As a result of his conversion David becomes aware of a new criterion by which to measure God's favor. Suffering is the just punishment for his sins, and yet God is mysteriously at work in it. Because it has a place in God's plan to bring sinners back to Him, there is hope in suffering. The Physician of souls knows suffering's medicinal value, as do those who receive His mercy.

---

14 Mt 7:21–23.
15 See John Paul II, *Dominicae cenae*, 4.

It is important to keep in mind that David is profoundly aware of the link between his suffering and his sin. The death of Bathsheba's son, the revolt of Absalom, and the humiliation of having to flee Jerusalem are directly related to his infidelities to God, his disdain of God's word. David has learned "to accept this temporal punishment of sin as a grace."[16] He perceives a mysterious fidelity of God is at work even in the midst of the consequences of his infidelity. David's faith is seen in his persistence in relating all to God. He especially laments before God, trusting that by humbling himself God will enrich him anew: "If we are faithless he remains faithful—for he cannot deny himself" (2 Tim 2:13). The greatest act of humility is to confess one's sins: "If we confess our sins, he is faithful and just, and will forgive our sins and cleanse us from all unrighteousness" (1 Jn 1:9). God's covenant is that the grace to become aware of sin will always be accompanied by the grace of faith in His mercy. God will never leave a sinner alone in the knowledge of his sins.

In this way, David's conversion is truly prophetic. It is Jeremiah who so keenly pinpoints the difference between true prophets and false prophets.[17] Both prophesy eventual victory and peace. But false prophets conveniently omit the place of darkness, purification, and suffering. In God's plan, the light, joy, and peace of His victory and abiding presence are the final outcome. True prophets know that these must be preceded by darkness, desolation, and the contradiction of His apparent defeat and abandonment. The calamities that Jeremiah predicts have a meaning in God's plan. They place God's people in a new situation of total dependence on God, so that they can experience anew His saving mercy. In this way they serve to reveal God's people to themselves, to make their sins so inescapably obvious that they finally humble themselves and turn to the Lord with broken and contrite hearts. This is all that God requires for the fulfillment of His promise, made through Jeremiah, to establish a New Covenant that consists in forgiving His people's sins and thereby writing His law on their hearts.[18] Jesus Christ is the true Prophet to whom all the other prophets bear witness. In His passion, death, and resurrection, He definitively fulfills the law that sorrow and desolation precede the joy of God's victory over sin. David's conversion is prophetic because it ratifies this law of true prophecy. Through his conversion David participates in the fulfillment of all prophecy in the paschal mystery of the true Prophet.

Every conversion likewise participates in Christ's fulfillment of all prophecy through His "conversion" from death to life. Whether it be occasioned by grave sins, like David's adultery and murder, or less serious sins, every conversion is a participation in Christ's suffering caused by sin, in His sorrow unto death,[19] followed by a participation in the joy of resurrection to new life. This is the essential meaning of Baptism: "If we

---

16 *CCC*, 1473.
17 See Jer 28:8–9, 15.
18 See Jer 31:31–34.
19 See Mt 26:38.

have died with Him, we shall also live with Him" (2 Tim 2:11), "For if we have been untied with Him in a death like His, we shall certainly be united with Him in a resurrection like His" (Rom 6:5).

David's first confrontation with a threat to his vocation is with Saul. As long as Saul pursues him, David lives under the sign of contradiction: God has called him to be king, yet Saul poses a threat to the fulfillment of the Lord's appointment. David learns to trust in God, and while this is good, it is limited to this external threat to his reign. Yet, the principle of trusting in God for the fulfillment of His promises, especially when they appear to be nullified, is the key lesson of this early stage of David's pilgrimage of faith. The son of Jesse will learn that there is another kind of threat to ruling as king. While his reign is secure from external enemies, it is threatened by a new menace, the interior enemy of sin. In terms of political power, David remains king, but in terms of fulfilling his vocation his lust and his pride bring his reign to ruin. The great king discovers that he is unable to fulfill the vocation to rule God's people as His representative because he is unable to rule himself. Only by humbly submitting himself and his vocation to the true King, Who alone rules over consciences, is David able to receive his vocation anew, restored by the mercy of God.

David's restored kingdom is a kingdom of mercy, and this is what makes him a prophet of the true King. Christ is the true King, and He rules by impressing His kingship upon us, making us participants in His kingdom of truth and mercy. He rules by enlightening consciences with the truth about sin and the truth about God's mercy. This is the truth that sets us free from hiding from God as Adam and Eve did, and from the fatigue of carrying the burden of guilt and groaning, as David did so long as he resisted confessing his sins. This freedom is the condition for fulfilling the fundamental law by which Christ governs His kingdom, namely, to love others as we have been loved by Him, and to do so by extending to them the same mercy that He has shown to us.[20] The glory of Christ's kingdom is self-effacing and self-sacrificing love "to the end" in service to those around us. And the greatest service is to fulfill the vocation to be light to the nations by bearing witness to the truth about sin and the truth about God's mercy, and thereby to invite all whom we meet to enter into the rhythm of God's transformation of darkness, groaning, and death into light, joy, and life. This vocation is always beyond us. It must constantly be received anew, and for this there is no more efficacious a means than to place ourselves before the throne of God's mercy by humbly confessing our sins, as we do at the beginning of every Mass at which we celebrate God's fidelity to answering our petition that His kingdom come.

Our royal vocation is constantly under attack. As long as there is some part of our being that has not been subjected to the reign of God, so long as there are faults that remain hidden, we live under a sign of contradiction.

---

[20] "A new commandment I give to you, that you love one another; even as I have loved you, that you also love one another" (Jn 13:34).

God calls us to be kings, yet something of the prince who wore the crown before Christ's rule clings to sovereignty. St. Paul names that someone "the old man" inside of us. Prior to Christ's enthronement in our hearts, our royal dignity, that is, our freedom, erected itself as absolute authority, accountable only to itself. Sin is a replay of Israel's desire to be like the other nations by acclaiming Saul as its king when in reality God's chosen people can have only one King, God Himself. To sin is to desire to be something other than God's chosen one, to take one's vision for happiness from other nations, and place one's freedom on the throne that is God's alone. Conversion entails the violent overthrow of the usurper of our own freedom in order to restore God to His rightful place as the only King Whose rule does not diminish our freedom but liberates, heals, expands, and perfects it. "It is right and just to entrust oneself wholly to God and to believe absolutely what he says. It would be futile and false to place such faith in a creature."[21]

David's story is one of violence, both exterior and interior. Whether it is Saul's jealousy, David's lust for Bathsheba and his treachery against Uriah, or the uprising of Absalom, the interior violence against God's truth in one's conscience is the cause of the exterior violence. As the torture and crucifixion of the true King attests, on earth God's kingdom is subject to violence. "The law and the prophets were until John; since then the good news of the kingdom of God is preached, and everyone enters it violently" (Lk 16:16).[22] To fulfill one's vocation by submitting to the rule of Christ entails the violence of conversion.

> This Kingdom and this salvation, which are the key words of Jesus Christ's evangelization, are available to every human being as grace and mercy, and yet at the same time each individual must gain them by force—they belong to the violent, says the Lord (see Mt 11:12; Lk 16:16), through toil and suffering, through a life lived according to the Gospel, through abnegation and the Cross, through the spirit of the beatitudes. But above all each individual gains them through a total interior renewal which the Gospel calls *metanoia*; it is a radical conversion, a profound change of mind and heart (see Mt 4:17).[23]

On earth, in faith, the kingdom of God is lived under the sign of contradiction. Christ's reign over consciences by the truth is constantly re-

---

21 *CCC*, 150.
22 Matthew's version is slightly different, but makes the same point: "From the days of John the Baptist until now the kingdom of heaven has suffered violence, and violent men take it by force" (Mt 11:12).
23 Paul VI, *Evangelii nuntiandi*, 10. See also John XXIII: "Indeed, penance is that counterforce which keeps the forces of concupiscence in check and repels them. In the words of Christ Himself, "the kingdom of heaven has been enduring violent assault, and the violent have been seizing it by force" (*Paenitentiam agere*, 10).

established by the violence of conversion that consists in taking sides with the truth against oneself by confessing one's sins and taking sides with the truth for oneself by entrusting oneself to the mercy of God. Paradoxically, the fruit of this violence of conversion is peace. Jesus, Who suffered the violence inflicted upon Him by sinners, who "in some way seem to lay violent hands on him,"[24] is the One Who imparts the gift of peace: "Peace I leave with you; my peace I give to you; not as the world gives do I give to you" (Jn 14:27).

It is vital for all who pray to know what they are asking when they make Jesus' prayer their own: "Thy kingdom come." That petition is answered through the violence of the paschal mystery and our participation in it through conversion. It is answered every time a person cooperates with God's grace by submitting to the truth of conscience, by accepting the judgment of truth about sin, and by confessing his sin with faith and hope in God's mercy.

---

24   *CCC*, 598.

About the Author

Douglas Bushman's teaching and writing in theology has been shaped especially by the Church Fathers' spiritual reading of Scripture, the theological methodology of St. Thomas Aquinas, and the pastoral orientation of the Second Vatican Council, as interpreted and implemented by St. John Paul II and Benedict XVI. He has exercised the gift of theology in service to the Church at virtually every level of the Church's life: parish, diocese (including programs of formation and courses for adults, catechists, permanent deacons, Catholic educators, and seminarians), Catholic schools, RCIA, and undergraduate and graduate degree programs.

Bushman has served as Lay Theologian for the parish of St. Charles Borromeo (Minneapolis), Director of Parish Mission for the Church of St. Joseph (West St. Paul), Director of Education (Diocese of Duluth), Director of the Institute for Religious and Pastoral Studies (University of Dallas), and Director of the Institute for Pastoral Theology (Ave Maria University). His last academic position was with the Augustine Institute (Denver), where he was St. John Paul II Professor of Theology for the New Evangelization. Currently Prof. Bushman's research and publishing focuses on the pastoral theology of the Second Vatican Council, the New Evangelization, and Catholic Spirituality.

Following his B.A. in Aristotelian and Thomistic philosophy (College of St. Thomas, St. Paul), he studied under the Dominican Pontifical Faculty of Theology at the University of Fribourg, Switzerland, who imparted a vibrant Thomism incorporating the study of Scripture, the Church Fathers, the best of the *ressourcement* theologians of the 20th century, Vatican II, and the best among post-Conciliar theologians.

Bushman is the author of *The Theology of Renewal for His Church: The Logic of Vatican II's Renewal in Paul VI's Encyclical* Ecclesiam Suam*, and Its Reception in John Paul II and Benedict XVI* (Wipf and Stock, 2024) among other works, he has contributed to the translation of the *Catechism of the Catholic Church* into English, and his articles have appeared in numerous Catholic publications including *Nova et Vetera, Homiletic and Pastoral Review, Lay Witness, Magnificat, Catholic World Report, Catholic Faith, Catholic Dossier,* and *The Catholic Servant.*